UNSOLVED NO MORE

A COLD CASE DETECTIVE'S FIGHT FOR JUSTICE

KENNETH L. MAINS

WILDBLUE
PRESS

WildBluePress.com

UNSOLVED NO MORE published by:

WILDBLUE PRESS

P.O. Box 102440

Denver, Colorado 80250

ISBN 978-1-947290-14-3   *Trade Paperback*

ISBN 978-1-942266-90-7   *eBook*

Interior Formatting/Book Cover Design by Elijah Toten www.totencreative.com

This book is dedicated to the people who have shaped and molded me into the person I am today: the family, the cops and the friends. It is also for the people who have the courage to stand up for what they feel is right, regardless of the consequences.

Focus – Inspire – Succeed

CONTENTS

PROLOGUE

"The challenge of politics and public service is to discover what is interfering with justice and dignity for the individual here and now, and then to decide swiftly upon the appropriate remedies."

Robert Kennedy

My old high school friends come up to me all the time and say, "Man you made it, I am so proud of you and your success." I find myself asking, what is success? Is success having a lot of money? If that is the case, I am not successful. If success is not having to worry about the mundane things in life such as car payments and insurance bills, I'm not successful. If success is waking up every morning and loving what you do for a living, then I will have to finally admit: I've made it; I am a success.

Yet I feel I am not anything but driven and passionate. I liken my success to any other occupation: a carpenter, a veterinarian or an actor. When you love what you do and you have a passion for doing it, you can attain the unattainable. I love being a detective; it is my passion. I am just a detective, yet I get to work doing the thing I have wanted to do my whole life. I get to solve crimes. I get to help people. More specifically, I get to solve the unsolved.

It wasn't easy to get to where I am. I have travelled an incredible journey, at least so I am told. I have fought, loved, laughed and cried. I have won wars and I have lost a few battles along the way. I try to make a difference because this life is too short not to try. Everyone has a gift – a gift that keeps on giving, long after you are gone and reduced to ash and your name is just words in cyberspace or a tombstone. I am always reminded when I lay down to sleep of an old quote, "Once the last person who knows you dies, you never existed."

My gift is determination and passion. I am determined to do what is right. I am determined not to become corrupt and unjust like some of the masses. I am determined to fight the good fight until I can fight no more. I am determined not to join the "politics" of society where egos are more important than solving murders.

I speak for those who are too afraid to speak. I speak for those who don't have the courage to stand up and shout, "That is not right!" I am determined to be the voice of the lost and the forgotten. Anybody who isn't already in the fraternity of lost loved ones will never fully grasp it. I have lost, as so many others have, so I understand.

To know how I ended up being called by some "the greatest cold case detective in the country," you must know where I came from and the trials and tribulations of getting where I am. I am not a professional athlete who is looked at with reverence and pride by our impressionable youth. In fact, I am what today's society seems to hate the most: I am a cop. Regardless of the stigma, the negative, the attitudes or the villainization, I continue to do my job, to protect and serve this great nation of ours. I am dedicated to this mission because that is what I am. That is what is in my blood. My DNA screams "detective"! My anguish implores that the unsolved be solved and I will do what is necessary to make that happen.

You will feel my anger for failures and those of our justice system and agencies that forget we work for the public and for the victims who cannot speak for themselves. You will feel the weight on my shoulders as I try to combat the corruption, politics and untruths within our justice system.

To know why cold cases and investigations are important to me and why I do what I do, you must know Kenneth L. Mains. To know why I take pride in the title "detective," you must know my upbringing, my mistakes and my characteristics. Conversely, you must know my weaknesses, my pet peeves and my sacrifices. All of these things are important in figuring out why I am passionate about the unsolved and being a detective.

You will see that success, no matter what your definition is, can be attained. I was a punk kid from a small country town who played every sport I could. Who loved the wilderness and hunting. Who adored his mother and father. But this punk kid from the country fought continually, drank to excess, rebelled against the establishment and got suspended from school repeatedly. This punk kid had a son when he was 17 years old and got kicked out of his home only to end up living in the back seat of a friend's car during his senior year of high school until he was able to secure an apartment. This punk kid went to high school part-time in order to work washing dishes at a restaurant to provide for that newborn son.

Yet through it all, I was able to continue marching forward toward my goals because I remained focused, inspired and prideful! Today, I am constantly approached by television executives, producers, authors and journalists. They want to know my story. I go to high schools and talk to students, hoping that my tale will inspire them to succeed. I am constantly being asked by family members of unsolved homicide victims to solve their cases. It is something that I cherish. I tell my story and use my skills and experiences to help others because that is what life is about. Inspiring other to achieve greatness—isn't that what we want our kids to believe in?

Don't be afraid of greatness; seek it out and embrace it. But always remember where you came from. Remain humble yet confident and treat everyone with respect. As one of my idols, Albert Einstein, once said, "I speak to everyone in the same way, whether he is the garbage man or the president of a university." I think if more law enforcement officials lived by this code, we would have a better relationship with the public.

Eventually, I became a United States Marine, the first in my family to become a college graduate; a police officer; an undercover agent for the FBI; detective for the district attorney; the chief narcotics enforcement officer in Lycoming County, Pa., as the drug task force coordinator; the founder of the greatest cold case organization in the world (AISOCC); an advisory board member at the Cyril Wecht Institute of Forensic Science and Law at Duquesne University; and an advisor at my alma mater. More importantly, through all those experiences, I became a good man. Strip away all those accolades, all those titles and what remains is someone who cares, loves and goes through every day with prideful integrity. That, to me, is all that matters in life.

Don't ever let anyone tell you that you can't do something! I am a living, breathing example of that. Success is attainable as long as you allow yourself the opportunity to learn, grow, experience and even fail. You will undoubtedly ruffle a few feathers along the way, but that is how you effect change!

We must, as a society, embrace change and evolve personally with this change. If we do not, the hardships that will undoubtedly occur will be forever embedded in our consciences without remedy or recourse. If we do not allow change to take place between what is right and what is wrong, our entire justice system is in peril and soon will become extinct.

*"Government's first duty is to protect
the people, not run their lives."*

Ronald Reagan

One thing that infuriates me, as it should others, is the arrest of innocent people. How can we arrest and convict an innocent person? Easily, because not enough time is given during the initial investigation. You are pressured to solve the case quickly and when you do that, shortcuts happen. When you rush, mistakes happen. That is why cold-case investigations are easier, I feel. You are not ever rushed. You can be meticulous, thorough and perfect.

It is my opinion there needs to be a standard for homicide investigations in general. Quality standards are used in labs, doctor offices and factories. Why is it we can arrest people and charge them with murder yet there is no quality control to make sure the right guy is arrested? A hard fact to swallow is that innocent people have been executed in the United States. Think about that for a minute. A person is charged, convicted and executed for something they did not do. It doesn't happen all the time because through time, safeguards in respect to death penalties have been put in place. Yet, one person killed by the government who was innocent is one to many in my book.

Innocent people are arrested all the time in the United States. Law enforcement does not want to admit this, but it is done. Most of the time, there is no malicious intent; it is just a mistake. We are humans and we are fallible. Yet, there needs to be someone— before it gets to the judge and jury—who examines the case. Because by the time it gets to the judge or jury, the person's life is already ruined, regardless of the verdict, regardless whether the charges are thrown out and regardless whether the charges are withdrawn. There needs to be an impartial and unbiased entity that examines all homicide cases before charges are filed. This would be a huge undertaking and I doubt it really could be implemented. As humans, we all see things differently. Two people can look at a picture and see two separate things. So, the reviewing of an unbiased panel of homicide cases would be very, very hard to implement.

The Innocence Project and others are touted, fairly or not, as being against law enforcement. This may be true for some, but for others, it is about the truth, exactly as it should be. The Innocence Project is a necessity if we cannot come up with another system that stops the prosecution of innocent people before they are charged with a crime. Once they are, their lives will be forever scarred. They will always be viewed upon as a murderer and people will treat them differently. Why? All because a detective followed the investigation down a wrong path without consulting anyone else on the case? It happens and there needs to be a way to curb this.

This could be curbed with a quality control for homicides—yet another one of my dreams for which I will have to fight. I get some mean looks from law enforcement when I bring this up, but I compare our jobs to a doctor. If a doctor screws up and a patient ends up misdiagnosed because of this mistake, the doctor is liable for malpractice. Now, that doctor surely did not wake up that morning with the intent of ruining the life and affecting the family of a patient. It was a mistake for which the doctor is held accountable.

A detective arrests someone for murder through a bad eyewitness and circumstantial evidence, which ruins the suspect's life and family forever when he is proved innocent. Where is the repercussion on the detective? Are we just supposed to say "Sorry," and move on with our everyday life while the wrongly accused person suffers? The detective is not held accountable for mistakes in the investigation that led to the arrest of the innocent person. Why? A doctor is, but a detective is not. Both made mistakes that changed someone's life in a negative way yet only the doctor is held responsible. To me, this doesn't make sense. You cannot arrest someone unless you are 100 percent sure it is the right person. There can be no doubt. Some will say that is what the jury is for—this angers me. We, as law enforcement, have to be held to a higher standard than this. We must be sure. Everyone makes mistakes, yet isn't it our responsibility as decent human beings to try to eliminate these mistakes?

If the government were to implement a quality control where all homicides to be charged were run through a neutral party or parties before going to the system, a lot of lives could be saved.

Some will say that is the district attorney's job, but prosecutors are not investigators, they are attorneys. Others will say that is what a jury is for. However, once the person's case reaches the jury, regardless of guilt or innocence, the person's life is already ruined.

It would be time-consuming and a lot of tweaking would have to be done, but that is the only way I see the problem getting solved. Even then, with a panel of professionals, there will be disagreement. Yet, much like how a jury operates, a conclusion would be made and it undoubtedly, would cut down on the number of innocent people being arrested. This is what should be done in America. Maybe this wouldn't work, but it could be a basis for something better. Will this ever come to light? Stay tuned America, because I'm working on it.

The justice system is not perfect and I don't know how to fix it. It convicts innocent people and it lets guilty people walk free. It's a system run by humans; therefore, it is fallible. People have committed homicides for centuries. People have gotten away with murder for just as long. That is life. Yet, I feel the gift I was given and the talents God has afforded me to have will allow me to help solve some of these unsolved homicides.

PREFACE

"Ken Mains is an experienced investigator with a vision. His drive and devotion to solve 'cold cases' have no parallel. Without Ken, these crimes would continue to collect dust in file drawers. I consider Ken Mains one of the top detectives in this country. I am proud to know him."

Dr. Werner U. Spitz, MD, FCAP, forensic pathologist

I believe solving cold cases and any crime really is just the art of deduction. You deduce possibilities to probabilities until the suspect shows himself or herself. That is how I solve cases or should I say, cases solve themselves. Maybe I believe in this theory because it is simple. Solving crime does not have to be difficult. It really is simple. The art of deduction—it is simple. I believe things are usually what they seem. Not always, but most of the time. I guess I like to keep things simple, not only in solving cold cases, but also in life. I subscribe to five simple rules in life:

1) Never give up.

2) Work harder than the next person.

3) Never put your own needs ahead of your children's.

4) Treat everyone with respect until it is time not to.

5) Traverse through this life with pride and integrity.

Those principles have allowed me to become the man I am today. Those principles allow me to persevere and inspire when others may have succumbed. Growing up, my heroes were always athletes, as is the case with most kids. I liked the strong, scrappy players. I didn't like the flashy, big-name athletes. I gravitated toward John Cappelletti, Rocky Bleier, Ray "Boom Boom" Mancini, Bill Mazeroski, Jack Dempsey, Jack Lambert, Rocky Marciano, Andy Van Slyke, Steve Prefontaine and Pete Rose, to name a few. They were the guys who didn't have all the talent in the world but they worked hard and "hustled," as my dad used to always say.

As I got older, my idols turned into thinkers and advocates including Albert Einstein, Robert Kennedy, Frank Serpico and Abraham Lincoln. I looked up to them because they were often ridiculed and even hated by some because they were trying to influence change in society to make other people's lives better. They fought to make this world a better place and I can relate to that. Why not fight to make the world a better place?

I continue to fight for change. I have fought against bad guys; I have fought against the good guys. I have fought with drug dealers and I have fought with my fellow law enforcement brothers. I have fought against political corruption and I have fought against the justice system because it was the right thing to do. In this world we live in today, someone has to be the voice of truth.

We, as police officers, have a difficult job already apart from the politics behind the scenes that always seem prevalent. We are teachers, educators, confidants and, of course, the assholes. It is a fine line when dealing with the good of society and then chasing down a drug dealer who just sold a bundle of heroin to a pregnant 18-year-old girl. It is something police have to juggle, being the good guy to being the whipping boy. In today's society, it is cool to hate cops. It is cool to disrespect us and criticize us. It is almost socially acceptable to push back against the "establishment."

Yet this has been going on since the Sixties. "Us" versus "them." Although today, it has a more violent tone to it. Not only is it socially acceptable to push back, it is considered OK to strike back without expected recourse. Since when is it OK to celebrate a cop's death or ask a cop killer to speak at a college graduation as Evergreen State College in Washington, Goddard College in Vermont and Antioch College in Ohio did when Mumia Abu-Jamal spoke there.

Abu-Jamal was sentenced to death following a high-profile trial in Philadelphia for killing Officer Daniel Faulkner, a 25-year-old patrolman who scuffled with Abu-Jamal's brother during an early morning traffic stop. His sentence was later reduced to life in prison without parole. Abu-Jamal was a member of the Black Panther Party at the time. It goes to show not only how society's values have changed, but also how disrespected police officers are today. Today, it is OK to sell drugs. People don't care as long as it doesn't impact them directly. They turn a blind eye because no one wants to get involved. That's the mentality of today's generation and it is disheartening to say the least. Everyone hates us until they need us.

We are very rarely thanked, but always openly criticized. Some never put themselves in our shoes. Some never wonder about the safety of our family and our kids while we are out protecting yours. Regardless, police officers will continue to do their jobs because that is what we do. We wake up every morning hoping to make a difference in someone's life all the while praying we will make it home safe to our own family at the end of our watch. We are the good guys; don't ever forget that. We cannot let a few small apples ruin the bunch. We have chosen this path because we are the wolves! Someone has to be brave enough to fight the good fight against the bad guys. Someone has to have enough courage to battle the evil in our society. We are the police officers of America and we are damn proud of it!

So what makes me so special, you are asking yourself? Why do I think I can solve cold cases better than anyone else? First off, I don't think I am special and never, ever would say I am better than anyone else. I will say that looking at cases from a different set of eyes will breathe new life into a cold case. I am just a man, no better than you or anyone else. I like to say I have a PhD in determination and master's degree in perseverance. I rarely talk politics or religion because it causes conflict between so many. I don't pay attention to the news or current events anymore because if it isn't about the good in society, I don't want to hear about it. Unless, of course, they are talking about cold cases—that is the only news I care about.

I shun social media because I don't care about what people made for dinner or that someone needs to feel relevant by getting "likes" on social media posts. In fact, I feel that social media gives too many people the freedom to speak when they shouldn't. I am all about freedom of speech, yet some people need to be careful of what they say because they are ignorant on a subject and their comments only spread false rumors and misinform the public. Everyone is now a keyboard tough guy or girl. They can sit in their parents' basement with no job or education and spout off on subjects they are not educated enough to speak on. Here is a perfect example. I used Facebook to show a picture of some heroin I got off some kids from my hometown of Penns Valley. I was letting the parents of the Valley know what was coming back into their town, so don't turn a blind eye to the heroin business because it affects every town, no matter how big or small. Trust me; as you will read later, I know personally about the devastation that heroin can do! So this is the comment I get:

Did you offer them help ??????? Or just put them in jail. Because if ya didn't offer them help then you didn't do a good job. Putting an addict in jail only hushes the demons till they get out. I hope the hell they get the help they need because if not the person you took this from is going to die.

My retort:

Ms. Bower – I'm not looking for a pat on the back and conversely I'm not looking for someone to second guess or criticize my job performance. I was simply warning parents in my hometown of Penns Valley to be aware of this heroin problem (Most already know). These individuals were selling heroin and the law calls for them to go to jail or be charged at a later date for this crime and I emphatically concur. Regardless whether they are feeding their own addiction by selling the drug or selling for profit because they are too lazy to get a real job, they need to go to jail and answer to these charges....that is the law and that is why we have laws. Maybe...just maybe my actions saved a life in Penns Valley, Bellefonte or Spring Mills because they were unable to sell these bundles of heroin to their customers because we took it off of the streets! Maybe you have me confused with a social worker or counselor.. I am not sure? My job is to enforce the law and take the drugs off of the street which I did. The drug dealer or as you surmise, addict, can get the help and counseling they need if THEY CHOOSE to help themselves inside a jail cell or once inside the criminal justice system. But to answer your question, "Did I offer them help"...... No, I sure didn't....guess I didn't do a good job...but thanks for your opinion!

So another uneducated, non-qualified person chimes in on the subject. By non-educated, I don't mean schooling. I mean that they are not educated on the topic they are spouting off about. They don't know facts. I could care less if someone has a PhD or someone dropped out in eighth grade—to me, they both are human beings in which I will respect as equals.

I agree with you Ms. Bower! When their family loses someone to it, or a close friend/family loses someone, maybe they will understand ur point of view! Cops now and days, are no good in my eyes! Yes they do their jobs n get that bad off the streets, but in today's world, murders n rapists get less time than someone who gets busted for drugs! Wtf is that? They are the ones who need to be put away for awhile! The addicts around weither they want help or not, should at least be offered to them! I know that addict has to want the help in order for it to work, I am a recovering addict myself frm many types of drugs! Maybe once they get in there, they will hav a change of mind n a change of heart! Ya never know less its offered! SMDH!! This world is going to shit n fast!!!

I quickly realized that no matter what you say, you can never win a war of words on social media. It's not worth my time. So, I responded one final time to get my point across and move on. It was shortly after this that I stopped using Facebook.

Megan – It is great that you can express your opinion; in fact that is what makes America the Country it is today. Let me address your opinions one by one and back it up with some facts though. First, you say, "When their family loses someone to it, or a close friend/family loses someone, maybe they will understand ur point of view!" Well I have... so I do understand, enough said! Secondly, you say Cops are "No good in my eyes". Well my only retort to you on this is that I bet you won't feel this way when you need one but let me tell you something....there are thousands of good cops in this world and your opinion is just that...an opinion and you are certainly entitled to that! Thirdly you suggest that murderers and rapists get less time in jail than someone who gets busted with drugs....this statement is just not accurate and totally ignorant. Although I agree the justice system is not perfect and there have been occasions in the history of the justice system that a drug dealer has gotten more prison time then a rapist or someone who committed a homicide; each individual case is different and you cannot make a broad statement and believe in general that drug dealers or someone who is caught with drugs does more time than a murderer or rapist.....simply not true. Again, I support people's opinions because everyone has a different background and ideology; so in essence how one person views or deals with life is different than others. Yet, I have opinions too. My opinion is that drug dealers break the law and need to be charged and put through the criminal justice system, period. Drug users, when caught with drugs such as heroin, need charged and put through the criminal justice system as well. Do you know why? Because they KNOW that possessing that heroin is a crime yet they CHOOSE to commit that crime and break the law! Sure you will say that it is because they have a disease and must have it... which may be true. But once inside the system, they then can CHOOSE to get the help they need. Yes, addiction is a disease but it cannot be used as an excuse to break the law. If that were the case, then a man who commits a rape could use the excuse that he is addicted to sex; therefore cannot be held accountable for raping women. So even though I don't offer them help because I am not a social worker or counselor and I, as a cop, is "no good" in your eyes, will continue to do my job to protect the innocent and I will continue to uphold the law to the very best of my ability... regardless of inexact opinions.

I just want to be left alone and solve cold cases. That's it. As I like to tell people, I am a very simple creature, yet with a very complex mind with an innate ability to solve the unsolved. But in reality, I am just a confident yet humbled, old-school man who gets to live out his boyhood dream of chasing the bad guys and investigating cold cases.

THE MAKING OF
A DETECTIVE

"You are not here merely to make a living. You are here in order to enable the world to live more amply, with greater vision, with a finer spirit of hope and achievement. You are here to enrich the world, and you impoverish yourself if you forget the errand."

Woodrow Wilson

As my friend and legendary homicide detective Lt. Joe Kenda would say, "To be a good detective, you must have a natural curiosity." I guess for me, my curiosity started when I was a young boy, maybe about 10 years of age. Cold cases and mysteries have always intrigued me. Back then, when I was a kid, it was the Loch Ness Monster and Bigfoot. I was always curious about why there were so many eyewitness accounts of these mythical creatures, but no physical evidence. No bones washing up on shore of the great Loch and no hunter taken down a Bigfoot while out hunting. Yet, the aura of these beasts still exists.

Then as I grew older, my curiosity for what happened grew to D.B. Cooper, Jimmy Hoffa and Amelia Earhart. How could these individuals of such "prestige" just vanish into thin air? Someone somewhere had to have seen or heard something. My curiosity for the unknown continues today with cases such as JonBenét Ramsey, Dr. Jeffrey MacDonald, the JFK assassination, Dr. Samuel Sheppard, the Zodiac Killer, the Black Dalia case and the Keddie murders. Can you imagine my excitement decades later when the History Channel asked me to do a television series with them to solve the Zodiac murders. Albert Einstein once said, "The important thing is not to stop questioning. Curiosity has its own reason for existing."

When I was younger, I would read "Helter Skelter" by Vincent Bugliosi and want to interview Charles Manson, Susan Atkins, Patricia Krenwinkle, Leslie Van Houten and Tex Watkins. Picture my exhilaration 30 years later when I received a handwritten letter from Mr. Bugliosi praising my efforts solving cold cases. That letter now hangs in a frame on my office wall to remind me of where I came from.

When I was young, I would read incessantly about these killers, trying to get inside their heads. Books about the Hillside Strangler, the Night Stalker and, of course, Ted Bundy were all lined up on the bookshelf in my room. This was all in an effort to learn more about how they lived, how they talked, how they walked and how they got caught. I wanted to know everything about them so someday I knew what to look for when I would be investigating others like them.

However, being curious about these mysteries and being able

to actually investigate these cold cases without limitations are extremely different. A dream came true in 2007 when I began to actually investigate the mysteries I was so enamored with since childhood.

I grew up in a middle-class home with my parents, older brother and younger sister. The environment was a joyful and yet structured one. My parents rarely drank alcohol (certainly never in front of us) or did drugs and were very loving and doting parents. I could not imagine growing up in a better home or environment. My father owned a successful electronic repair shop and my mother was a housewife who raised the kids. I loved and enjoyed sports growing up. I was an avid wrestler and played baseball, basketball and football. I was particularly close with my father growing up and we would often be seen practicing baseball together and watching my favorite television show, "Unsolved Mysteries."

However, at age 15, things began to change in my life. I still read my true crime books about Charles Manson, Ted Bundy and Jeffrey MacDonald, wishing I could investigate these crimes. Yet, now my attention turned to alcohol, parties and chasing women. Not unlike a lot of male adolescents I might add, but I seemed to do everything in excess. My zeal for playing baseball or watching "America's Most Wanted" with my family had waned, replaced by women, alcohol and fighting.

Maybe a lot of youths go through these trying times. It is teenage angst that sometimes derails a dream. My dreams almost got derailed many, many times. I got involved with a girl who came from the wrong side of the tracks. My parents knew that. They could tell by looking at her. I thought I was a teenager in love. It took me years to figure out lust is not love.

HIGH SCHOOL

I grew my hair long and looked for fights to live up to a reputation my older brother had created. I lived on the edge while constantly searching for the next party. I was always looking to solve my problems with fists before words. I was cocky, arrogant and thought I knew it all. I was always taught by my father not to start a fight and not to swing first if I did get into a fight, but to finish the fight. I had a different philosophy when it came to fighting—always swing first to catch your opponent off guard in order to win. To me, that was the whole purpose of fighting.

My father, a United States Marine Corps and Vietnam veteran, did not approve of these changes in his son. However, he tried very hard to let me "live" my own life and make my own decisions. He hated that I had long hair and earrings. That was not his vision of a son. He hated that I was spending all my time with my girlfriend and not on the baseball diamond. Although I tried very hard to cling to my family and the sports that I loved so much, the party scene and my bad choices began to tear me away from my family, as it does to a lot of teenagers.

It is almost unfathomable to think back now, decades later, that my father and I are so much alike. I handle situations as he did, I think like him and I for sure look like him. I look back and realize what he and my mother had done for their kids. You take so many things for granted growing up. Looking back, I know now that they were without question the greatest parents I could have ever hoped for. My mother is the warmest and most giving woman I ever met. She routinely sacrificed her happiness for her family. My father is and always will be my idol. He is simply the greatest man I have ever met. I would not be the man I am today without the values and morals my parents instilled in me. They taught me that I could do anything I wanted as long as I worked hard. Yet, I was just a punk kid at age 17, thinking I knew everything.

At that age, I was kicked out of my home after a disagreement with my father. I had recently learned I was about to father a child with this "bad choice girlfriend" and this led to tension between father and son. He was afraid that this would derail his young son from his goals. It was a logical inference, but it was something I had zero control over. I was going to be a father; I just had to deal with it and continue to march on.

I lived in my friend's car for a week while still attending high school before I was able to secure a small apartment. I only went to school for half of the day during my senior year in high school and worked the other half at a restaurant washing dishes in order to support myself and my soon-to-be born son. This precluded me from playing any organized sports and only led to more drinking and partying. I eventually graduated from Penns Valley High School in Spring Mills, Pa., in 1992, second from last in the academic class standings. I always scored extremely high on my standardized testing, but I just didn't put forth the effort. Never brought my books to class and would sleep in class. I basically got by because I could pass the tests without studying.

My report card from my senior year showed that I missed 30 days of school and was tardy 15 other times. I was suspended, in school and out of school, on at least five occasions for various infractions. Although I knew I wanted to be a detective and investigate mysteries, I sure didn't prepare myself very well during my time in Penns Valley High School. I look back now and shake my head at how I treated some of the teachers. I was disrespectful because I didn't pay attention and slept in class. I even went back to my high school 20 years later and apologized to three of my teachers who were still there. So, imagine my bewilderment being asked back there 20 years later to talk to the students about following your goals.

> *"But the person who scored well on an SAT will not necessarily be the best doctor or the best lawyer or the best businessman. These tests do not measure character, leadership, creativity, perseverance."*
>
> *William Julius Wilson*

UNITED STATES MARINE CORPS

After graduating high school, my goal was set on one thing: I had always wanted to be a United States Marine. The dress blues, the swagger, the high and tights. I wanted to follow in my father's footsteps. He was my idol regardless of any disagreements we may have had growing up. I wanted to be just like him. He is the epitome of a role model and in my mind, he is the greatest man alive. But being a Marine—that was always the plan. I knew the reputation of the Marine Corps. Everyone knows the reputation of the Marine Corps. The Marine Corps takes all the bad asses and makes them indestructible killing machines. They are the best of the best and only the top percent can be Marines. These were all things instilled in me growing up about the Marine Corps. There was never another option. Boot camp at Parris Island was a huge eye-opener for me. Here I was in a room of teenagers who think they are bad asses. All of them are thinking they were the toughest in the room. I remember the drill instructors telling me to get off their bus—the rest is just a hazy memory.

I recall my dad saying to me the night before I left for boot camp, "Don't let them know your name. Don't stand out because you will have it twice as hard. Just do what you are supposed to do, no more no less." I listened and the tactic worked until halfway through boot camp.

Pugil sticks is an event that all Marines enjoyed. You are taking a stick and beating another person legally. What isn't to like about this form of aggression release?

On one hot day in August 1992, my platoon, 3106, had our first pugil stick event. The drill instructors matched their favorites and watched the fights as if they were betting on cockfights in Mexico. There was one event in which there was an octagon set up in the middle of the woods where the fight would take place. Each fighter would start out about 50 yards away in a clearing and run up separate paths and enter the ring to fight. Whomever got to the ring first had the advantage because they could surprise the other fighter.

As I waited my turn to enter, I started to creep ahead on the trail, trying to gather as much of an advantage as I could. My drill instructor whispered to me, "Start going." I started to move forward well before the whistle sounded and I had a good seven-yard head start up the path when the whistle finally blew.

I was always a fast runner so as I sprinted to the ring. I beat my opponent by about 10 seconds. As I entered, I saw the instructors and other spectators standing on platforms so they could see into the pit. I saw the doorway where my opponent would be entering into the ring. So, I crouched down next to the opening and waited for him. It was quiet, but I heard the unmistakable sound of footprints coming, leaves crunching beneath his running feet and someone breathing heavy. It was getting closer and closer. I saw the tip of his black combat boot and before he knew what hit him, I sprung up with all of my 140 pounds and hit the Marine under his chin with all of my might. He went down like he was shot. Out. This guy was out, snoring. It was the first time I ever knocked someone out cold. You could hear nothing. It was absolutely silent, unlike the cheering and hollering I was hearing before I entered the ring. It was complete and utter silence that seemed to last forever as I stood over my fallen foe. Then, all of a sudden, I heard my drill instructor say, "Who the hell are you?" I said—rather, mumbled—with my mouthpiece still in, "Recruit Mains, sir." He screamed, "Mains? That was fucking awesome." He gave me the platoon guide iron to carry home that night. Well, guess what—they knew my name now and boy, did they mess with me.

Anytime the drill instructors wanted to demonstrate anything, they would yell, "Mains, come here." Once, I was demonstrating how to do pull-ups and the DI made me pull myself over the metal bar, grab my belt loops and hold on. So I had this metal bar digging into my armpits for five minutes as all my weight was suspended onto this bar. Very painful and I was bruised for a couple of weeks. I realize now that when they picked on you, it was because they liked you. I find myself doing the same thing to people I like today.

On the rifle range, I was pulling targets down as my DI was walking past. I leaned backwards to get out of his way. He stopped in front of me and looked around to see if anyone was watching. As I was leaning backwards, he punched me square in the chest with all his might. He then looked me in the eyes and nodded. I nodded back. It was a sign of respect, nothing malicious, and I knew he was doing it to signal his approval of me. It is hard for some people to grasp this, but that was our way, the Marine Corps way.

However, it wasn't all cheery for me at boot camp. I recall the first week we got mail. It is the only thing you look forward to. We didn't receive mail for a while and when we did get it, everyone had numerous letters from home that first night. I got zero. I recall sitting on my footlocker watching everyone tear open their letters and smile reading about things back home. I didn't get a single letter and I felt as alone and sad as I ever had up until that point in my young life.

Eventually, when I wrote home and told my family how I didn't get any letters, they came in droves. My dad wrote me and sent me newspaper clips of sports scores every day. My mom, who wasn't the best speller, swallowed her pride and wrote me letters. My brother, sister and grandparents also wrote. My high school friend Jason Brooks took time out of his day to write me. I started to feel appreciated again and that I wasn't forgotten. Being away from my friends, family and newborn son was a crippling feeling but it was just another fight I had to win in order to obtain the goal. It was a truly magical experience to get those letters. The content of those letters were of no consequence, it was just that they wrote to make me feel better. That is what family does and that is why I love my family so much. They never realized how much those letters meant to me.

The very last day of boot camp we went on a six-mile run. About three miles in, the drill instructor called me out to do the cadence. It was such an honor and I was so shocked at this. I wasn't a rah-rah guy, never was and never will be. I kept quiet and just did my job to the best of my abilities. Yet, people noticed. That is when I knew what it took to be a leader.

I was stationed at Camp Lejeune, N.C., for my entire four years of service. The majority of the tour was with the II Marine Expeditionary Force (II MEF) Special Operations Training Group (SOTG).

SOTG consisted of a small, elite group of Marines who trained other units and made them Special Operations Capable (SOC). I possessed a secret clearance level and would gather and disseminate intelligence to my commanders while handling administrative duties for the entire unit. Some of the finest human beings I ever met in my life were on that beach in Onslow, N.C., with me! Matt West, John Buffin, John Bates, Carl Ake, Hannon Hardy (RIP), Nick John, Fernando Piza, Gerald Walters, John Lynch, Mike Holiday and last, but certainly not least, Lt. Col John Muth III (RIP).

I excelled in the Marine Corps and was routinely sought out for complex tasks and to assist high-level commanders. I received letters of commendations from many enlisted commanders and officers alike, including a high-level brigadier general who praised me for my work ethic, confidence and perseverance. That general, Martin Berndt, with whom I would lift weights in the morning, would be the same person who rescued Air Force Capt. Scott O'Grady when his jet was shot down behind enemy lines in Bosnia on June 2, 1995.

The Marine Corps was the absolute best thing that ever happened to me. It taught me discipline, courage, work ethic, leadership and accountability. Those were all attributes my father had already instilled in me, but the Marine Corps reinforced them.

However, my penchant for getting into trouble was still lurking around me constantly. One night while out, underage, drinking at a bar, I had swapped cars with my fellow Marine brother John Bates. Bates was as tough as they come. He was a special operations recon Marine who fought tough-man contests before the UFC was popular. His nickname was very appropriate, "Bad Man." This guy was built like a bodybuilder and could legitimately kick some ass in and out of the ring. I remember watching a tape of one of his fights and he hit this guy so hard it almost snapped his neck. I remember a bunch of us Marines sitting around this small television watching it and we kept rewinding it to see "Bad Man's" punch.

Anyway, I took his BMW this night with the personalized license plate SHINKICK. He in turn took my Jeep Wrangler to go to Myrtle Beach. My friend Hannon Hardy and I were driving back to our barracks on the beach after a late night at the bar where we imbibed in way too many adult beverages. I was driving "Bad Man" Bates' BMW at a very high rate of speed. As I pulled off the road into a dirt tank trail to urinate, I saw a gaggle of headlights come upon me. I then heard the sound of a voice coming across a speaker: "Driver, with your left hand, open the door and step out. Walk backwards toward the sound of my voice."

It was the military police and I just saw my entire career flash in front of my drunken eyes. I was thrown down and a knee placed on the back of my head while I ate the sand that my face was pushed into. I recall the police officer say, "Do you know how fast you were going?" I remained silent as the sand was matted to the side of my face.

My blood alcohol content was 0.14 percent, well over the legal limit of 0.10 percent. Not to mention I was underage and wasn't even able to legally drink alcohol. To top it off, I was clocked at 108 mph in a 45 mph zone.

Although I was sentenced to a suspended military probation period (as long as I didn't get in trouble in the next six months, it would be wiped from my record and I would receive no punishment), it didn't account for the encounter and temper of "Bad Man" Bates.

Bates busted into my room shirtless, muscles popping and said, "What the fuck, dude, going 108?" I looked at him calmly and, with my heart racing and a bit of confusion, said, "What? No, it was 78 miles per hour, dude." He said, "Oh," turned and walked back out the door. I was so close to being shin kicked and beat down and I would have deserved it. However, some quick wit and thinking saved me a possible beating.

I was still getting into trouble. Why couldn't I just stay out of trouble? I guess because I was thinking like legendary Marine Chesty Puller, who once said, "Take me to the brig where the real Marines are."

Working for SOTG was different than the other units. We were a small special operations unit and we didn't follow the rules as others had to. We PT'd (worked out and ran) on our own, lived alone and no one bothered us. Others had to get up at 5 a.m. and meet in formation to PT—we did not. We were "special" and did what we wanted. We lived on Onslow Beach as well with the Marine Corps Force Recon Unit. Everyone looked up to us, but oftentimes bad-mouthed us because they were jealous of what we had and what we could get away with. This prepared me for how others perceive people whom they are jealous of. It is a common thread among society to be jealous of something you cannot have. As my career advanced, I saw this jealousy first hand. It wasn't the last time I would be faced with these preconceived opinions.

*"I come in peace. I didn't bring artillery. But
I'm pleading with you, with tears in my eyes:
If you fuck with me, I'll kill you all."*

Gen. James Mattis, USMC (ret)

POST MARINE CORPS

In 1996, I returned home to Pennsylvania after being honorably discharged from the United States Marine Corps. I was changed; the Marine Corps has that effect on people. I was definitely more mature and focused, but I was still young. I immediately began to hang out with those same characters I had left in my wake four years ago. Most of them hadn't changed; they were still working dead-end jobs and blowing their paycheck on booze on the weekends. I joined right in to the fray. The street fighting and party scene was back as I again donned long hair and earrings to accompany me with my bottle of Yukon Jack. I wasn't an alcoholic by any stretch of the imagination. I rarely drank alcohol during the week and saved it for the weekend. But it was definitely done in excess. Everything I have ever done in life was done to excess. Yet, being back home after four years was even worse this time around because I had an even greater reputation to uphold. I was not spending a lot of times with my son, just the weekend overnights. Yet, even when he was with me for those two or three days, half that time I was out at the bars, leaving him with my parents. Looking back, I struggle with this and sometimes cry when I am alone, wishing I could go back and change my young thought process.

I was known as a bad ass before I left for Parris Island on Aug. 28, 1992, and my reputation and expectations tripled when I was a Marine. If I was in a bar with my brother or friends and some drunken patrons were getting loud, I was expected to shut them up. If a fight broke out in the bar, I felt I had an obligation to be in the middle of it. That was me, a hard-drinking, hard-partying fighter. Hell, I was a United States Marine. My drill instructors used to instill that into our heads, every single night.

Fighting always seemed to follow me around. It was a reputation I got from my older brother. He was known to be a great fighter and he had earned that reputation. I, however, had not really earned it when it was bestowed upon me at a very early age. The reputation came because of my brother. I remember going to high school and seniors would come up to me and call me "Little Mains" and say, "I bet you can fight like your brother."

Reputations are a funny thing. They allow you to be something you're not. That reputation makes you feel good until it comes time that you have to live up to that reputation. You either enhance that reputation by winning in dominant fashion or you lose it in one fast swoop. Fortunately, I never lost it. I recall upperclassman trying to make kids fight me and I would go along with it like a puppet, trying to live up to the reputation. Deep down inside, though, I didn't really want to fight. I was scared because I didn't know how yet. Eventually that changed, not the scared part because you are always scared, but eventually, I found out how to fight through the experience of fighting.

Fighting was a way to keep the reputation and allowed me to feel safe. After a few big fights, people got intimidated and I didn't have to worry much anymore. That is until the next guy who has just an established reputation as you comes along. Then you fight again. Eventually, as much as I liked the reputation as someone who you didn't mess with, I grew to hate it as well. It is funny because when I go back home, I still carry that reputation decades later. But because of that reputation, you become less liked or trusted because people may see you as mean and that is the farthest from the truth. Yet, there is always someone bigger and badder than you are or who you are perceived to be. Always. I was just lucky not to run up against someone who was better at the time.

Yet, regardless of reputations, I was never going to be a professional fighter. Mike Tyson had nothing to worry about because the punk kid wasn't coming after him. I always knew I wanted to be a detective and investigate unsolved cases; this never changed since childhood. I also was aware I wouldn't accomplish that living alone in the middle of the woods partying with people who were going nowhere in life. These were people who were not necessarily bad people, they were good people who just had no desire to be the best and I wouldn't settle for anything less. As Oregon and track and field legend Steve Prefontaine would famously say, "To give anything less than the best is to sacrifice the gift." I believed in this wholeheartedly. I had a gift to investigate the unsolved. I wasn't going to let it go to waste.

I finally realized that if I wanted to fulfill my boyhood dream of becoming a detective and investigate cold cases in law enforcement,

I had to go to college and further my education. As much as you think the military helps you—and it does—it is not a substitute for a college education. So, in 2000, I put myself through college at the Lock Haven University in Lock Haven, Pa., studying criminal justice. I routinely made the dean's list for academic excellence while maintaining an above-average GPA. Not bad for someone who graduated second to last in his high school class. It just goes to prove that when you want something, it is easier to learn because it is not forced on you. I wanted to learn and it was something I needed in order to make a better life for my son and me. I remember my friends used to pick on me growing up because I would read a different encyclopedia every night. Where else could you find that amount of varied information on different subjects? To me, it satisfied my curiosity for the night and it allowed me to become well versed in my educational upbringing.

In 2003, while in my junior year of college, I took my first and only police exam. It was for the Williamsport Bureau of Police in Williamsport, Pa. I placed second out of approximately 75 applicants and was offered the job. Initially, I was hesitant to accept the position because I had not finished college yet and knew it would be hard to pick it up again if I did decide to leave. After speaking about the situation with my father, whom I still maintained a close relationship with and is my biggest inspiration, I decided to take the job as a police officer for the Williamsport Bureau of Police Department.

It was a decision that quite possible saved my life and hopefully impacted others. This decision forced me to behave or at least forced me from my hometown and from the peer pressures located there. Yet, as usual, my proclivity to go home and hang with my "boys" almost derailed this dream before it could barely get started.

While still on probation with the Williamsport Police Department as a new hire, I went back to my hometown to hang out with my old friends and have a few drinks. A stupid decision to drive home to sleep in my own bed almost cost me a career. I was pulled over by a fellow police officer. He felt I was incapable of safe driving and I could have probably gotten arrested for driving under the influence. When he asked for my driver's license, I showed him my badge. He went back to his car as I sat and waited, believing my career was over. However, the cop emerged from his patrol car and asked me where I lived. I told him Williamsport, which was about 45 minutes from where we were sitting along the road. He put me in the front seat of his patrol car and drove me home. No questions, nothing spoken, just took me home. I don't know who the police officer was, but he saved my career. Was it a cop sticking up for another cop? You bet it was. Was it the right decision on his part? I don't know, but I am still extremely grateful for what he did for me that cold night in 2003.

Because of that incident, I stopped going back home to hang out with my friends. I learned that if I wanted to follow my dreams, I had to get away from that town. This decision gave me a career in law enforcement and allowed me to stay focused on my goal of being a detective and investigating the unsolved. I very easily could have been on the other side of the law with all the partying, fighting and bad choices. Then, once a dream is crushed, it is way too easy to give up on the world. I would hope I would not have … but I don't know. I can say, scoring that high on the police exam, getting that job and that cop taking me home when I should have been arrested definitely had an impact on where I am today.

I left college in 2003, without my coveted degree. In 2011, I finished what I started and obtained my criminal justice degree. In addition, I began my master's degree in forensic criminology with an emphasis on criminal profiling. Because of my parents' emphasis on never quitting and finishing what you start, I was able to become the first person in my entire family history to graduate from college. Since then, I have had a niece who has graduated from college and is doing what she loves. I would like to hope part of that is because she saw her uncle do it.

"What you get by achieving your goals is not as important as what you become by achieving your goals."

Henry David Thoreau

So, in January 2003, I left for Harrisburg to begin formal training to become a police officer. This concept, me being a cop, was looked upon in disbelief by some. I was no angel growing up and into my early twenties. But I always felt that the experience on the other side of the tracks would help me relate to crime and, in some cases, the criminals themselves. So, it was a bit ironic at the Police Academy, I was elected class president and was appointed as the first-class lieutenant in charge of the entire class. I can assume I was chosen because I was older and had more education than most of the others. I was 29 at the time, had been in the Marine Corps for four years and had three years of college under my belt. At the end of the Police Academy, my most humbling award was being voted the "Best Leader" by my fellow academy recruits.

I think I earned a lot of respect after being called upon to assist in a demonstration of defensive tactics by the tactical instructor. He called me up to demonstrate a particular finishing move to utilize when wanting to take down a bad guy. After you lock up, or grab hold of each other, he would basically knee the side of your thigh, on your femur, a very debilitating move that will bring most anyone down. Well, after he started to demonstrate it and I didn't go down as he expected, the instructor became embarrassed. I wasn't trying to embarrass him; I just don't give in easy. He began to knee me harder and harder while attempting to get me to drop to the ground. He kept kneeing me, saying, "Go down, just go down." I whispered into his ear as he was kneeing me, "I don't go down for anybody."

"Pain is temporary; pride is forever."

A Marine Corps motto I believe in

Eventually, he tired out and was left staring at me as he just shook his head. The entire class began to clap as I was helped back to the locker room. My thigh ballooned up and was black and blue for a week. How he did not break my leg is beyond me, but through the beating, I got much respect. I wasn't trying to be tough; I just couldn't change a philosophy that had been instilled in me since birth in order to appease the ego of an instructor. I don't give up, I don't quit and I don't go down for anyone. That is my mentality.

After graduation from the Police Academy, I worked as a patrolman for the Williamsport Bureau of Police from 2003–05. The new uniform, the gun, the radio strapped to your hip. The shiny boots that never again will look that shiny, the police patch and short haircut. It was almost like being in the Marine Corps again—almost! One thing that was different ended up being the very thing I missed the most: brotherhood. This department did not have it. It was cutthroat, dysfunctional, cliquey and sad.

However, it took me a few years to learn the bad and dysfunctional aspects about the department. In the beginning, I didn't know what the word "political" meant. I just wanted to arrest the bad guys. I just wanted to be a detective. However, in order to do that, you must start somewhere else. You have to work your way up to detective. It is something not given; it is earned. This means you must start in patrol. Just as every Marine is a rifleman, every cop is a patrolman. Patrol is the backbone of any police department and I loved the aspect of hunting down the bad guy. Patrol was great, but my eye was always on detective and investigations.

I remember my patrol commander, Lt. Glenn Ardrey, telling me that I was a phenomenal investigator for my relative inexperience. He even requested that I work investigations for the patrol shift. There was talk to specially assign me to the Detective's Unit as a patrol officer. This ruffled some feathers because I was a new officer. Of course, the Fraternal Order of Police (FOP) quashed that idea. The union argued it took a paid position away from another officer who should be promoted to that position and it wasn't fair to me to be doing detective work getting paid as a patrolman. I didn't care. I just wanted to investigate and I wanted to tell the FOP to mind its own business. It wasn't long before I realized that the FOP controlled the police department.

Early on in my career, I was given the nickname "Serpico" by my sergeant. I am not sure if he meant it in a negative manner, but I took it as a compliment. He was referring, of course, to Frank Serpico, a New York City police officer whose career was well-documented in Peter Maas's best-selling biography and in the Academy Award-nominated film, "Serpico," in which Al Pacino portrayed him. Serpico's career as a plainclothes detective working in Brooklyn and the Bronx to expose vice racketeering was short-lived, however, because he swam against the tide of corruption that engulfed the NYPD during the late Sixties and early Seventies. Not only did he consistently refuse to take bribes for "looking the other way," he risked his own safety to expose those who did. In 1967, he reported to appropriate officials "credible evidence of widespread, systemic police corruption."

It was not until April 1970, however, when The New York Times published an explosive story, that Mayor John Lindsay took action and appointed the Knapp Commission to investigate. As a consequence of his testimony before the commission, Serpico was ostracized by his peers and, many believe, ultimately set up to be shot during a drug raid in which he was seriously wounded and his fellow officers did not call for assistance. He resigned from the NYPD and spent the next 10 years living abroad, recovering from his wounds, traveling and learning.

Although my experiences within the criminal justice system and police department were not identical, they were similar in a way. I felt ostracized all of the time because of my penchant for saying what I felt and standing up for what was right, regardless of the consequences. I believe I was given that nickname because that is how I felt. We, as police officers, need to be held to a higher standard and we cannot be hypocrites! If that means being a "whistleblower," so be it. The public deserves that from its public servants.

I never cared what others thought, I just wanted to investigate and be a detective. I was assigned burglaries as a patrol officer. I was assigned equivocal deaths—deaths that were not classified as natural, suicide or homicide—as well as drug deaths. I was also assigned to do crime scene work. These assignments pissed off other guys because it pulled me off patrol and it short-handed them on shift. I never liked that because I felt that we needed more guys on shift to answer calls. When you run from call to call, you never have time to get your reports done for the shift, which becomes a domino effect and you feel that you are always behind. It is also, more importantly, a safety issue as well. If something bad happens—and it can at any given moment—you want guys on the street to keep the public and your fellow officers safe.

I remember being shorthanded on patrol once and hearing police dispatch a unit to a section of town that I was not currently patrolling. It was a very busy night and we were running all over the place answering calls. The call was for a drunk in the middle of the street shouting profanities. It wasn't my call and I didn't have to take it, but I was close and I didn't mind helping out my brother officers. There are some officers who purposely do not get to the scene first because they don't want to write a report. They will circle the area until they hear another unit radio that they are on scene. Yes, there are lazy cops who do this.

On this particular call, I arrived on Maynard Street in Williamsport looking for this unruly and loud man. It did not take me long to spot him. He was walking down the middle of the street at about 10 p.m. with cars beeping their horns at him. I activated my lights and approached the gentleman. I asked him what he was doing. He walked at very fast pace toward me, got right in my face and said, "Jesus saves." As much as I would have loved to listen to his religious ramblings, the odor of an alcoholic beverage on his breath told me that it was time for this guy to be put to bed.

I grabbed his left arm and managed to get a cuff on him telling him he was under arrest for public intoxication and disorderly conduct. He looked me straight in the eyes and said, "You are the devil," and swung his right hand at my head. Wow, I thought, this guy was just spewing rhetoric about Jesus saving and now I'm the devil. As he swung, I instinctively ducked and punched him in the face. He continued yelling religious oddities at me all the while I'm telling him to stop resisting that he was under arrest. He kept yelling and swinging and I kept ducking and hitting him in the face, but he wasn't dropping. Not only wasn't he falling down, he was talking to me while I was hitting him. I felt like Joe Frazier fighting Ali; the guy wouldn't shut up no matter how much I was hitting him. I had a hold of the one cuff and I would pull him toward me, then I struck him in the face, adding an extra level of impact and ensuring he wasn't going to get away.

Eventually, I got worried. It was the first time it flashed in my head that my life was in danger as a cop. I just wanted to arrest this guy and move on with the rest of my shift. But now, I was in a life-or-death battle with a guy who wanted to physically injury me. I was able to reach my radio with my free hand and ask for help. I said out of breath, "County, send me another unit."

The sound I heard within the next minute was a sound I will never forget! That sound alone made me proud to be a cop. It was the sound of police engines. The revving of engines. Cops were coming to my aid and they were coming fast. I heard them coming. A police engine has a distinct sound and I will never forget that sound coming to my aid. This was the first and probably only time I felt "the thin blue line." I felt the camaraderie for the first time. The one thing I missed more than anything leaving the Marine Corps was the camaraderie.

But on this day, as I was hitting the man in an effort to survive the assault, I was getting tired. There is nothing worse than getting tired in a fight. Especially a fight that could end with your life being taken. I was exhausted and this guy was still swinging and wrestling with me. I saw headlights and heard a car door open and the rattling of handcuffs from a distance. That "thin blue line" was coming to save me. Yes, I thought to myself, back-up has arrived. Just at that exact time, I hit the guy one final time and it knocked him backward and he tripped over a railroad tie. As I fell on him to knee him in the head, I missed and caught his ear. It came off. I remember thinking, "Wow, I just ripped this dude's ear right off his head. Wild."

We had one female officer on the force at that time. Of all the people I wanted to be there to help me control this guy, it wasn't her. But as fate would have it, she was the first one there to help me and she jumped right in the mix. Not only did she fight, she deployed a whole can of pepper spray in the guy's face and where his ear used to be. I was able to get the other cuff on him and by then, other units had arrived. The battle lasted no more than four minutes, but it felt like an eternity. As I watched him get loaded into the ambulance, I remember the supervisor say to me, "We knew it must have been bad if you called for help." Not surprisingly, the guy was wanted in another state for assaulting a police officer.

A few days later at the preliminary hearing for this guy, he came up to me in the hallway and apologized. He said he was smoking crack and taking PCP that night. I shook his hand and told him I had no hard feelings; he was the one who had to live with one ear the rest of his life.

Yet incidents like this will have critics and pundits saying, "Well, wasn't there another way to solve this, without physically assaulting the man?" My answer is yes, I could have shot him and most likely would have been justified. The streets are a mean and dangerous place. I received the Gallantry Star Medal from the Williamsport police after a guy tried to stab two of my fellow officers and me when we attempted to take him into custody. We could have shot him and it would have been justified. Fortunately, we used pepper spray and a few punches to disarm him without anyone getting seriously hurt. When the police tell you to do something, you do it. When we try to legally arrest you, don't resist. If you run or resist, someone will get hurt. If you do get hurt, there should be absolutely zero sympathy for you and the media should not put you in the spotlight as an unsuspecting victim because the police legally tried to arrest you and you resisted. Maybe we should just let all the criminals resist and run from us and only arrest the ones who turn themselves in; maybe that will solve the problem for all the critics. The bottom line is do not resist the police and everyone will go home unharmed. That is life in patrol—mean, dirty, dangerous and always scrutinized.

DRUG TASK FORCE

In 2006, I was hand-picked by the chief of police and captains of the Williamsport Bureau of Police and assigned to the Lycoming County Drug Task Force as an undercover officer. I grew my hair out (once again) past my shoulders, pierced both ears (once again) and played the drug part by going to bars every week, drinking to excess and making connections to the drug trade. This all came pretty natural to me, but was no doubt a risky endeavor both professionally and personally as there is a fine line between good and evil.

One of my first undercover experiences made me probably the most scared I have been doing drug work. I remember buying an ounce of cocaine from a middleman who was cooperating with us. I went to his small two-room apartment and he let me in. He was about 300 pounds, naked and in a wheelchair. He had open sores all over his body and his ceiling had blood on it from junkies cleaning their needles.

Regardless of his appeal, he made a call to the drug dealer for me. The black male arrived a short time later, handed naked guy the coke, who in turn gave it to me. Simple, easy, no issues, done deal.

I took the coke back to the office and put it in evidence. After doing the reports and required paperwork, I had the bright idea, "Well that was so easy. Let's go do it again." So I called the naked wheelchair guy up again and told him to set up another deal. He said, "It has only been two hours. You couldn't have done all that coke. He will know something is up." I said, "Let me worry about that."

So, I proceed back to the apartment where I just was a couple of hours ago. I am wearing a wig because I just got assigned to the drug unit from patrol and I yet to grow my hair out. When I entered the small apartment, there are two females in their twenties blowing lines of cocaine off the dining-room table. So I sit down—mind you, it is 10:30 a.m.—and I crack open a beer. I asked naked guy if he called the "hook." He said he did and he should be there shortly.

I had two officers doing surveillance from across the street, about 100 yards away. As always, I told them that if shit went sideways, I would throw something through the glass window—a chair or a person, it didn't matter which. That would be their cue to come get me.

About halfway through my beer, the door opened and in walked the drug dealer. He was followed by another thug, and another, and another and another. "Oh, shit," I was thinking to myself.

Remember, I am in a small, two-room apartment that can only fit about four people and now my dealer just came in with his whole crew. As I looked at each one coming in, I recognized three of the four as dealers I had arrested while on patrol only months before. My heart sank. As they stared at me and nodded their heads, I just knew I was done.

The crew and the middleman went to the kitchen to talk. As they talked, they turned and looked at me while I sat and nervously drank this piss-warm beer, trying to blend in with the party girls.

The drug dealer called me into the room and I see gun butts in the waistbands of two crew members. All I could think of for some reason was that they were gonna pull my hair and my wig would come off. The things you think of in a pressure situation like this always amazed me. Trying to think ahead, plan for everything and have an answer for whatever they ask or whatever happens.

He said, "You want another ounce? What happened to the shit you just got?" I said, "Man, I took that shit back to Lock Haven at the college and sold it already. I had people waiting for that."

He nodded and told me to hold out my hand. I said, "Why, what's up?" He reached into his coat pocket and pulled out a solid, softball size rock of cocaine and grabbed a butter knife off of the counter. He then proceeded to break rocks off into my opened hand, without weighing or bagging it. He said, "Look about right?" I said, "Yup."

The crew walked out and I felt a huge relief. The girls who saw this whole deal go down now became my best friends. It is obvious I just became a whole lot more attractive with an ounce of cocaine in my possession.

They wanted to know where I was going and could they come party with me. I was feeling a lot of relief and I had let my guard down a bit. I didn't realize I was still dealing with drug addicts who had probably been up for 24 hours and paranoia was creeping into their subconscious.

I said, "No, I gotta leave and go sell this. I'm not really a user, just a seller." One of the girls said, "OK, well, if you change your mind, here is our numbers." I took their numbers and said, "Be careful when you leave here." She looked at me immediately and said, "Why did you say that?" I said, "Um, because if you are fucked up driving, you don't want the police to fuck with you." Her paranoia was now full-blown, "Are you a cop? That is something a cop would say." I said, "Shut the fuck up. Do I look like a cop, you crazy bitch? I'm out of here." So I left before my luck ran out.

Once I met with my surveillance team, I told them to take down the girls when they left because they were good looking and I knew they would make good snitches. Drug dealers love selling to good-looking drug addicts.

So, they waited on them to leave, which was a few hours later, and pulled them over. Both had cocaine; the mouthy one thought she was slick and had it hidden in the drawstring area of her hoodie, but we found it.

When she saw me at the police station, she didn't recognize me. I put the wig on in front of her and she couldn't believe it. I smiled and walked away. That is narcotics.

Although this professional life was excelling, the lifestyle and drug assignment took its toll on my personal life. My wife left and divorced me in 2007. If that weren't enough bad news, my unit, the Lycoming County Drug Task Force, was being investigated for possible corruption. I had only been in the unit for five months before an investigation got under way because my lieutenant and police chief decided to take a drug dealer's confiscated truck to Canada for a fishing trip. The very same truck I helped confiscate. It is funny, at the time they were two of the people I looked up to very much, especially the police chief. He was a fellow Marine, he treated me with respect and he led by example. He was a great, great role model. But he was arrogant. He felt he did nothing wrong. He honestly felt that it was OK to take this confiscated truck on vacation because he was just a passenger. Not only did they take the truck on a fishing trip out of the country, they installed a trailer hitch on it to haul a personal boat. Wow, talk about arrogance. That is what happens when you have no one to keep you in check; you start to feel like you can get away with any and everything.

Then lie about it. That is exactly what the lieutenant did by saying he took the truck to talk to the Royal Canadian Mounted Police about drugs. Wow. Just take your medicine and move on. Don't dig yourself in deeper by the lie.

The mayor at the time who hand-picked the police chief demoted him and put him back on patrol as a supervisor (his last rank before becoming part of the administration). The district attorney, who was friends with my lieutenant, recused himself from the investigation and turned the matter over to the Attorney General's Office. That says a lot about that man's integrity. He could have easily swept that under the rug, but he did the right thing. He should be commended for that.

My direct supervisors, a corporal and lieutenant, were eventually arrested for various crimes while assigned to the Lycoming County Drug Task Force. My corporal, a squared-away, super-fit good cop, someone who does the job with integrity and respect, was arrested for covering for his lieutenant and taking a television from a drug dealer to use it at home. My corporal was fired from the police department, but worked out a deal that included collecting his full 20-year pension. Not bad for a guy who was arrested and convicted of a crime while working to uphold the law.

I recall being in a bar when he was awaiting trial on the charges. A bunch of us cops were on one side of the bar and he was alone on the other. None of the other cops liked him, never did really because they felt he got things handed to him too quickly and was assigned to the drug unit. They were basically jealous of him, but his arrogance was radiating as well. I, too, would come to feel that very wrath later in my career. Yet I went over to talk to him because that is the type of person I am. I don't care that everyone else shuns you. You are still someone I looked up to and respected. We hung out together, drank beer together and had each other's backs. I wouldn't be a man if I didn't talk to him. So I went over and shook his hand and asked him how he was doing. I hadn't seen him for a few years at this point, as this whole trial process was being strung out. We talked, but I immediately noticed his arrogance had tripled since I last talked to him. He had always been somewhat arrogant, but most cops are. But this was above and beyond.

So, I cut the conversation short by saying, "Hey, I just wanted you to know I am thinking about you and you were a good cop. I looked up to you." He said, "Damn right I was a good cop. I was the best cop in North Central PA."

Whoa. Really? OK, well, I just saw something come out of him that made me ill on the spot. He said, "You know you rode my coattails." I became immediately offended and pissed off. Here I was coming over trying to make him feel less uncomfortable given his situation and surroundings, offering my empathy and support, and he went there. I said, "Well, if you have something against me, we can go outside and settle it." My old high school mentality came out. That mentality reared its ugly head when alcohol was involved. He just looked at me and didn't say a word, so I went back over to the non-suspended cop section of the bar to continue with my beer.

This was a guy who I called every Christmas after the investigation into him started just to make him feel good and he tried to belittle me. I guess maybe he was just drunk, but those feelings usually come from a place deep inside and alcohol just has the ability to reach in and pull them out. I have lost no sleep over what happened to him.

My lieutenant ended up going on trial and being convicted of some forgery type of charges. He basically confiscated a drug dealer's car and then sold the cars to his friend who in turn sold the cars back to him. Not all the time, but he did it a couple of times and a couple of times is twice too many. It was certainly unethical and obviously criminal. During the trial, he acted as his own attorney and cross-examined me on the stand about my time in the drug unit and whether I ever saw him do anything criminal. I spoke truthfully as I always do. Afterward, in the hallway, he shook my hand and thanked me saying, "Thanks for telling the truth, a lot of the other guys didn't." I told him, "That's all I can do and all I will ever do." He was found guilty and fired from the Williamsport Bureau of Police.

There is no such thing as a crooked cop; you're either a crook or a cop." Frank Serpico

Looking back, I view things differently than I did then. None of the three were railroaded. They all had the very same qualities that bring down most who decide to exude that characteristic: hubris. All three were great cops at one point in time; I will never deny them that. But they all got fair punishment for the black eye they gave the Williamsport Police and Lycoming County law enforcement.

So, while the investigation was ongoing, all of the narcotics unit officers who were assigned to the unit were removed—except one.

I was the only police officer who did not get arrested or removed from the unit, although no one else had anything to hide, either besides the two afore mentioned supervisors. My peers and superiors knew my integrity was above reproach and I was asked to stay and somehow keep the unit running. "If you don't have integrity, you have nothing. You can't buy it. You can have all the money in the world, but if you are not a moral and ethical person, you really have nothing," Henry Kravis said once. He is 100 percent correct.

I recall once having been asked to destroy some evidence that was taken from drug dealers. There was a huge pile of things including clothing, CDs, electronics, papers, phones, etc. We had court orders, so it was all going to the dump and completely legal. There was a cell phone I was getting ready to throw into the dump, but it had a cover on it. The phone was the same model as my work phone and I needed a cover. This was going into the dump, so what the hell, I took it. I put the cover on my phone and continued working. About 15 minutes later, the phone was lying on my desk. I was typing a report, but I glanced up and saw the phone with the new cover. I got up, took the phone cover off and threw it in the garbage. I remember specifically saying to myself right then and there, "That's where it starts."

With the help of Lycoming County Det. Ed McCoy, whom I have a tremendous amount of respect for, from the District Attorney's Office, we took on the work of six investigators to keep the unit running and continued to arrest drug dealers and make the community safe. My integrity was never compromised or brought into question and I excelled in this new position. McCoy let me run the show. Although on paper he was in charge, he knew little about drug work. He never came in and said, "This is the way it is going to be." He relied on me, just as a good supervisor does. We made it work and he was a great partner. We ran the drug unit the way it should be, with cooperation from all law enforcement in the county. We made everyone feel a part of it, not just four or five guys running roughshod over the city. But drug work is not for everybody. All cops have their niche. Traffic, investigations, administration, interviews—we all have a niche. My niche in

2006 was undercover drug work. Yet my goal was still detective and cold cases.

I ended up returning to the drug world and taking over the head role within this unit in 2016. I was chosen to run the narcotics unit for the county as the Lycoming County Drug Task Force Coordinator even though I stated I would never go back to that world. It was a difficult decision for me to make for many reasons. First off, I did not like doing drug work anymore because you get burned out. You arrest drug dealers who run and fight you and a year later, they are back on the street and you are arresting them again. It gets to be a joke. Second and most important was the death of my only son. Many people do not know the son that I had in high school died. I stave off embarrassment that my only son was using heroin. I fend off shame that I couldn't stop it. I had to swallow my pride in order to help others.

Three years later as I am writing this book, the pain is still there, a constant reminder to me of being a failed father. I stand there, looking intently into the mirror—staring into the eyes that will not allow me to forget. I continually shake my head, a constant reminder of despair and disbelief. How did I let this happen? How could I not know? I'm a cop, for God's sake—even more than that, I was a narcotics officer for many years working with the Williamsport Bureau of Police, FBI and DEA. I know drugs—inside and out. Hell, I've been qualified as an expert on illegal narcotics in the courts of the Commonwealth of Pennsylvania. I've arrested hundreds of drug dealers and users alike. I've preached this to him. I've showed him literature and examples of what happens when you do drugs. I have told him the type of person you will become if you do drugs. I shake my head and say out loud, "I freaking told you!" How did this happen?

Not my boy!

Not my boy, who would flash up and down the basketball courts and make others look like amateurs when they tried to defend him. I recall sitting there watching him overtake a game by himself. He was masterful, if not brilliant, on that court. I was never prouder of anything in my life. Pride has a way of making your stomach tighten and your jaw hurt from smiling. It made tears run down my face. That's my boy! As I close my eyes, tears streaming down my face … I still see him. Smiling, playing and running around without his shirt with a ball in his hand. The warm summer breeze gently blows his light brown hair as he sheepishly asks, "Dad, wanna play catch?" I see it as if it just happened yesterday, in slow motion, that coy smile emanating off his beautiful face. That impressionable twinkle in his eye looking at me with admiration. That's my boy.

I open my eyes and stare back into that mirror. Those tough, haunting eyes stare back at me. They exude confidence and determination to the outside world, but they hide the pain and anguish lurking deep within.

Yet I answer my son out loud while looking back into the mirror, "Of course I wanna play catch … you're my boy!"

That is why I chose to come back into the drug world and arrest drug dealers and other heroin users. Because I know there are thousands of parents out there who feel my anguish. Heroin can take hold of anyone, regardless of race, religion or upbringing. I am a living, breathing example of it.

I used to think regret was a wasted emotion. Regret is something I will forever carry with me until the day I die. No matter what anyone will ever say or what anyone will ever do, I will always carry this burden on my shoulders. It is a father's job to protect his child. I failed.

I failed.

Regardless of what any counselors, friends and family say, I failed as a father and no one will ever make me feel any different. This is something that I will carry around me until I join my son in death. This is the punishment that has been doled out to me by the gods and I accept those consequences. Yet I have chosen to take that failure and feed my fire and passion to do right in this world for others—and my only begotten son.

LEADERSHIP

It was my desire to lead men into battle that overcame my doubts

I had as a failed father going back to work in the narcotics unit. I could not lead my son, what makes me think I can lead others? It is this self-doubt I had to face in order to succeed as a leader. I was there from 2006 to 2008 as an undercover officer, but his time I would be the one in charge of the unit. In addition, my two best friends from the Williamsport Police were assigned to the unit. Jeremy Brown and Justin Snyder didn't need anyone to lead them into battle; they were well versed on the topic themselves. However, they did need someone who thought as they did and had the same warrior mentality. It was a perfect match.

Being in charge of your friends is a hard job in itself. Joe Kenda told me when I called him for advice not to be their friend, be their boss. It was sound advice, but how to do that when you're already friends with them, I thought. You have to rely on them to do the right things and produce so you don't have to discipline them. It is a very fine line maintaining friendship and running an effective unit. Not to mention the other six detectives that you hire and eventually form bonds with. However, it is the person who can balance friendship and make the right decisions for the unit and the community who will become an effective leader. Leadership is something I work very hard to maintain. To lead men and women into battle and know that they trust you with every decision is a responsibility I revel in. You must lead by example. A leader has to be willing to do what they task their men to do. A good leader also surrounds themselves with good talent. People who will tell him when he is wrong, not people who are "yes men." A good leader must always be the first one to work and motivate them to be the best. People will get comfortable in their environment and that is when the work becomes sloppy. A good leader must at all times rein them in when they start to get to loose. You never want to micromanage and when you hire good employees, you never have to. But you do have to give them enough slack to let them build confidence in themselves. Every now and again, you will have to settle them down or discipline them, but when they respect you, there are no hard feelings—it is what needs to be done.

A great leader will build confidence in their men and women by reminding them that second place isn't good enough for them; they can be better than that. A great leader doesn't allow internal conflicts to spill to external units. What happens in-house stays in-house. That is how camaraderie is built and that is how you get a team to trust you as a leader. Nothing is ever swept under the rug, but a leader disciplines his men/women, never having someone else do it. It is little things like looking them in the eyes when you discipline them and patting their back when you praise them. Both have to be done in order for them to not become too comfortable. It keeps that fire in their belly and reminds them as to why they chose this profession.

Another underappreciated art of leadership is the ability to make decisions. A leader must be able to make quick, but not hasty, decisions and stick with those decisions. If that decision doesn't work, the leader must own up to it and not blame anyone else.

That is why I love leadership. I loved when I was following a great leader and know now that I am fortunate enough to lead others. It is an art and it is something you either have or don't have. It is a natural instinct to keep marching forward in the face of adversity for a leader. Others will crumble or subside. It takes a strong leader to fight through all the battles with his men in order to accomplish the mission. It allows you to succeed and that is what is most important about leadership—to succeed.

UNDERCOVER WITH THE FBI

Undercover work is a way of life. The earrings, the long hair, the stale beer breath in the morning. Waking up beside whatever cop groupie hung on you long enough the night before. It is a way of life! Yet most cops at the Williamsport Bureau of Police didn't get that, especially the older ones. If you were not suffering in a patrol car as they were, they talked behind your back—well, most of them. They wanted you to be as miserable as they were!

In 2008, the Federal Bureau of Investigations (FBI) approached me. They were recruiting me. The FBI was recruiting me. I was astonished. The FBI asked if I was interested in working for its Safe Streets Task Force as an undercover agent. I initially declined the offer because I was content working in the Lycoming County

Drug Task Force, but then realized that working for the FBI was something that I just couldn't pass up and quickly reconsidered. Here I was going to be working for the premiere law enforcement entity in the world. A punk who fought too much, drank too much and barely finished high school was now going to be working with the FBI! J. Edgar was rolling over in his grave.

I recall going into the office every morning and looking at the plaque on the secure door and seeing, Office of the Federal Bureau of Investigations. I could not believe I was working for the FBI. I would literally shake my head in amazement going into the office and smile because I loved it! It was during this time I got a small taste of the mafia. The mafia or *La Costra Nostra* (American mafia) has ties to Lycoming County going back several decades. You doubt this? Well, you are not the only one, as the local police departments didn't believe it, either.

Although I was working undercover for the FBI investigating violent crimes and in particular illegal narcotics, I was more fascinated with the mafia's connection to Lycoming County. I was able to access records with the FBI that bolstered my assertion that the mafia existed in Williamsport. In particular, I was able to research famed mafia boss Russell Bufalino and his connection to Jimmy Hoffa's disappearance. Hoffa, the union leader who was enemies with Robert Kennedy Jr. and had mafia ties while head of the Teamsters, was last seen on July 30, 1975. This isn't anything new, but Bufalino's ties to Williamsport and the established people in the small town was new to me. The amount of influence that the American mafia had in that tiny town of Williamsport still amazes me to this day.

It was my investigation into a small-time drug and prostitution case that led me to the mafia-related activities in Lycoming County. That is how investigations begin and fester to something larger. It is like a tree and the investigation starts at the roots. The roots are the drug dealers and prostitutes. But as your investigation deepens, the investigation goes up the tree to many branches where you uncover larger players and conspiracies. It was on this tree I found the mafia and political figures. It was on those branches I saw the crooked attorneys, government officials and corporate payoffs. Through painstaking research, interviews with various witnesses (including a retired judge) and hours spent going through old newspaper clippings on microfiche, I absolutely, 100 percent confirmed the mafia's existence and influence in Lycoming County.

An old-time mafia associate confessed he killed Hoffa on orders from Bufalino. Frank "The Irishman" Sheeran was a labor union official who was accused of having links to the Bufalino crime family and who has claimed to have killed Hoffa on orders from Bufalino.

"I Heard You Paint Houses" is being turned into a Hollywood movie and Robert De Niro is confirmed to be teaming up with longtime partner in crime Martin Scorsese. Joining them in the movie will be two other actors that you might have seen in quite a few mob flicks: Al Pacino and Joe Pesci. It is crazy to believe that all of this has ties to Lycoming County in a roundabout way as both Bufalino and Sheeran have documented stays in Williamsport and Lycoming County. Bufalino's attorney also served as Lycoming County's solicitor. Why was the mafia in Lycoming County? Let's just say they had a vested interest in the political scene there. Most of my investigation into this political corruption within the mafia is classified with the FBI; therefore, I will not explain it in great detail. However, as a kid who was always fascinated with cold cases and unsolved crime in general, it was an eye-opening investigation into the shady underground of politics and *La Costa Nostra*.

I was pulled from my FBI assignment by the Williamsport Bureau of Police before any further investigation into political corruption or mafia related crimes could be fully investigated. My investigation was left in the hands of the FBI for whom I was working for at the time. Unfortunately, I don't think it was ever followed up on and that, too, has become a cold case of sorts. It was shortly after this I left the Williamsport Police Department to work for the Lycoming County District Attorney. Again, there were just so many incidents that occurred while I was a member of the Williamsport Bureau of Police that left a bad taste in my mouth. I thought I was getting that military camaraderie back when I joined the Williamsport Bureau of Police. I was wrong. That doesn't exist there; at least it didn't while I was there. There are cliques, but not the solidarity of united brotherhood—it just doesn't exist there.

I recall being in the watch commander's office during shift change once. An officer who had ruffled feathers because he did what he wanted to do and didn't fall into the clique category made a traffic stop on the interstate of an 18-wheeler. This was this officer's forte; he liked messing with these big rigs and he was good at it. Yet, other veteran officers didn't like it and didn't like him. After a few minutes, he was on the radio calling for assistance. Apparently, this truck driver didn't like the way he was being talked to and it became physical. One veteran officer who was in the room with me leaned back, crossed his feet and said, "Fuck him. Trucker fucker anyhow," as I was bolting from the room in an attempt to get to this officer, whom I was having some disagreements with at the time as well. I couldn't believe that the veteran officer said what he said and didn't go to help his brother officer. It appalled me and still does to this day. I left that department and never looked back.

THE DISTRICT ATTORNEY'S OFFICE

The District Attorney's Office was run by Eric Linhardt during my tenure there. He was a private defense attorney who eventually went on to become Lycoming County's chief prosecutor. I butted heads against Linhardt when he was a defense attorney. In fact, he was the only attorney I did not like. I didn't like him for two reasons. One, he called me a liar once when he cross-examined me for five hours on a traffic stop in which I confiscated two guns and drugs off of a local star basketball player. During his closing arguments, he told the judge that I wasn't credible, which made my blood boil. You can take everything away from me, but my integrity is something I cherish and will never be compromised. I will never lie on the stand and I will never jeopardize my integrity—period. For him to do that made me extremely pissed off and I let him know it. During deliberations, he ran into me in the hallway and said, "Don't take it personally, officer." I went off on him, letting him know that I do take it personally because it is my life. I live and breathe being a cop and to question my integrity is something that I cannot take lying down. He got the message. Second, I hated him because he was the best attorney I ever faced, bar none. So, it was ironic that he hired me as one of his detectives. He was a fair, determined man for whom I have *much* respect. Although he plays politics more than I like, he still is the best district attorney I have seen and the citizens of Lycoming County should be grateful they have such a dedicated individual putting the bad guys away.

It used to infuriate me when defense attorneys would question a cop's integrity unless it was warranted somehow. I found out why once when I was on stand for a drug trial during my undercover days. A female sold me crack cocaine. I gave her money; she put the drugs in my hand. In addition, my partner, Officer Jeremy Brown, was across the street in a van videotaping the transaction. It was as clear-cut case as there is in the drug world.

During trial, her attorney cross-examined me and said, "Isn't it true you lied about who you were to my client? Isn't it true you lie all the time to people, pretending to be someone else? So you're a professional liar, isn't that correct, Officer Mains?" I answered, "I guess I am."

The jury almost came back with a not guilty verdict, according to one of the jury members. They actually believed the defendant because she had come in with her church supporters and reverend and that I was a professional liar. None of that changed the fact she sold crack cocaine to me and we got it on videotape. It shows how misled juries can be. The defense attorney ran into me in the hallway and said, "I'm so sorry, Kenny. It's all I had." I smiled because to me, it was a compliment. My case was so good, she had to attack my credibility and say I lied about everything. She knew I didn't lie.

While assigned to the District Attorney's Office, I created and maintained the Cold Case Unit with Linhardt's blessing. I was the only member of the unit, so it was very easy to maintain. Yet, it wasn't without hardship as other police agencies did not seem to take to kindly to this kid "interfering" with cases that belonged to them. Police are very territorial about their cases—even if they are not being actively investigated. It's all about jurisdiction. On Dec. 19, 2014, while working for the District Attorney's Office, I received a tip about a cold case murder of a child.

Based on that tip, I began a review of this case. In a stroke of bad timing, the local newspaper had called me to do an article about cold cases in the county at the same time as I was reviewing the case in order to determine if the tip had any credibility.

The next week, on the front page of the Sunday edition of the Williamsport Sun Gazette, was my picture along with the child's saying that I was investigating the case. Wow, did this open up a can of worms for me with the jurisdicting police agency. The head of its criminal investigations called my supervisor, the district attorney, Eric Linhardt, explaining his displeasure. He said I was trying to embarrass his agency and that I was out of line for commenting about their case.

After a meeting was held with the police agency and district attorney (without me), Linhardt instructed me not to interview anyone regarding this case. I smirked at him when he said this and told him that was not gonna happen. I gave him this very realistic scenario: A man comes to my office, the office of the district attorney, and says he would like to talk to me because he has information on this particular homicide case. Do you seriously want me to tell the informant that I cannot take his information but instead tell him to drive five miles to the jurisdicting police agency's station and tell someone there? How completely asinine is that?

First off, the person coming forward with the information is already under enough pressure and he is probably hesitant to talk to begin with. He mustered up the courage to come tell someone information that may help solve a cold case and I tell him I can't speak to him because it isn't my case? This is a joke! What happens if the informant changes his mind after I send him away without taking his information? What if I just tell him, "Hey, let me take your name and number and have the police agency that has the case call you?" What happens when the police agency calls him a day or two later and the informant says, "Oh, I don't have nothing to say," because he changed his mind. You *must* strike while the iron is hot; when an informant is ready to give information, you take it. That way, if he later changes his mind, it doesn't matter because you already elicited the tip.

So, I told Linhardt that I respect him and I will listen to him, but the police agency that has this case has lost its god-damned mind if the cops there think I will turn away a person giving information on an unsolved homicide case! Linhardt smiled and shook his head in amazement of my defiance.

It is my belief that many cases, especially homicides, go unsolved because of egos. These egos are those of the detectives and investigators who have jurisdiction over the cases. They feel that it is their case and no one else should interfere, even if they are not doing anything to move the case forward to a resolution. This drives me absolutely insane with anger.

I caught so much heat from this police agency for trying to help solve this murder that it almost pushed me out of law enforcement. Even though I was being pro-active and trying to generate tips in order to solve a case, they saw it as a slap in the face, as if I were trying to overshadow them. Wait a second, guys; we possibly have a murderer who abducted a little girl from her house, killed her and he is still walking our streets. He could come in your very house and take your daughter, but you don't care? Well, goddamnit, I care and I won't cower down to you or any other agency that doesn't do what is right for the victims.

One thing is for certain, being a cop changed a lot for me on that day in February 2015. I no longer saw all police as wanting to do the right thing. Yet as I stated before, that is not all police, just some. What I saw that day was jealous, paranoid, ego-driven cops who did not have the best interest of a dead 10-year-old girl at heart. They instead were worrying about me and how I was trying to make them look bad—according to them.

I have never seen such complete and total disrespect from an organization that is supposed to protect and serve. Now don't get me wrong, there are so many great police officers in that organization who I have worked with and a few bad apples do not ruin the bunch. However, on this specific case and this specific instance, they disgusted me as a detective and as a human being.

It is so easy for people to just go with the flow and not create waves. Think about your job. The people who come in, show up on time, leave when they're supposed and do no more and no less. They are never messed with. They do the bare minimum, nothing above and beyond. They will never stay late or go the extra mile. They are the status quo.

But people who are pro-active, go above and beyond, come in early and stay late are ridiculed. Oh, those people just ass-kissers or just grandstanding, trying to make us all look bad. No, maybe they just enjoy their job and are passionate about it. Maybe they were taught that you do things to the very best of your ability. Maybe they just want to do the job with vigor and enthusiasm. But no, people want to knock them down because they are jealous and they are not strong enough to do what they do. It takes a very strong person to take this ridicule and continue doing the right thing. It takes a very strong person! "The man who is anybody and who does anything is surely going to be criticized, vilified, and misunderstood. This is a part of the penalty for greatness, and every great man understands it; and understands, too, that it is no proof of greatness. The final proof of greatness lies in being able to endure contumely without resentment," American philosopher Elbert Green Hubbard said.

Investigating these cold cases is what I wanted to do my whole life. I had finally made it. Regardless of ridicule. Regardless of dirty looks. Regardless of being alienated. I obtained my goal. Achieving goals is very important for successful people. A person who grows and prospers should always have goals. My goal was to become the best cold case investigator in the world and solve cases! Some people have said I have succeeded in accomplishing this goal. I say, I can still learn to be better! Once, while investigating a cold case homicide, I got stuck. I had never gotten stuck in an investigation before. It was then I decided to create a cold case organization like no other.

THE AMERICAN INVESTIGATIVE SOCIETY OF COLD CASES

The American Investigative Society of Cold Cases (AISOCC) was born in March of 2013. While investigating the 1994 cold case murders of Gail Matthews and Tamara Berkheiser, I became stuck. It is a detective's worst nightmare. It is a horrible feeling. You feel lost, desolate, failed and alone. I felt that I had nowhere to turn for help because no single person or group entity had invested the time and passion I had into the case, so why would they even care. If I could not find anyone else to assist me in my search to find a killer, I was going to start my own organization and staff it with a multi-disciplinary field of educated professionals whose sole purpose is to help law enforcement solve cold cases. I envisioned having the absolute best crime fighters in the world under one roof, battling the staggering amount of unsolved cold cases. I wanted the cream of the crop and the foremost names in crime fighting. I wanted the American Investigative Society of Cold Cases to always be the place where law enforcement would go when they could not solve a case. I wanted there to be an organization that brings together the elite of the elite to review and ultimately solve previously unsolvable cold cases. I wanted that organization to be the American Investigative Society of Cold Cases.

For a person who loves sports, it was like assembling the greatest team of crime fighters of all time. I was like a college football recruiter, making my pitch to the talent and hoping they would decide to become a part of my winning tradition and join my organization. I wanted a team that consisted of a seasoned homicide detective, DNA expert, criminal profiler, crime scene expert and reconstructionist, forensic psychiatrist and psychologist as well as a forensic pathologist. I needed these different disciplines because I wanted people to see the cold cases through a different lens. A homicide detective may see something different than a forensic pathologist and vice versa. That was extremely important to me when creating this organization. We had to get different viewpoints because ultimately that will generate new leads. This was the foundation that I wanted. Once I had that established, I could expand.

"Change is the law of life. And those who look only to the past or present are certain to miss the future."

John F. Kennedy

Following unsolved mysteries and true crime as I have my entire life, I knew who the best of the best in cold-case investigations were already. However, I researched others who I didn't know off the top of my head but I wanted. I read their publications; I talked to their peers and read newspaper articles about them. When I found the professionals I felt were qualified as being the best in the business, I began calling, emailing and soliciting them. I wanted to know if they wanted to be a part of this elite and one-of-a-kind cold-case group of crime-fighting all-stars dedicated to solving the unsolved. Almost everyone I contacted wanted to be a part of this endeavor because they, too, cared and were passionate about these cases as I was.

Today, I consider myself a United States Marine Corps veteran and a detective. I use a unique and particular combination of forensic science, criminal investigation, forensic psychology, victimology, crime reconstruction, crime scene assessment and criminal profiling to solve cases. You have to have a good foundation in all of these disciplines to be a good investigator. I am the president and founder of the AISOCC. In this capacity, I have reviewed hundreds of cold-case files with the best investigators in the world who are an integral part of my organization to include such great crime fighters as Dr. Henry Lee, Dr. Cyril Wecht, Dr. Werner Spitz, Lt. Joe Kenda, Dr. Mary Ellen O'Toole, Mark Safarik and Dr. Robert Keppel, among many others.

Throughout my law enforcement career, I have investigated a variety of criminal activity to include illegal narcotics, financial, property and white-collar crimes. I have been recognized by the Pennsylvania courts as an expert in the area of illegal narcotics. I have also investigated numerous violent crimes including robberies, homicides, cold cases, equivocal or undetermined death and missing persons. Additionally, I have investigated public and political corruption and the intricacies of criminal organizations such as the Blood and Crips street gangs as well as the American mafia or *La Costa Nostra*.

My law enforcement career has consisted of working as a member of the Williamsport Bureau of Police, Lycoming County Drug Task Force, DEA, Federal Bureau of Investigations and the Lycoming County of Pennsylvania's District Attorney's Office.

During my tour with the United States Marine Corps, I was assigned primarily with the Special Operations Training Group (SOTG), II Marine Expeditionary Force with a concentration on administrative intelligence.

I hold a bachelor of science degree (BS) in criminal justice from Lock Haven University and have taken master's level course work in forensic criminology with an emphasis on criminal profiling. I hold professional memberships in the American Academy of Forensic Sciences, the Mid-Atlantic Cold Case Homicide Investigators Association and the Pennsylvania Homicide Investigators Association.

I have had professional training in criminal law, criminal investigations, forensic criminology, criminal profiling, medicolegal death investigation, cold case analysis for law enforcement, undercover narcotics investigations, advanced crime scene investigations, sex-related homicide investigations, practical homicide investigations, among many others.

In addition, I am an advisory board member at the Cyril H. Wecht Institute of Forensic Science and Law at Duquesne University, Lock Haven University and am a second opinion provider for the National Organization for Parents of Murdered Children. As a second opinion provider, I look at cases for parents who feel their loved one may not have died in the manner or circumstances that were originally classified or told.

I have been bestowed a number of awards to include Police Officer of the Year by the Williamsport Bureau of Police and the Gallantry Star for Acts of Distinguished Bravery by the Williamsport Fraternal Order of Police. I am also a three-time recipient of the Williamsport Bureau of Police's Officer of the Quarter Award.

I personally have reviewed, investigated or assisted on more than 100 homicides, equivocal deaths, suicides and cold cases. Lastly, a punk kid from Centre Hall, Pa., who was never supposed to amount to anything because of all the obstacles, fought his way to accomplish those goals and succeed where it matters most—in life.

These are the credentials that I bring forth the following book and assessments as it relates to cold cases and being a detective.

Mains FBI Undercover 2008

Mains USMC 1992

Card given to little boy dying of cancer who asked for police cards. I Gave him my personal lanyard.

Mains and son 2003

COLD CASE DETECTIVE

"Kenneth Mains is an experienced and hard-working detective. He has a vast amount of knowledge in criminal investigation, human behavior and forensic evidence. I had some excellent working experience with him."

Dr. Henry Lee, world-renowned forensic criminologist

Cold Case. Just sounds chilling, doesn't it? What is a cold case? There are many definitions, some more technical than others. The simplest definition is a case that does not have definitive resolution. That could be an unsolved homicide or it could be that someone is in jail and convicted, but there is serious doubt to the likelihood the person is actually responsible for the crime. Yes, there are innocent people convicted in America.

Regardless of one's definition, one thing is universal when it comes to cold cases, they are cold for a reason. They are cold because they are difficult. The offender was lucky, smart or a combination of both. They are cold because the offender kept his or her mouth shut and didn't need to brag about the crime. They are cold because the leads dried up and the case got overrun by other cases.

I can tell you that most detectives never forget an unsolved murder they investigated or were a part of in some way. The unsolved murder will stay with them long after retirement. They would like nothing better than to see the case solved. They would love to dust off their boots, pull out the old gun belt, get back in the fight and re-investigate the case. That is why cold cases never go away— someone will always care. When I work cold cases, I love to reach out to those original detectives. I speak to old detectives every single chance I get. Not only do they have a wealth of knowledge, they still have that fire to see the case solved. They can tell you things that are not in a report. They can tell you a movement or look a suspect gave during a specific question. Subtle things like that will often go unnoticed or at the very least not end up in a report. However, that veteran detective never forgot and he wants nothing more than to share that information. You just have to be willing to go get it.

I had worked for the Williamsport Bureau of Police in Pennsylvania for about four years and never heard the name Dawn Miller or knew we had a cold case within our department. Little did I know this girl, whom I never met, and the cold case it embodied, would change my life forever. It was just a name that came up on my Google search when I was researching missing persons in my area. But there it was, staring at me as with a purpose. Dawn Miller. Missing. Cold case. What an incredible journey it has been since that day in 2007. My journey really began the very next day.

That next day, I asked my captain about Dawn and her case. He stated that he never heard of her and he, too, had no idea we had an active missing person case. I asked if I could investigate the case. I was told, "You are a narcotics officer, not an agent." I told the captain that I would investigate it on my own time. He grudgingly granted me permission. That day, the cold case of Dawn Miller started to warm up.

I received the report from our records department, all two pages of the initial report with a few pages of follow-up investigations. Within one week, I had two suspects who I had no doubt murdered this girl. It was very clear this girl was not a runaway as portrayed. This poor girl was murdered and no one did the proper investigation necessary to convict the two individuals responsible. The system had failed her, but I was determined to bring justice to her and her family because that is why I became a cop.

Although this was the start of my foray into actual investigations of cold cases and the politics behind the scenes, it was not my last. In fact, it only got better—or worse. After solving the Miller case, I was looking for the next challenge.

I was unaware how challenging, demanding, consuming and political it was going to be. It started like this:

I was doing a lot of drug work with the FBI, as it was so much easier than with the state and county government. I mean, it is easier to make arrests and prove those arrests in courts. The reason for this is because number one, you have the leverage of federal time. Nobody wants to do federal time as a drug dealer because the sentences are longer—way longer. Number two, you can get telephone information from a drug dealer's number just by issuing an office subpoena. No court order, no search warrant, nothing. The federal government is much more relaxed getting documents than the state government. Just that you suspect a phone number is associated with drug activity is all it takes to get the phone records. It was heaven for a drug investigator. But these types of cases with the FBI take time. You have to connect the dots and indict everyone.

However, my passion was still with investigations and cold cases.

There was another unsolved murder in the city of Williamsport like no other. It was the murder of Gail Matthews, 23, and her 5-year-old daughter, Tamara, in September 1994. This case was very different than the Dawn Miller case because everyone knew about these murders and the proclaimed "insolvability" of the case.

The problem, I felt, was simple: it was a cold case and no one was actively working on the case. Most people felt they knew whom the offender was, but law enforcement didn't have enough evidence for a conviction. There had been two grand juries convened and two arrests of the suspect. Each time, the suspect was let go and charges dropped. I thought to myself, "I could do it. I could solve this crime and put the person responsible in jail where he belongs." I had law enforcement people telling me I should look into it. But who was I? Sure, I solved one cold case, but this was different— this was larger and a lot more complex. However, it seemed I had someone other than myself who had confidence in me: Linhardt, the district attorney of Lycoming County. I was still working for the Williamsport police and assigned to the FBI, but Linhardt wanted me to investigate the murders of Gail and Tamara. A very fair, professional and smart man. Someone who gained my respect while working for him later in my career. My cold-case career was unfolding before my eyes. He called me to his office one day and asked if I was interested in solving this case. I told him I was and I had already been reading reports about the case on my own time. He requested that I investigate this horrible murder and I obliged.

I would not break my chain of command, though, and so I approached my new captain, explained to him my interest in the case and that I was requested by the DA to investigate it. I was told, "No." I begged, "I will do it on my own time like before." Again, I was told, "No, you are not an agent." I said, "This case can be solved." Again, I was told "No." I told my captain that "just because I do not have a title in front of my name, it doesn't mean I cannot do the job as good as or better than an agent." The captain assured me that I was the best person to investigate it and he had confidence in me, however, I could not investigate the case and that was final.

This came from a captain for whom I had very little respect. It was because this captain had zero integrity and, to me, that is the number one attribute not only a leader should have, but all people should have. He had none.

It just so happened that within a few months, there was going to be an opening for a detective working for the district attorney of Lycoming County. I was completely dismayed at the decisions, unwarranted promotions, backstabbing, alliances, jealousy and lack of leadership within the Williamsport Bureau of Police. I decided at that moment that I was not going to allow another victim to be forgotten about and I made the toughest decision of my life. If the Williamsport Bureau of Police was not going to allow me to investigate this cold case, I would resign.

I am of the belief that a successful organization is made by placing a person into a position they enjoy and are good at. The benefit of this is twofold. The employer succeeds because his employee is happy and is turning out good work, which in turn benefits the leadership, which ultimately in police work, benefits the community.

This is not the way the Williamsport Bureau of Police was set up. It has since become better because it brought in good outside leadership from the state police. I felt, as others there did, that you're just a number, just a cog in the ever-changing wheel. You're just a number, just a line item on a budget and overtime list. The day I resigned, I received a bottle of Jack Daniel's and a Liberty Bell plaque from my co-workers at the FBI. I received nothing from the Williamsport Bureau of Police. My six nominations for Officer of the Quarter, three Officer of the Quarter Awards, Gallantry Star Medal and Officer of the Year awards didn't mean anything. Don't get me wrong, I don't feel that I am entitled to anything; I just say this to illustrate my point about the substandard leadership and impersonal working environment there. Thankfully, it has gotten better.

My new position with the District Attorney's Office had a positive side: I could investigate the Matthews case and other cold cases. The negative: I would have to take a pay cut—a huge pay cut.

I recall getting a phone call from a Williamsport police detective before I made a decision on the district attorney's position. He said, "No matter what you decide to do—run a restaurant, stay in law enforcement or change oil—I have no doubt you will be successful. You will be successful at anything you do, Kenny, because that is how you're made." That has always stuck with me because it proved that others saw me as someone who strives to be the best.

So, I took a 50-percent pay cut, to investigate the cold case of Gail and Tamara and leave the bureaucracy of a substandard police department with no leadership or vision because it was the right thing to do.

I continue to investigate those murders. They are my white whale. They are my nightmare. The impact of speaking to Gail's mother and younger sister is a feeling I cannot shake. When they cry, I cry—on the inside. I can't show weakness, ever. It is what I am; it is how I am made. Inside, I am torn. I am living their own personal hell because I do care.

I have investigated the murders of Gail and Tamara nine years now and I believe I know who was responsible for this heinous act. However, knowing, proving and convincing a jury of peers are very different things. Hell, you can't get 12 people to agree on what color the sky is and you expect them to convict someone for a double murder of two beautiful and innocent people, especially after the police already arrested someone else for these murders twice. I will continue to investigate the case until I die. That is the only way I know how. Gail deserves that. Tamara deserves that. Their families deserve that. One of the hardest things I have ever done in my life was to speak at a memorial on the 20-year anniversary of their deaths. Gail's mother and sister asked me to speak. I didn't want to. It's not for me to speak on their behalf. Yet, I felt that everyone involved deserved to hear from me. So I did. This is what I had to say:

> *For those who don't know me, my name is Detective Kenneth Mains and I work for the District Attorney's Office and I am the lead and sole investigator in the deaths of Gail Louise Matthews and Tamara Marie Berkheiser.*
>
> *There are a couple of issues I want to address tonight first and foremost.*

First, I thank all of you for coming. The support shown by all of you is overwhelming. It shows that this community and all of you still care ... you care about this case and these victims and their families. It shows that Gail and Tamara are not forgotten.

Secondly, I want to talk about how these murders have become almost like a local legend ... a folklore or myth, especially to the younger people that do not remember Gail or Tamara. We cannot allow that to happen. We cannot allow that to happen because when that happens, their murder and their lives become a story that isn't real, just words on a computer screen or newspaper as many of you may have read today. Well, I'm here to tell you, it is real. It is as real today, as it was 20 years ago. Please don't forget that!

I'm not here to discuss specifics about the case; that is not what this is about. We can do that after the vigil, one on one if you have questions. This time, this moment is to celebrate the life of Gail Matthews and Tamara Berkheiser and ultimately and sadly, mourn their deaths.

But I will talk briefly about what happened on September 2nd, 1994, at 812 Center Street, here in Williamsport, about three blocks over. At 10:37 a.m., Lois Matthews and her friend, Sara Horn, placed a frantic 911 call after Gail did not show up for work and after the horror they witnessed inside that home.

I've listened to that 911 call ... many, many times, looking, searching for clues. But the only thing I can glean from that call was the pain, the despair, the terror and the uncertainty in Lois Matthews' voice as she frantically asked for help. That voice, that terror and that despair will never ... ever ... leave me. I see that today, 20 years later in her eyes when I talk to her. I see the void inside of her and it is gut-wrenching to see. Every week when she or Gail's sister Julie calls me, I hear it in their voice. It is that same terror, frustration and despair that was so evident 20 years ago.

I began investigating these murders in 2010 when I initially went to my supervisor and requested to investigate this case. I was told "No" ... because I didn't hold the title of "detective."

Even when I requested to investigate the case on my own time, I was again told "No."

However, just like Lois Matthews, I didn't take "No" for an answer. To me, this case needed investigated and it needed investigated more thoroughly than ever before and it would require a detective that would be willing to sacrifice a bit of his own life in order to do so. I was and I still am willing to make this sacrifice—not only for Gail and Tamara, but also for the family and friends of Gail and Tamara.

Eventually, I was personally requested by the district attorney, Eric Linhardt, to investigate this case as a member of his staff. I accepted this because that was right thing to do. In fact, I took a 50% pay cut in order to investigate this case because it was the right thing to do. But tonight isn't about me. In fact, it never should be or will be about me. It should be and always will be about Gail Matthews and her daughter, Tamara.

You know, one thing I've realized the older I get and that is that life isn't about me. It's not about me as an individual. It's about what can I do to help others. How can I make someone else happy. It could be as simple as giving a badge to a 10-year-old boy who wants to be a cop or as difficult as solving a 20-year-old murder. Regardless of what it is, we do these things because we are good human beings and we care. That is what life is truly about, helping others.

People can say what they want about all the investigators who have worked on this case in the past 20 years, but I'm here to tell you they all had one thing in common: they cared. Bill Miller cared. Jack Yanni cared. Jean Stump cared. Dave Ritter cared. And let me tell you something, I care. If you question that, please talk to Lois Matthews or Gail's sister, Julie, or Gail's best friend, Shawna. I have no doubt they will tell you above all else ... I care.

But ultimately, caring alone does not solve crime and caring alone won't solve this crime. Dedication, determination, people coming forward with information and the advances in forensics will solve this crime. That and a little bit of luck.

There are three things that I think a good detective needs in order to be successful in solving cases and that is passion, determination and a bit of luck. One thing I can tell you standing right here today is that this case has two out of those three elements. The passion and determination is overwhelming. Just look around. It is the luck part that has been missing. There have been many nights when I have looked to the sky and said, "Come on Gail, help me out here." All I am looking for is that one lucky break. It hasn't come yet. But don't give up hope, because I will never give up hope. Nor will Gail and Tamara's family and friends.

One of the very first things you do as an investigator in cases like this is what is called victimology. You want to learn everything you can about the victims. Once you do that, it will ultimately lead you closer to who is responsible for the murders. While doing this, I met Lois Matthews, Gail's mother. I met Eric Berkheiser, Tamara's father. I met Julie Stroble, Gail's sister. I met Shawna Bartholomew, Gail's best friend. I met them and countless others and through those meetings, I learned what Gail would do, and what she wouldn't do. I learned what Gail liked and what she didn't like. I learned what Tamara would do in certain situations and what Tamara wouldn't do.

I learned that Gail was very particular about her hair and that she hated to cook, even though she was employed as one. I also learned how Tamara was a fussy eater and loved to ride her bike and play in the yard with other kids. It is through those interactions that I got to know Gail and Tamara as if they were a part of my family. They have become a part of me. I see them every single day. Not only in the picture that is hanging in my office that I touch with my two fingers every single morning, but also in my mind. It is there ... in my mind where I see them ... laughing ... playing and enjoying life.

A good detective will always work the case forever in his mind, he will always be thinking about the case and the victims in his mind. At least I know I do. When I am at Lowe's, I think about the case. When I am at dinner, eating with my family, I think about the case. When I am lying in bed, I think about the case. I think about this case every single day of my life.

I think about why something looked the way it did in that house on September 2, 1994, 20 years ago today, at 812 Center Street or why a person said what they said during an interview that didn't make sense to me. I see it, I breathe it and I have lived it every single day of my life for the past four years. I can't help it. That's how I am made; that is my genetic makeup, it's in my DNA. That's why I am a detective.

Just last month, I took my family to Knobel Groves. As my young daughter was on a ride, I watched her and my mind immediately went to a home video I saw of Tamara on that very same ride only months before her death 20 years ago. It is those moments that allow me to never forget and never give up on the pursuit of justice.

You all are here because Gail Matthews and Tamara Berkheiser and their families mean something to you. The Matthews and Berkheiser families are a strong, tough bunch. Above all else, they are a family and that word family still means something to them, as well it should. This tragedy has brought them together, closer—as it has a lot of you.

I know it has brought me closer to two very strong women here tonight in Lois Matthews and Gail's sister, Julie Stroble. One thing I know for sure is that right now, Gail Matthews is looking down and beaming with pride knowing her baby sister, Julie, has followed in her footsteps by turning out to be such a great person and such a great mom, just like Gail. Both Julie and Lois are two remarkable individuals and I am very proud to have gotten to know them through these past couple of years. Those two have made me smile and they have made me shed a tear or two, but most of all, they have provided me with invaluable memories of Gail Matthews and her daughter, Tamara Berkheiser.

They remember Gail and her laugh, the crinkle in the corner of her eye when she smiled. They remember Tamara running around the house with loose change in her pocket spilling out into the floor. Those are the memories they have. Someone took Gail and Tamara away from them and all of us in September 1994, 20 years ago today. Yet, they cannot take away those memories. It is those memories that will allow

Gail and Tamara to live forever. Not as words. Not as just names and pictures on a computer screen, but as they should be remembered—as living, breathing, loving, and caring human beings.

I ask each and every one of you to think of Gail and Tamara as living, breathing human beings and not pictures and words in the newspaper or on a Facebook post because they are more than that. They were someone's daughter, someone's sister, someone's niece and someone's friend. That is how they should be remembered and that is how they deserve to be remembered.

The most important thing I want to stress tonight is this. As long as I am breathing air, as long as I am alive, this case will be investigated with passion and determination. I owe that to Julie Stroble. I owe that to Charles Beakley. I owe that to Shawna Bartholomew. I owe that to Dale Matthews. I owe that to Ricky Matthews. I owe that to Scot Beakley. I owe that to Galen Matthews. I owe that to Eric Berkheiser and I owe that to Lois Matthews!

*But lastly and most importantly, you **damn well better believe** I owe that to Gail Louise Matthews and Tamara Marie Berkheiser and I **will not let** them down.*

Thank you.

When I was done, there wasn't a dry eye. Then as I walked away, I heard someone yell, "We love you, Detective Mains." I will always remember that. I said, "I love you guys, too." It was a very, very touching moment in my life that I will forever cherish and remember.

Yet it is crimes like this that make you question God and faith. I don't ever talk religion or share my beliefs, maybe because it is one mystery I cannot solve. But I do know without an intelligent designer, you cannot have an intelligent design. It is that reasoning I believe Gail and Tamara will get justice for their untimely and unjustified deaths someday.

There are some people in law enforcement who just don't like me, mostly I feel, because of their own insecurities and jealousy and because I often take the side of what is right, not what is popular.

If the truth lies in the defense's arguments, I will say as much. Some cops are just pro-law enforcement and that is the bottom line. They don't care about the truth because it is all about the prosecution. I am not that way. I don't hate defense attorneys because they are defense attorneys. I don't hate drug dealers just because they are drug dealers. I remember arresting a drug dealer once and him thanking me for being fair with him. I told him, "Just because you are a drug dealer doesn't mean you are not a good person." You do what you do, I do what I do and most of the time, you win. Today, I won; that's all." I am about the truth!

One of my field training officers, who is now a lieutenant for the Williamsport Bureau of Police, Brian Womer, would always say, "Don't mistake my kindness for weakness." I loved that.

Some hate because I stand up for myself and others who don't conform. Regardless, you have to have pride and confidence in yourself. If people want to ridicule you for your beliefs, they are not worth your time. I have learned that people will never always agree with you or your beliefs. Yet you cannot let the hate or negativity stop you from doing what you believe. You cannot be scared to ruffle feathers if that is what it takes. I have noticed over the years that those same people who hate me—and I have never even talked to them—eventually meet me and get to know me, they change the hate to respect and that is all you can ask for in this world.

However, there are the few, the ones I care about who do get it. One cop once told me over a few beers, "There is just something about you that makes people gravitate to you. You're an inspiration. I can't explain it, but I would follow you into battle anywhere." That was a bold and humbling statement that will always stick with me. Especially since it came from a cop I respect and admire and now works in my former position with the FBI.

There are many people who do like me and what I stand for. However, the most important thing to me is that they respect me and my work, and most do.

> *"I'm not concerned with your liking or disliking me.*
> *All I ask is that you respect me as a human being."*
>
> *Jackie Robinson*

I stopped caring about what people think a long time ago, because you will never please everyone. I realize that I come from a humble background and I will never forget where I have come from. I stand for integrity, courage, dedication, perseverance and passion. I enjoy helping others and leaving an impact on this life before I leave it. There are many others who feel the same way I do. They work hard at their craft, perfecting it in order to effectively help others. Doctors, social workers, mothers, fathers and yes, police officers.

I remember turning in my badge and gun to the property guy my last day working for the Williamsport police. Beside me was my partner from the drug unit and one of my best friends, Jeremy Brown. Brown was always beside me when I needed it. Always! If you looked up the word loyalty, Brown's picture would be there. You couldn't ask for a better partner and friend. The property officer asked me, "You sure you want to do this?" I remember feeling hesitant because I didn't know what I was going to do next. As I walked out to my car and was standing in the heavy rain unpacking, a car stopped in the middle of the road and backed up. A man got out of the car in the rain and walked up to me and shook my hand and thanked me for my service. It was the mayor of Williamsport. I remember that and I will always take from that the little act of acknowledging someone's efforts will often impact someone. I will always appreciate that little gesture. However, I knew fate would lead me to my next endeavor just as it had intervened in my life in November 2002 when I took my police application to the police department.

On a cold day in November 2002, I was dropping off my police application that I just got done filling out. It was the last day to turn it in. It was also late in the day, close to 4 p.m. when the secretary leaves.

Before she left, I gave her the application. She flipped through it in order to make sure I had everything filled out properly. She stopped, looked up at me and said, "You didn't get a doctor to fill this out?" I stated that I had not; I filled out my medical history. She said that I had to get a physical and the doctor had to sign these pages. I looked at the clock, she looked at me and I said, "Well, I guess you can throw it away because I can't get a physical because the deadline to have this turned in is in 30 minutes." She said, "Hold on," and placed a phone call. She hung up and said if I went to the Divine Providence Hospital about five minutes away, they would give me the physical and I could turn in the application. I did and the rest is history. Fate. Crazy how things worked out. I should have never even made the deadline for the application.

A few months later, I was given the polygraph examination. I failed. I went home and was contemplating my life over a cold Yingling beer and got a call from the chief of police. He asked if I could come back in and take the polygraph again in the morning. "Sure," I said.

I passed the polygraph and the rest is history. Fate. Nobody takes that polygraph twice. Did I lie? Not exactly, but I wasn't totally forthcoming with my background, therefore causing me not to do well on the test.

So, I knew when I turned that badge and gun in that day that I was making the right decision. Fate. I would wear a badge once again.

I have always believed in standing up for what you believe in, no matter the consequences. There are some people who just don't like me, mostly I feel, because of their own insecurities and jealousy and also because I stand up for myself and others and don't conform. There are some people who love me and what I stand for. However, the most important thing to me is that they respect me and my work, and I think most people do. I stopped caring about what other people think a long time ago, because you will never please everyone. I realize that I come from a humble background and I will never forget where I have come from. I stand for integrity, courage, dedication, perseverance and passion. I enjoy helping others and leaving an impact on this life before I leave it. It is those attributes that allowed me to chase my passion as a detective and eventually to investigate cold cases.

All those years watching "Unsolved Mysteries" and reading about how Dr. Henry Lee would investigate unsolved homicides was now about to involve me. It was my passion and it still is to this day. Cold cases, solving the unsolved and helping others while doing it. That, to me, is what it is all about.

Gail Matthews and daughter Tamara Berkheiser

Mains explaining a cold case for television
producers and law enforcement officers

Detective Mains speaking at vigil for Gail Matthews and Tamara Berkheiser. Gail's mother is also in photograph.

HOW TO INVESTIGATE
A COLD CASE

"Ken Mains is a professional investigator with a stellar reputation and is motivated by the best possible reason: he wants to give a voice to all the tragic souls who have been silenced. Ken has established relationships with the top professionals in many fields related to criminal investigations and utilizes their knowledge in his work. I cannot think of a better choice for cold case investigations."

Lt. Joe Kenda, legendary homicide detective from the television show "Homicide Hunter."

As I stated previously, I love old detectives. I worked with two who were the epitome of old-school detectives. I have much respect for both of them. I loved listening to their stories. They were full of knowledge gained through experience. They both were a cop's cop! Been there and done that type of guys. They cared about getting the job done regardless of how long it took. I always listened to both them, even when I realized early on they didn't know everything. They knew more than I did, that's for sure, but you have to filter what you take in. When they tell me a guy is innocent because of the way he reacted to a picture of the victim being flashed across his face, I laugh on the inside. They believed wholeheartedly the suspect should have reacted one way and since he didn't, they can base a conclusion. I called bullshit. Or that a guy is isn't a suspect because he showed up early for the interview. I laugh. I listen—because I show respect. But, I still laugh.

I don't care if you investigated 1,000 cases and in 999 of them, the guy reacted the same way or the "guilty" suspect showed up late or on time but never early—there is always that 1-percent chance. So don't base your conclusions off of that. You have to qualify that statement and not make it an absolute. You say, "I don't think the guy is guilty because of this and that based on the totality," but never say never based off one response or lack thereof.

Yet, when they would say they had a hunch, I listen more than usual. Because after you work this job long enough, hunches are sometimes all we can go on and more often than not, they are right. They will never hold up as evidence but hunches are just like luck. Ask any detective; we will take luck over skill any day of the week.

When I begin investigating a cold case, they are all the same. No one murder case takes precedence over another. As Dr. Werner Spitz, the famed forensic pathologist, once said when he reviewed the assassination of President John F. Kennedy, "When people are on the autopsy table, they are all the same." For me, it is much of the same.

I sit down at my desk with a cup of coffee, notepad and a pen. I read the case file and jot down anything and everything that stands out to me. Anything that just redirects my attention from the story,

I annotate. You must look at the case with unbiased eyes. Not as a cop, not as an innocent—as a natural observer. I read it like a story and let it talk to me. I let the story become a visual in my head. Once I am done, which may take a couple of days, I re-read it. This time, I become a little more meticulous in my approach. It no longer is a story; it is fact and fiction. I re-read a sentence a couple of times or I start to write down times, names, stories that may or may not have rational explanation. I start annotating timelines and alibis. I start marking asterisks by people or things that pique my interest.

After this, I re-read, re-read and re-read the report again before I do anything else. I want to know the case like the back of my hand. I want to know that victim. I want to know what that victim would most likely do given a certain circumstance. I also want to fill my brain with every fact about the case so when I am in a room with a bunch of people talking about the case, I have an answer to every question that is asked of me. If famed pathologist Dr. Cyril Wecht asks me a question, the worst answer I can give is, "I don't know." I learned this lesson quickly in the Marine Corps. The correct answer is and always will be, "I don't know right now but I will find out." I have seen detectives who have investigated cases not remember the date of the homicides. Are you kidding me? If that investigator were working for me, I would fire him. Now I understand if you have 150 homicides under your belt, but a small town like Williamsport, Pa., there is no excuse. It simply means you don't care enough to remember.

After I have read the file numerous times, I then start working the leads that I have jotted down. I start interviewing people from my notepad that I felt may have information or can shed light on the case. It gets my blood pumping. I get excited reading a case file. I see things unfolding in my brain. The smells, the culture, the looks, the fear, and the pain—I feel it all. Not literally, of course, as I don't believe in psychics or any of that. But I do believe in letting the facts tell you a story of what happened and who is responsible. You couple that story with inductive and deductive reasoning in order to get to the truth.

A cold case is unique because it gives the investigator something the original investigator never had: time. Time is an undefeated opponent. No one beats time. Yet, time gives me an advantage.

> *"Patience and perseverance have a magical effect before which difficulties disappear and obstacles vanish." – John Quincy Adams*

Sure, original investigators have the best chance of solving the case because they have the best chance to interview people when things are fresh in their minds. They also have the benefit of having to notice fresh abrasions, bruises and scratches on people that a cold case investigator doesn't have. However, it is a tradeoff. Cold cases can be worked at a leisurely pace with no interruptions.

What people who are not cops fail to realize is why cases become cold. Detectives do not have the luxury of only working a homicide case. When a homicide occurs and is assigned to a detective, the current caseload doesn't stop. The homicide takes priority, but the caseload continues to pile up on the desk. The robberies, the burglaries and the frauds continue to come in.

Detectives work those homicide leads until they reach a dead end and their supervisors remind them about the other cases that are piling up on the desk. That is how a case becomes cold. It gets pushed to the side after leads dry up and the detective has to get back to the other cases.

A cold-case detective doesn't have that problem, so in some ways, my job is easier. Sure, when I review a case I think, "Boy, I wish I were the original investigator on this," and I criticize some of their actions, but the bottom line is hindsight is always 20/20.

Another aspect of time that benefits a cold-case investigator is that over time, relationships change. Couples break up through the passage of time and friends have falling outs with each other. This benefits me because I can go to them now and re-introduce them to the crime. I want to bring all those memories and emotions flooding into their brains when I knock on their door. I am bringing something to them that most of them have suppressed deep down inside and they would never bring it up willingly had I not knocked on that door 20 years later.

Sometimes, it is the suspect's door I am knocking on, whether

I know it or not. Usually, I treat everyone as a suspect in a cold case because the simple fact is, I don't know who committed the murder. I don't let them know this; I treat them like a friend or a witness and I'm just there gathering information. But I watch them; I observe them keenly. Their actions, their demeanors, their responses, these actions—done consciously or subconsciously— are what I am noticing.

I don't make any conclusions off of these, but I do note them. Some people are nervous when a cop comes knocking on their door, whether they have something to hide or not. Some people will fidget with their hair or tap their foot because it is what they do, not because they are hiding information on a 20-year-old murder. However, it is something I take note of because it gives you an insight to this person's normal behavior.

"Human behavior flows from three main
sources: desire, emotion and knowledge."

Plato

Studying human behavior and listening more than talking is the best way to interpret verbal and non-verbal cues from a suspect. I knew of a veteran detective who would sit silent with suspects for long periods of time before the suspect would begin talking, unprovoked. The detective did this with me and I fell for it. I couldn't take the silence and it made me talk. It is very, very effective technique that I incorporate into my interviews.

Revisit the crime scene, no matter what. One of the most shocking aspects of my foray into cold-case investigations came from a re-visit. You can gauge nothing from photographs. I stared at crime scene photographs, video and had driven by the Matthews house hundreds of times. However, I never went in the house. Big mistake. During my investigation into the Gail Matthews murders, I was constantly bombarded about the next-door neighbor being involved. This was because people couldn't understand how she didn't hear any the victims screaming or struggling for their lives. So, I revisited the scene of this heinous crime 18 years after the fact.

I was aghast of how incredibly small the entire house was, especially the bedroom where the bodies were found—Gail and her daughter, Tamara, both strangled and void of life. I could never get the correct feel for what those victims went through until I was in the very same room their last breaths were taken. I was floored, shocked and frightened. They had nowhere to run. They were killed in a room that was basically the size of a large closet. I never got the feeling of the room size by those pictures or videos; I had to go and stand there for myself.

I stood in the neighbor's bedroom where she was during the time I believed the murders took place. I had another detective stand in the room where the murders took place and where the bodies were recovered. I began to scream and yell and thrash about. After a few minutes, the detective in the other room called me and asked if I had started. I told him I had been yelling and screaming for a minute or so. He heard nothing. Myth debunked. The other detective was now a believer as well. Those small details have to be done in order to confirm or move on to another suspect.

One thing I tell young investigators is something I learned through trial and error: do not manipulate the facts or the evidence to fit your theory. Don't overthink it. You make this mistake when you have tunnel vision on a person of interest or suspect. You try to make everything fit or you look too deep into something when it has zero bearing on the case. An example of this is I had a father whose daughter was murdered. When I looked at the case decades later, I was looking a photograph of him. I observed a picture of a tattoo he got in remembrance of his daughter. The tattoo had his daughter's date of birth and the date she died. The only problem is, the date of death was two days off. I immediately jumped on this as a big break in the case. I theorized he put the different date on the tattoo because he couldn't bear to put the date he killed her on his body for eternity. She had died on the first of the month and he had the third. Looking back, I was just so focused on this guy and was looking for anything and everything to justify my opinion that he was responsible for the murder. Lesson learned.

One of my idiosyncrasies when I work a cold case is to keep a journal of everything I have done in the case. This is unlike the police report that you turn into your supervisors that is a lot more detailed. This is just a synopsis of things I did. The reason I keep this is twofold. One is because I now have a quick reference to go back to in order to determine if and when I did something regarding the case. Another is thinking down the road. Always be preparing for trial and anticipate what the defense is going to do or say before you even make an arrest.

I keep this journal so that I know what I did and there is never a question. Yes, this journal is discoverable—and the defense attorneys and their clients can read it—but it doesn't matter, because you are putting facts into it, not conjecture. The journal also saves me from flipping through hundreds or thousands of police reports to find a date of when I did something.

Next comes the fun part of solving cold cases: deduction. You have your list of suspects. You can now start eliminating based on solid alibis. Next, you can deduce further because of crime scene assessments and the nature of the crime. You eliminate based on known commodities until the suspect shows himself to you. This is a simple process, but it takes years of trial and error to perfect. You cannot simply eliminate a career burglar as a suspect from a murder/rape case because nothing is missing from the crime scene. Yet, you can draw inferences and move around your suspect tree a bit. You create a suspect tree much like a family tree.

I then start looking at the evidence to see if it matches up with any of my suspects or if I can start eliminating based on evidence. At the same time, I can look to see what can be retested as new technology becomes relevant. Regardless of all the previous mentioned methodologies, there is really only one trait that matters.

Dedication is something that cannot be learned. It is a trait you either have or do not. It comes with passion for the job in which you are doing. When I investigate a case, everything else takes a back seat to that mission. I can't turn it off. I may not have a master's degree in DNA, but I promise you that I have a PhD in determination. You can't quit. You can't give up. You must push through any obstacle in your way to be successful as a cold case detective and in life.

*"It's not that I'm so smart; it's just that
I stay with problems longer."*

Albert Einstein

The best professional compliment I ever received was when I was told by two different and well-respected police officers, Brett Williams and Justin Snyder, on separate occasions mind you, "If I was ever lying dead somewhere on a street corner, I would want you standing over me investigating my death." As an investigator, I could not ask for a higher, more humbling compliment then that!

While I currently work for the district attorney, I do consulting services as well. When I get hired by law enforcement and victims' families to review their cases, I become obsessed with it. Everything else becomes secondary. Especially for the victims' families, I am there for them 110 percent because they deserve that. They deserve that respect. It is my job to give it everything I can to help them find that elusive term: closure.

The challenges of cold-case investigations and homicides are plentiful but one is always head and shoulders above the rest: turning it off. I have preached this before. Going to bed at night and continually thinking of ways to solve the case or who may have done it or what you could be doing better to solve the case. For me personally, you never turn that off. I think all great homicide detectives are like that; you never turn it off and you can't separate your personal life from work. Those victims stay with me when I am eating dinner with my family. The crime stays with me when I am grocery shopping, which is just how it is, I just can't turn it off.

After I meet the parents of a murder victim, I want to do nothing more than to solve the case and bring them closure. You feel their pain, their desolation and despair. You can see it in their eyes as they put their entire faith in you. They want you to rid them of this sickening feeling of loss and solve the case. That, my friend, is called pressure. That, my friend, is cold-case investigations. Welcome to my world.

CRIMINAL PROFILING

*"The investigation, analysis, and resolution of cold cases
in real life is more complex and challenging than what is
portrayed in the world of fiction. Experience, dedication,
perseverance, and keen intellect are necessary for successful
outcomes. Kenneth Mains possesses all these qualities
and utilizes his acquired skill to help bring closure and
comfort to puzzled agencies and grieving families."*

Dr. Cyril Wecht, world-renowned forensic pathologist

Criminal profiling is the process of identifying behavioral tendencies, personality traits and geographic location, demographic or biographic descriptors of an offender based on the characteristics of a particular crime. The primary goal of criminal profiling is to narrow the field of possible suspects to a more reasonable number from the hundreds or thousands of possible suspects. It is a tool, not an absolute. Sometimes, it works. Sometimes, it doesn't and it should never be used as an absolute. I have seen some very good assessments, but I have also seen some that were horrible and wrong.

Former FBI profiler Mark Safarik is great and I love reading his assessments. He wrote one on a case I was reviewing with him and I was impressed with his work. Another person whose assessments I think are great is Anthony Meoli. Both come from different backgrounds, but both do outstanding work. The reason is because they do not guess. The both backed up their assessments with facts and not conjecture. They explain why they see something the way they do. I have seen criminal profilers not associate their name with their work. To me, the only reason would be because you can't substantiate your assessments.

I am not a criminal profiler. I never have claimed to be such. Others in that field take great pride in being called a criminal profiler, people including John Douglas, Jim Clemente, Mary Ellen O'Toole, Robert Ressler, Mark Safarik, Richard Walter and Brent Turvey. Some have better résumés and reputations then others. When they do what they do to help victims and law enforcement in order to solve the crime, I am a fan of theirs. When it is done to promote, bash or create a hardship for others because of personal vendettas, I get angry. Again, some people will hate or despise others for no real reason—that is life. Yet these criminal profilers will use inductive and deductive measures to create a profile of what type offender committed the crime. Although I do subscribe to the deductive art in criminal profiling, I like to use that in conjunction with the statistical side or inductive profiling.

I like to say I am more of a "crime scene assessor," of which all detectives are or should be. We look at the scene in order to give us indicators as to who committed the offense. When I started my master's degree, my first course was criminal profiling. Although I found the course rather easy and obtained the grade of A-, it left me feeling that profiling is an art. Like most art, it should be used in conjunction with other variables in order to create a masterpiece. That is why I don't call myself a profiler. Many individuals make that mistake and throw around the term "profiler" very loosely. I have had discussions with true criminal profilers and it makes them very angry. I use crime scene assessment along with other facets of investigating in order to solve crime.

A perfect example is finding the murder weapon at a crime scene. A knife is placed on a shelf in a closet that is 7 feet high. The area is carpeted. The shelf is filled to the very top of the ceiling with various articles and clothing. The knife is on top of all of these items. There is no chair in the room and no indentations in the carpet from a chair. From this alone, you can deduce that your suspect is most likely over 6 feet tall because he didn't throw the knife up there and no chair was used. That is crime scene assessment.

I was asked once to create a criminal profile for a famous unsolved case. I chose to write about "who" D.B. Cooper was. This isn't a profile as much as it is a crime scene assessment. Now this is much different than a murder scene, but you take what evidence you know, incorporate it into your experiences and known facts in order to assess the crime. Below is an example of how you can take a known fact and mold it into a working theory that will eventually lead you to a suspect by deduction. Again, using the art of deduction, the suspect will show himself.

For those who do not know, a man hijacked a Boeing 727 aircraft flying between Portland, Ore., and Seattle, Wash., on Nov. 24, 1971. He requested $200,000 in ransom and then parachuted to an uncertain fate. Despite an extensive manhunt and an ongoing FBI investigation, the perpetrator has never been located or positively identified.

The suspect purchased his airline ticket using the alias Dan Cooper, but due to a news broadcasting miscommunication, he became known in popular lore as "D.B. Cooper." Hundreds of leads have been pursued in the ensuing years, but no conclusive evidence has ever surfaced regarding Cooper's true identity or whereabouts. The only solid clue to the enduring mystery was the discovery in February 1980 when an 8-year-old boy named Brian Ingram uncovered three packets of the ransom cash, significantly degenerated but still bundled in rubber bands, as he raked the sandy riverbank to build a campfire. FBI technicians confirmed that the money was indeed a portion of the ransom—two packets of 100 bills each and a third packet of 90, all arranged in the same order as when given to Cooper.

The incident began mid-afternoon on Thanksgiving Eve, 1971, at Portland International Airport. A man carrying a black attaché case approached the flight counter of Northwest Orient Airlines. He identified himself as "Dan Cooper" and purchased a one-way ticket on Flight 305, a 30-minute trip to Seattle.

Cooper boarded the aircraft and took seat in the rear of the passenger cabin. He lit a cigarette and ordered a bourbon and water. Eyewitnesses recalled a man in his mid-forties, between 5 feet 10 inches and 6 feet tall. He wore a black lightweight raincoat, loafers, a dark suit, neatly pressed white collared shirt, black necktie and mother of pearl tiepin.

Cooper passed a note to a flight attendant sitting nearest to him in a jump seat attached to the aft stair door. She, assuming the note contained a lonely businessman's phone number, dropped it unopened into her purse. Cooper leaned toward her and whispered, "Miss, you'd better look at that note. I have a bomb." The note was printed in neat, all-capital letters with a felt pen. It read, "I have a bomb in my briefcase. I will use it if necessary. I want you to sit next to me. You are being hijacked." The attendant did as requested and then quietly asked to see the bomb. Cooper cracked open his briefcase long enough for her to glimpse wires coated with red insulation and a large cylindrical battery. After closing the briefcase, he dictated his demands: $200,000 in "negotiable American currency," four parachutes and a fuel truck standing by in Seattle to refuel the aircraft upon arrival.

Cooper appeared familiar with the local terrain; at one point, he remarked, "Looks like Tacoma down there," as the aircraft flew above it. He also mentioned, correctly, that McChord Air Force Base was only a 20-minute drive from Seattle-Tacoma Airport. He was described as calm, polite, and well-spoken. "He wasn't nervous," the attendant told investigators. "He seemed rather nice.

He was never cruel or nasty. He was thoughtful and calm all the time." He ordered a second bourbon and water, paid his drink tab (and insisted the attendant keep the change) and offered to request meals for the flight crew during the stop in Seattle.

Cooper rejected the military-issue parachutes initially offered by authorities, demanding instead civilian parachutes with manually operated ripcords. At 5:24 p.m., Cooper was informed that his demands had been met, and at 5:39 p.m., the aircraft landed at Seattle-Tacoma Airport. Cooper instructed the pilot to taxi the jet to an isolated, brightly lit section of the tarmac and extinguish lights in the cabin to deter police snipers. Cooper was then delivered a cash-filled knapsack and once the delivery was completed, Cooper permitted all passengers and senior flight attendant Alice Hancock to leave the plane.

During refueling, Cooper outlined his flight plan to the cockpit crew: a southeast course toward Mexico City at the minimum air speed possible without stalling the aircraft at a maximum 10,000-foot altitude. He further specified that the landing gear remain deployed in the takeoff/landing position, the wing flaps be lowered 15 degrees and the cabin remain unpressurized. Cooper and the crew discussed options and agreed on Reno, Nev., as the refueling stop. Finally, Cooper directed that the plane take off with the rear exit door open and its staircase extended. Northwest's home office objected on grounds that it was unsafe to take off with the aft staircase deployed. Cooper countered that it was indeed safe, but he would not argue the point; he would lower it himself once they were airborne. At approximately 7:40 p.m., the 727 took off with only Cooper, the pilot, two flight attendants, the co-pilot and a flight engineer. After takeoff, Cooper told the flight attendants to join the rest of the crew in the cockpit and remain there with the door closed. As she complied, she observed Cooper tying something around his waist. At approximately 8 p.m., a warning light flashed in the cockpit, indicating that the aft stair apparatus had been activated. The crew's offer of assistance via the aircraft's intercom system was curtly refused. The crew soon noticed a subjective change of air pressure, indicating that the aft door was open.

At approximately 8:13 p.m., the aircraft's tail section sustained a sudden upward movement, significant enough to require the pilot to bring the plane back to level flight.

D.B. Cooper had jumped into the cold, black night, never to be heard from again. Aboard the airliner, FBI agents recovered 66 unidentified latent fingerprints, Cooper's black clip-on tie and mother of pearl tie clip, and two of the four parachutes, one of which had been opened and two shroud lines cut from its canopy, presumably used to tie the bag of money to himself.

To date, none of the approximately 9,700 remaining bills has turned up anywhere in the world. Their serial numbers remain available online for public search.

In late 2007, the FBI announced that a partial DNA profile had been obtained from three organic samples found on the clip-on tie left behind by the hijacker. That partial DNA profile might or might not be Cooper's. Touch DNA is a very tricky and delicate subject. DNA will not always solve your crime; it should be treated as another lead.

The Bureau also made public a file of previously unreleased evidence, including Cooper's 1971 plane ticket from Portland to Seattle and disclosed that Cooper chose the older of the two primary parachutes supplied to him, rather than the technically superior professional sport parachute.

In addition, from the two reserve parachutes he received, Cooper selected a "dummy"—an unusable unit with an inoperative ripcord intended for classroom demonstrations, despite the fact that it had clear markings identifying it to any experienced skydiver as non-functional.

So, who was D.B. Cooper and where did he go? The first question is not as easy to answer as the second, but here is my assessment:

- D.B. Cooper was a middle-aged white male in financial disarray. Cooper was probably a gambler, whether large or small. I base this on the fact he pulled off a daring, systematic and unprecedented act that may or may not have been because he was in desperate need of money.

- Cooper had no living family or he did not correspond with his family. Thanksgiving is one of the most suicidal times of the year. Often, acts of desperation are committed around this time. His choosing of this date to commit this crime is not by accident. It was because he was desperate and probably depressed.

- He was *not* a skilled parachutist and may have never jumped before in his life. A skilled parachutist could have made the jump in the pitch-black night, in the rain, with a 200-mph wind in his face, and into a −70 °F wind chill. A skilled parachutist would not have done so wearing loafers, suit and a trench coat and would have picked better weather for the jump. He also would not have chosen to jump with the older and technically inferior of the two primary parachutes supplied to him.

- Cooper was vaguely familiar with the practice of "jumping," but very familiar with airplanes, especially the Boeing 727. This leads me to believe he worked on or around these particular planes and chose the 727 because of the aft stairwell.

- He was a planner, though not meticulous. He did not simply carry a briefcase and state he had a bomb, he made a realistic bomb replica equipped with wires and batteries. He brought the ransom note. He knew exact coordinates, altitudes and speed to which instruct the pilots. These were not written down, so he either memorized them or knew this through experienced learning. That would show planning. However, he didn't bring proper clothing for the jump, which leads me to believe he was desperate.

- He was probably not in the military or was in the military and kicked out. He was familiar with the military and their tactics. He may have had had a brother or good friend in the military or his father may have served in the military as well. I base this on the fact that Cooper planned, but didn't plan enough. He had the forethought to have details in place, but not enough. In other words, he knew planning was important, but didn't care enough to follow through 100 percent with the proper planning. He didn't want the military parachutes that were presented to him, opting instead for the civilian. This may because he did not trust the military, based on experience.

- He lived in or around McChord Air Force Base or surrounding area during the time of the crime or at some point in his life. He was too familiar with distance and time it takes to travel to and from this area to not be intimately familiar with the base.

- He had spent time in Canada or at least a portion thereof. Although Dan Cooper is a rather common American name, the alias Dan Cooper most likely came from a popular comic book series of the 1970s featuring the fictional hero Dan Cooper, a Royal Canadian Air Force test pilot. One cover from the series depicts test pilot Cooper skydiving. This is a coincidence I cannot ignore. Because the Dan Cooper comics were never translated into English nor imported to the U.S., it is possible that Cooper was Canadian and found the comics in Canada, where they were also sold. In addition, the comment Cooper made in his demand for "negotiable American currency" is peculiar and no one stated that Cooper had an accent. This being said, Canada would be his most likely country of origin if he were not a United States citizen.

- Lastly, but the easiest to determine is that D.B. Cooper died during the commission of this crime. Given the fact that none of the money ever showed back up in circulation and part of it was found deteriorated on the banks of a river, it is probable that he died during the jump. He was obviously not dressed appropriately, was not skilled in the art of jumping and had the adverse weather against him. It is probable he landed in a body of water and drowned when the parachute pulled him under in the pitch-black night or died shortly thereafter from hypothermia.

Although, the more I think about it ... maybe D.B. Cooper had a jeep waiting for him in the vast wilderness where he jumped and landed safely. He then discarded some of the currency to make it appear as if he died during the jump. Cooper then drove himself out of the forest, to a hunting cabin where he smoked a cigar and drank a fine bourbon while he fantasized about the legend he just created.

D.B. Cooper courtesy of FBI

ACTUAL COLD CASES

"Kenneth is an experienced investigator and trusted friend and colleague. His organizational skills and ability to gather a team of national experts in all fields related to violent and sexual crimes is phenomenal. I have a tremendous amount of respect for his investigative insights and his integrity as an honest and hard-working professional."

Jim Clemente, former FBI criminal profiler and writer from the television show "Criminal Minds"

This is it. This is why I was put on this earth. Cold cases. The unsolved. The cat-and-mouse game. Thinking like the offender, yet reacting like the victim. Wondering, searching and calculating the behaviors, reasons and magnitudes of the case. You have to be it. You have to feel what they felt, think like they think and execute like they execute. In order to effectively solve a cold case, you have to exhort every ounce of passion, dedication and determination from your pores. You have to bleed, sweat and piss passion. You reach inside yourself and pull out your own inner demons, your scarred childhood and insecurities and turn them outwardly into palatable experiences that will help you solve this case.

There is a huge difference between cases that I actually investigate and others in which I am requested or hired to review. I am contacted all the time—even before the creation of the American Investigative Society of Cold Cases—to assist on cases. Most of the time, it is by family members of loved ones murdered who have yet to find that closure they so desperately desire.

The biggest difference is the access to the entire case file. Any good investigator will request and need access to the entire case file in order to do an accurate and concise review. Without this, not only are you gambling with your findings, but you are also undermining the original investigators' work, opinions and summations. I do not like to do this. It is easy to look at everything in hindsight and second-guess.

With that being said, sometimes working without the entire case file and access to all of the evidence cannot be done. However, it needs to be done with a disclaimer. The person requesting the review needs to be informed that the findings are based off of the limited information available at the time of review. If other information becomes available, it could change your ruling, theories and summations as well. If they can accept this, then there is little harm in helping.

So here I will present several cases in which I personally investigated and reviewed. There are some in which I had the entire case file available to me and others that I did not. I think it is easy to ascertain which is which. I tried to include a variety of cases: equivocal deaths, missing persons, whodunits and others in which the perpetrator is known but the case is not provable.

DAWN MARIE MILLER
MISSING PERSON

*"I can't say enough about the efforts of this man
to solve a case that nobody else cared about. It is
heartwarming to know that in a world where there
is so much violence and hatred, that there are really
good people like Ken who do care. You hear so much
about bad cops, but you never hear about the good
ones that really care. Ken is one of those who do."*

Sandy Northern

This is the case that changed my life. This is the case that got me started as a cold case investigator, Dawn Marie Miller. A name to be forever etched into my soul. As I had stated previously, I had worked for the Williamsport Bureau of Police for about four years by 2007 and never heard of the name Dawn Miller or even knew the department had an unsolved missing person's case. Usually, there will be a missing person's flier posted around the department, regardless of how much time has passed. I had typed the words "missing person" and "Williamsport" in the Google search engine and Dawn Marie Miller was introduced into my life. I had no idea at the time it would forever change my life.

I received the report from our records department, all two pages of the initial report with a few pages of follow-up investigations. It was easy for me to decide where to start: the last two people to see her alive.

I don't know exactly how this case slipped through the justice system other than to say there were jurisdiction problems and I believe laziness had something to do with it initially. Dawn was from Williamsport, but she was visiting her new boyfriend in Bellefonte, Pa. So you had investigators from Lycoming County (Williamsport police) and Centre County (Bellefonte police) telling Dawn's mother that each other's department was responsible for handling the missing persons case. Critical time was lost during these weeks of pushing off the work.

Once Dawn's mother went to the newspaper to report her daughter missing—that's right, she had to go to the newspaper—then the Williamsport police decided to take the missing person report and start an investigation. However, for some reason, one in which I do not fully understand, a proper investigation did not commence. If it did, I never received more than two pages of the investigative reports.

Within one week, I had two suspects who I had no doubt murdered this girl. It was very clear this young woman was not a runaway as portrayed. This poor girl was murdered and no one did the proper investigation necessary to convict the two individuals responsible. The first page of the report detailed how Dawn's boyfriend, Gregory Emel, and his nephew were the last to see her alive and drove her from Bellefonte to Williamsport to take her home. Upon returning, Emel had a fresh scratch on his face, which he claimed was from a jagger bush. Are you serious? What investigator believed that story? Apparently, a few did because he got away with murder for 20 years until I was able to put the pieces together decades later. The facts of the case are this:

On or about Oct. 24, 1992, Dawn was last seen leaving the Academy Apartments in Bellefonte Borough, Centre County, with two men: Emel and his nephew, John Easton, which is not his real name. Dawn has never been seen or heard from again.

Dawn's family, being unable to locate her in the following days, reported her missing to the Bellefonte police department and also the Williamsport Bureau of Police. Dawn lived in Williamsport at the time, but was visiting Bellefonte Borough. An official missing person investigation was initiated through the Williamsport Bureau of Police on Dec. 14, 1992.

During the initial stages of this investigation, it was learned that Dawn had traveled from Williamsport to the Academy Apartments in Bellefonte to be with her boyfriend at the time, Emel. Emel was staying at the Academy Apartments, apartment number 3-7, with Easton and his then-girlfriend, Bonnie Gardner.

It was determined during the initial investigation in 1992 that Emel and Easton left the Academy Apartments with Dawn on or about Oct. 24, 1992 at approximately 8 p.m. Emel and Easton returned between 11:30 p.m. and 2 a.m. without Dawn.

In December 1992, Sgt. Curly Jett of the Williamsport Bureau of Police interviewed Emel and Easton. Sgt. Jett stated that he actually drove the men f nm rom Bellefonte to Williamsport in an attempt to show the officer where they had dropped Dawn off. According to Sgt. Jett, they could not pinpoint a location.

After no further leads were developed in this investigation, it eventually turned cold. In January 2008, after reviewing an Internet website for missing persons (www.network.org), I came across Dawn's missing persons information. I then sought and received permission to reopen and investigate the disappearance, as long as I did it on my own time. I was told I was a "dope cop" and couldn't investigate on normal work hours. I requested to do it on my days off and after work and was finally granted permission.

This was my very first "mystery" to investigate and had unlimited access to. I had dabbled before I was a police officer with the disappearance of Carrie Culberson from Blanchester, Ohio, but this was different. I wasn't just talking to private investigators or peripheral players; I was actually in the game.

In January 2008, Agent William Weber of the Williamsport Bureau of Police and I interviewed Michael L. Williams. Williams becomes an integral part of the solving of this case. He was the one who always insisted that Dawn was murdered. He knew and he never quit trying to tell everyone about what he believed happened to his friend Dawn Miller. Williams lived at the Academy Apartments in October 1992 and was friends with both Emel and Easton. Williams also was married to Easton's sister, Janice. Williams frequently hung out with the Emel and Easton during this time period. According to Williams, a couple of days before Dawn's disappearance, he overheard Emel and Easton referring to Dawn: "She's gone like history" and "We're gonna drop her off the Earth." He heard Easton state, "We are gonna roll her up in a rug." Emel also told him "if Dawn is pregnant, it's not my kid." These are all statements that tie into the totality of the entire scenario. These statements alone do not prove anything, yet it gives the detective an avenue to go down. It gives the detective a new lead and ask any detective, that's all we want is to have another lead.

Williams stated that on or around Oct. 24, 1992, he was told by Emel and Easton that they were leaving to take Dawn back to Williamsport because "she was getting on their nerves." Williams then observed Emel and Easton return to the Academy Apartments several hours later with various scratches and soiled clothing (a facial scratch on Emel, dirt/blood on Easton's pants). Williams confirmed that neither Emel appeared in such condition prior to leaving the apartment with Dawn.

The next day, Williams saw Emel and Easton throwing Dawn's belongings, including her purse and backpack, into a dumpster at the Academy Apartments. This backpack, according to Williams, contained a journal that Williams observed Dawn writing in. When Williams asked why they were doing this, Emel said, "She's not coming back," referring to Dawn.

Williams also said in November or December of 1992, Emel and Easton took him to a wooded area near Howard, known as the Howard Reservoir, in Howard Township, Centre County. There, Williams overheard Dawn asking Easton if he "remembered the spot." Williams was disturbed by the "weird" content of the conversation between Emel and Easton. Williams was also disturbed by the fact that Easton vomited in this same wooded area at that time. Williams believed this area had something to do with Dawn's disappearance.

In November 2001, Williams called the Bellefonte police department with this information he believed to be relevant to the case. Williams had long tried to alert police to Dawn's disappearance, but was rebuffed continually. Williams stated that he watched as Emel moved his belongings out of the Academy Apartments shortly after Dawn's disappearance. When Williams asked Emel what he was doing, he said, "I'm not coming around here anymore." Williams also indicated that when Emel returned from having dropped Dawn off in Williamsport, he observed a scratch on Emel's cheek and blood on his leg. Why wasn't this stuff relayed to the police I kept thinking to myself? Williams claimed it was. He also stated that Easton appeared to drink more alcohol, do more drugs and become more violent after Dawn disappeared. I know this to happen to individuals who commit murder. They become guilt ridden and try to drown their conscience in cocaine and beer. It doesn't always work.

Williams said that in June 2002 he asked Easton how he "could do that to that girl," referring to Dawn. Easton responded by attacking Williams, grabbing him by the throat and whispering into his ear, "Do you want to die like her?" This is another example of his violence and not wanting to be reminded of what he did. During another altercation with Williams, when Williams accused Easton of being involved with Dawn's disappearance, Easton again grabbed Williams by the throat and stated, "I'll fucking kill you. I've done it once. I can do it again." He does this strictly as a form of intimidation. Again, for some unknown reason, this information was never followed up on. No police department was working on the case. It took me going to Bellefonte police department a decade later and going through files in a basement to find this information. It goes to show that if you want something, don't take it at face value it isn't there; you have to dig. It also goes to show there was no communications between the two police departments. This happens a lot when multiple jurisdictions are involved with a missing person case. After Dawn's mom reported her missing in 1992, there was absolutely no follow-up after that fall.

Williams wouldn't let Dawn's disappearance go. He knew that Dawn was murdered and he knew who did it. He could not believe that the police were not taking any action. Dawn was simply slipping through the cracks of the criminal justice system that was supposed to protect her. In fact, the investigators allowed her to be forgotten because they did a substandard investigation. I don't like to call out police because I know the struggles, but I will when I see it. I saw it up close and it is pitiful what they did in this case and to this girl.

In January 2008, Williams led Agent William Weber and me to this location where Emel asked Easton, "Do you remember the spot?" This wooded area is approximately 14 miles from the apartment where Dawn had been last seen and approximately one mile from Emel's residence.

After some additional digging in the Bellefonte Police files, I found a one-page report in which Emel went to an area in the woods and threatened suicide. No big deal, right? I mean there are a lot of people who commit suicide in the woods. Yet, when I looked closely, two things jumped out to me. First was the date. Second was the location. Again, alone these details mean nothing, but when you couple them with the totality, it begins to add up and paint you a picture. This location is where on Oct. 23, 1993 (the one-year anniversary of Dawn's disappearance) Emel was taken into custody after threatening suicide. This location is where Emel told Williams he would take Dawn to park. At this point, I know something happened at this spot. Too many coincidences that add up. Emel is heard asking, "Do you remember the spot?", the date coincides with the anniversary of Dawn's disappearance and it is an area where Emel was known to go parking with Dawn. Something took place at this spot. The location holds a significant meaning to Emel, which is why he goes to this location one year after the disappearance and threatens suicide.

In January 2008, I interviewed Gardner, Easton's girlfriend who shared an apartment with him in October 1992.

Gardner stated she had a long-term relationship with Easton and knew him to be extremely violent. She said Easton had beaten her up to six times a day for years during the relationship. Once, she said, he strangled her with a cord in front of Dawn's brother, Joseph Miller, and a mutual friend.

Gardner stated she remembers Dawn being at her apartment with Dawn in October 1992. She stated that one evening, sometime around dark, Emel and Easton stated they were taking Dawn back to Williamsport. Gardner asked to accompany them, but Easton refused to let her. Gardner stated that this was unusual behavior because Easton was controlling and always took her with him everywhere he went. To me, this is one indication of premeditation. They knew what they were going to do to Dawn when they left those apartments.

Gardner saw Easton and Emel return to the apartment between 11:30 p.m. and 2 a.m. Gardner said she Easton immediately went into the bathroom, at which time she heard water running and concluded that Easton was washing his hands. Gardner said she then saw Easton leave the bathroom and whisper into Emel's ear, after which both men went into a bedroom and shut the door. Gardner heard Emel and Easton whispering to each other. She found this behavior odd, as they had never before acted in this manner.

When Easton and Emel came out of the bedroom, they observed Dawn's backpack, which had been left at the apartment. According to Gardner, this backpack contained a journal in which Dawn often wrote. Easton and Emel threw the backpack into the dumpster, where Gardner saw it the next morning. Gardner noticed that Emel had a single scratch down the left side of his cheek and Easton had a scratch on his left arm. When she inquired as to what happened they both explained that they had gotten a flat tire after dropping off Dawn in Williamsport; they said a tire rolled over an embankment and Emel received the scratch from a briar jagging his face as he retrieved the tire. Gardner asked both men where Dawn was and Emel stated, "Maybe a trucker or black guy nabbed her." This statement is given only hours after Emel was last seen with Dawn. Dawn wasn't even declared missing yet; so the statement is odd and indicative of someone who knows her fate already.

Gardner stated that Emel is Easton's uncle, but Emel did whatever Easton told him to do. She stated that Easton and Emel hung around together frequently up to that day. However, after Dawn disappeared, Emel and Easton rarely were seen together. Again, this is another indication to me that they were the correct suspects. Oftentimes, people who commit a crime together will distance themselves from each other after the crime.

In February 2008, I interviewed Joseph Miller, Dawn's brother. Miller stated he had confronted Easton a couple of days after Dawn disappeared. Miller knew Easton very well and considered him a friend. Miller asked where his sister was and Easton became evasive in his answers and would not make eye contact with Miller. Again, this is indicative of someone who feels guilty. Easton then stated that he dropped her off at a convenience store in Williamsport. Miller stated he observed two scratches on Easton's neck and several on Easton's left arm. Miller asked Easton how he obtained the scratches and Easton told him, "I fell."

In May 2008, Trooper David Aiello of the Pennsylvania State Police, who helped me extensively with this case, interviewed Jamie Lynn, Easton's former wife. She stated that Easton was an extremely violent guy and a bully. She stated that he would hit her all the time and pick fights with people just to fight. She described Easton's rage as "uncontrollable."

In June 2008, Trooper Aiello interviewed Matthew Rupert, who lived with Dawn from about 1993 to 1994. Rupert overheard Emel saying to another person, "That's OK; I've made women come up missing before." Emel had been drinking and was angry at the time. In June 2008, Trooper Aiello interviewed Jodi Noll, who also lived with Emel around 1993 to 1994. According to Noll, Emel once said something to her about "making me disappear like another woman." So now you have two witnesses who have heard Emel state he has made a girl disappear before.

I finally felt ready to interview my number one suspect, Emel, regarding the disappearance of Dawn. Remember, he had only been interviewed once in 20 years and there had been no pressure put on him. In his mind, he had gotten away with this murder. He looked confident; he wasn't at all nervous. Of course, we had gotten him to the interview using a ruse. We told him he needed to come update his Megan's Law information. Greg had been convicted of inappropriately touching his young niece and had to register under Megan's Law. So he just figured that is why he was there. Then this longhaired, earring-wearing police officer from Williamsport showed up in the room with a picture of Dawn and a notepad. I shook his hand and said, "Greg, I'm Officer Ken Mains from Williamsport. Greg's demeanor changed rapidly. I showed him a picture of Dawn and asked him if he knew who that was. He stated, "It looks like Dawn Miller." He squirmed in his chair, looked at the door and became nervous. I knew I had him.

Emel stated that he knew Dawn and had had a sexual relationship with her in October 1992. He stated the reason he took Dawn back to Williamsport on the night in question "because she was getting on everyone's nerves and people in the Academy Apartments were threatening to beat her up." To most people, and maybe to himself, Emel was trying to concoct an alibi or excuse. But to me, as a skilled interviewer with experience in how the criminal mind thinks, I saw him as a guilty man trying to deflect culpability off himself and divert my attention elsewhere away from him. He stated he took Easton with him because he did not know his way around Williamsport. He did not remember the date, day, time or where they sat in the vehicle.

When I asked about the possibility of Dawn being pregnant, Emel specifically remembered "she wasn't pregnant because she was on her period, because she borrowed a maxi-pad from Bonnie that night." Gardner does not recall this incident. Emel also remembered getting a flat tire on the way back from dropping Dawn off at her house in Williamsport. Emel explained that he received a scratch while retrieving a tire that had rolled over an embankment. When asked what happened to the backpack that Dawn left at the apartment, Emel insisted that the cops retrieved it. When asked if he had blood on his pants upon his return to the

Academy Apartments after having dropped off Dawn—as reported by a witness—Emel explained, Easton "had blood, I mean red paint on his pants. It was from a job he had done earlier in the day. Do you really think that if we did something to this girl we would return with evidence?" When asked about the Howard Reservoir area, Emel stated, "I used to go parking there with Dawn."

I hit him with the questions, rapid-fire, one right after the other. I did this to throw on the table what I had. I wasn't going to be like past investigators and believe his lies. I knew I had the right guy and I wanted him to know that I knew that. Though at times visibly shaken and making the statement "Don't you think I feel guilty about this whole situation?"

Emel denied any involvement. I didn't get a confession. I did get was his attention.

At the same time I was interviewing Emel, Troopers Aiello and Brian Wakefield interviewed Easton. I brought Emel and Easton in on the same day and set it up so they passed each other in the hallway—to put additional pressure on them. Once they saw each other, they knew why they were there. In addition, it lets me tell one or the other that the person in the other room just ratted them out and told me everything. Sometimes this works, sometimes it doesn't. Yet, it is an effective tool when it comes to interviewing multiple people who have information about each other or the crime that was committed.

Easton initially denied any involvement in Dawn's disappearance. During this interview, Easton maintained that he was sleeping in the back seat of Emel's vehicle when they took Dawn home the night she disappeared. Easton stated that the whole night was a blur, but he remembers getting a flat tire after dropping off Dawn in Williamsport. It was no coincidence that both remembered the flat tire. It isn't because it happened; it is because that was their story to cover the scratches. That is why they remember that story. Over the past 20 years, they knew if questioned, to give that story. Hell, it worked in 1992, why wouldn't the cops buy it now?

He stated he was drunk and stoned during his time in the car with Emel and Dawn. He denied having anything on his pants such as blood or red paint and stated he had no scratches on his body after returning from dropping off Dawn in Williamsport. When asked why he did not allow Gardner to accompany them to Williamsport that night, Easton admitted that it was strange for him not to take her along because, "I took her everywhere with me back then."

In the hallway, I had a polygrapher waiting and I offered both men the chance to take a polygraph. The reason I did this was because it is easy for your suspect to agree to a polygraph and come in on a date that is scheduled. Then they don't show. I planned to have the polygrapher there, waiting, so the suspects have no way out if they agree. Both declined. However, Easton agreed a few weeks later. In April 2008, Agent Stephen Sorage of the Williamsport Bureau of Police conducted a second interview with Easton during a polygraph examination. Easton stated, "If anybody had done anything to her (referencing Dawn), it would have been Greg, because I was in the back seat sleeping." When Easton was given a scenario where two individuals were present when Dawn was hurt and possibly murdered, what did he think should happen to the two individuals? Easton stated that the first person should go to jail and not get a second chance and that the second individual should get help and a second chance. When asked what he believes had happened to Dawn, Easton said, "She probably ran away to start a new life." Everyone else interviewed in this case believes Emel and Easton had something to do with Dawn's disappearance. All believe she is dead. However, when Easton is asked what happened to Dawn, he states, "I think she ran away and started a new life" and Emel states, "She ran away with a trucker." Come on, really? These two amateurs just made my job easier by their stupid statements. Easton failed the polygraph. Not only did he fail, he gave classic answers to the questions stated above. On all those questions, he was given an out and he took it. To me, because of how he answered these question...I knew I had the right guys.

On Oct. 15, 2008, Gregory Lynn Emel committed suicide in Centre County by hanging himself from a tree. I remember getting the call from my Bellefonte partner and friend, Det. Matt Rickard. It was bittersweet feeling for me. He was dead and I wasn't too terribly upset about that, but I may now never find out what happened to Dawn. Emel was a coward, plain and simple. He took the easy way out instead of facing the wrath that was about to be unleashed upon him by the justice system. The other half of me said, "Oh, well, one less sexual predator and murderer off of the streets."

So, shortly after this, Trooper Aiello and I interviewed Kali Green, Emel's niece who had lived with him for the past year. Kali stated that Emel would "bawl his eyes out" when talking about Dawn and stated that he was going to commit suicide because of the renewed police investigation and the financial difficulties that came with it. Kali stated that Emel predicted that after he killed himself, "Police would then only have Easton to blame." Kali stated Emel used a stun gun on her and tried to incapacitate her in order to sexually assault her a day before he committed suicide.

In October 2008, Trooper Aiello and I interviewed Teri Emel, Easton's wife at the time. She stated that in April 2008, Emel told her that the police were trying to blame him for Dawn's disappearance because "she was pregnant to me." Easton admitted seeing Emel kill Dawn in Emel's car.

Where was Dawn? Well, my biggest break in this case occurred when I stumbled upon a report from the Bellefonte Police Department's archives. This report was written, filed and never linked to Dawn's disappearance.

As I stated previously, on Oct. 24, 1993, exactly one year after Dawn's disappearance, Emel went to the same location where he had taken Dawn to park and where he had taken Williams and Easton and was "acting strange." Emel called Jennetta Johnson around 2 a.m. and asked her to meet him at a wooded location. He was taken into custody with razor blades in his pocket.

I don't believe in coincidences. I knew that something significant had to have happened at that location where Emel went to "threaten" suicide. That is either where Dawn is, was or was last alive. That is where we had to begin our search for Dawn's. However, this area was not documented properly in the police report, so I had to track down the retired police officer who took the report and Emel's roommates. Both gave different locations as to where this took place and the police officer couldn't even remember the incident.

I learned that in addition to this suicide threat, Emel was seen by roommates leaving the Bellefonte apartment after midnight on other occasions between the years 1993 and 1994. This was odd behavior, even for Emel, so the roommates followed him on one occasion.

Emel traveled to the Jacksonville quarry alone and is confronted by the roommates, so the roommates followed him one time to a wooded area near a quarry, where Emel emerged from the woods sweaty, out of breath and irate that they had followed him. He told them not to tell anyone he was there and, they recalled, acted extremely suspicious and "weird." The Jacksonville quarry, where Emel had led them, is half a mile from where Williams led me earlier and said Emel asked Easton if "he remembered the spot." Both locations are within one mile from Emel's home. To complicate matters, Emel lived in front of a cemetery—a perfect location to dispose of a body. All he had to do was wait until a fresh grave was dug and throw a body in on top of it.

So, where is Dawn? What happened? Well, the only person alive who knows that was the person sitting in the back seat of the car on that fateful night in October 1992.

Throughout the investigation, Trooper Aiello and I talked about numerous methods we thought were best to get Easton to confess to the homicide and tell us what happened to Dawn. Once Emel committed suicide, we figured that Easton would feel isolated and have no one else to blame.

Trooper Aiello came up with a brilliant move. He suggested that we get a search warrant for Easton's DNA. My first statement was, "For what? We don't have a body." As soon as I said that, I knew what Dave was thinking immediately. He knew it would scare him and he would *think* we did find her body. Easton would then want to put the blame on Emel. I didn't care who took the blame at the time, as I knew both were responsible for her death. But getting Easton to blame Emel was something I felt he would do and boy, did he ever fall for this ruse.

It wasn't easy getting the search warrant, as we had to get a Centre County judge to buy into what we were selling. When we presented the judge with what we had, he looked up from the paperwork and asked the same question I had a couple hours earlier. "Why do you want his DNA if you don't have a body to compare any DNA to?" Dave's answer was perfect, "Because we might someday, judge." It wasn't a lie; it was a perfect answer … because we might someday.

So, we got our search warrant and proceeded to Easton's home. I knew that once we got him in the car, he was done. I knew from all the background research I had done on him that he was weak minded. He was your typical bully who solved problems with violence because he wasn't smart enough to solve problems any other way. I knew when he didn't have his uncle to lean on anymore, he would crumble. He was like a lot of other criminals who are behind bars, a false exterior that masks the evil and scared inner child.

Once in the car, I sat in the back seat with Easton. Pundits and critics of police will say that I did this to place pressure on Easton. Maybe they are right. However, there is one thing I did know for sure. I knew how Dawn died sitting in front of Easton one night in 1992 in a car and I wasn't about to suffer the same fate as she did.

Before we pulled out of the driveway, I said to Easton, "I can't believe you are going to take the rap for your dead uncle." There was a long pause of what seemed like minutes, but it was probably about 10 seconds before Easton blurted out words that still echo in my brain today. "All right, I'm gonna level with you guys. Greg did kill Dawn." I will never, *ever* forget those words. It was if all the weight had been lifted off my shoulders. The ruse worked, as we knew it would. It worked to perfection. Easton kept talking without us asking any questions. One thing I know is when a suspect starts talking, do not interrupt. He talked until we were almost at the hospital where we were taking him. No questions were asked of Easton; he just spoke. In legal terms, this can be described as "excited utterance." Excited utterance is admissible in court because you are not questioning the person.

Once there, Trooper Aiello stopped the car. We gave Easton his Miranda warning and asked him to repeat what he had just told us. Of course Dave, always prepared, had a tape recorder on him and began to tape the confession. This is the transcript of what Easton said happened to Dawn:

The time is 1615 hours. It is Monday, October 27th, 2008. Trooper Dave Aiello and Detective Ken Mains. With us in the car is (John Easton). We're in an unmarked state police car in the parking lot of Centre Community Hospital, Centre County. Detective Mains, I'm going to ask you to hold that. Put it about 18 inches in front of (Easton) so we can pick up his voice. (Easton), I'm going to go ahead and read you your rights. I want you to understand these. I gave the date and the time already and the place. My name is Trooper Dave Aiello. This is Officer Ken Mains. You have an absolute right to remain silent. Anything you say can and will be used against you in a court of law. You have the right to talk to an attorney, to have an attorney present with you during questioning. If you cannot afford to hire an attorney, one will be appointed to represent you without charge before questioning if you so desire. If you do decide to answer questions, you may stop at any time you wish. You cannot be forced to continue. Do you understand this statement of your rights about answering questions? Do you understand that?

Easton	*Yeah.*
Trooper Aiello	*Do you wish to talk with us now?*
Easton	*Yes.*
Trooper Aiello	*All right. We've been talking off tape here just for a little bit in the car. Informally, you indicated that you had some information relative to Dawn Marie Miller and her disappearance. Before we go any further, you'd indicated you had some information. We're going to stop, give you your admonishments and we're going to get this on audio. Do you understand you're being audio recorded?*
Easton	*Yes.*
Trooper Aiello	*Okay. Detective Mains, do you want to go ahead?*
Det. Mains	*Um, just tell us exactly what you had stated previously. What you observed and what you*

	seen happen the night that you, Dawn Miller and Dawn left the Academy Apartments back in October 1992.
Easton	*We were driving down the road and Greg just starting going—started going nuts and started beating on Dawn's head.*
Det. Mains	*With an object or his hands?*
Easton	*With an object, out of his car.*
Det. Mains	*What happened next?*
Easton	*He drove up into a set of woods. Like I said, I can't recall where.*
Det. Mains	*But you believe it was Howard?*
Easton	*I believe it could have been Howard.*
Det. Mains	*Okay, what happened next?*
Easton	*He ... he was like, dude, you gotta help me, man. He says this chick's ... you know, she's pregnant to me and I can't have this, so we gotta fuckin' kill her and this and that and that and there thing. I'm like, no. This is not right. No. And he pulled her out of the car and drug her about 20, 30 feet and he's like, help me start digging a hole. We gotta get— we gotta get rid of this evidence. So I started helping him dig a hole. I didn't know what else to do. I was afraid for my life basically.*
Det. Mains	*Okay. And this place where he pulled off of the road, was it a main road or a—*
Easton	*It was like a back road.*
Det. Mains	*Was it dirt or was it concrete?*
Easton	*It was a regular paved road.*
Det. Mains	*Okay. And he pulled off to the side of that road and went about 20, 30 feet you say?*
Easton	*Yeah.*

Det. Mains	What side of the road was it on? Right or left?
Easton	Um, I think we were heading ...
Det. Mains	He pulled her and she was in the passenger—
Easton	We were heading down this way I think, so he pulled in this way.
Trooper Aiello	You're indicating to the right.
Easton	That would be to the right. Yeah.
Trooper Aiello	Dawn was seated in the right front passenger seat?
Easton	She was up here, yeah.
Trooper Aiello	Greg was driving?
Easton	Right.
Trooper Aiello	Where were you?
Easton	I was in the back seat, like probably in the middle like, kinda.
Trooper Aiello	Whose car?
Easton	It was Greg's car.
Trooper Aiello	Do you know what kind of car?
Easton	I haven't a clue.
Det. Mains	You get out of the car, you pull her—do you both pull her out?
Easton	No. Greg just dragged her.
Det. Mains	Okay, he pulled out and he took her to which side of the vehicle?
Easton	He just started dragging her to the front of the car.
Det. Mains	So it was in front of the car?
Easton	Right.
Det. Mains	He didn't cross over?
Easton	No. He just kind of like, drug her up—up a

	hill.
Det. Mains	*Okay. Was it up an embankment? Like heavy?*
Easton	*It wasn't very steep. It didn't appear to be, anyways. I mean, it may have been a 10% grade.*
Det. Mains	*Okay.*
Easton	*Maybe 15% grade.*
Det. Mains	*And that's where she, uh ... and that's where he buried her? On that embankment?*
Easton	*Yeah.*
Det. Mains	*Did he place anything there?*
Easton	*No.*
Det. Mains	*You know, like a marker of any sort.*
Easton	*Not that I know of. I don't know.*
Det. Mains	*Okay.*
Easton	*If he did, he didn't—he didn't tell me about it.*
Det. Mains	*Okay. Um, and you indicated that the grave was probably knee-height if you were standing in it.*
Easton	*Yes.*
Det. Mains	*And about how wide?*
Easton	*Probably two-and-a-half, three-foot.*
Det. Mains	*Okay. And she fit in there?*
Easton	*She just went down in it, yeah.*
Det. Mains	*Okay. And then you guys buried her. Put anything else on her? Rocks or anything like that, or it was just dirt?*
Easton	*Just whatever come out of the hole went back in.*
Det. Mains	*So there was a mound?*

Easton	*There had to have been a little mound, yeah.*
Det. Mains	*Okay. Then what happened when you guys leave?*
Easton	*We went to Bellefonte and he went to a car wash and he started washing everything off real good.*
Det. Mains	*Inside or outside?*
Easton	*Doing the in—he washed off the inside of his car in here and he washed off the object that he was using and then we left. He took me home. Actually, I walked home because I lived right up over the hill.*
Det. Mains	*Okay. Did he—he kept that object then? He didn't throw it away?*
Easton	*As far as I'm—I believe he did, yeah.*
Det. Mains	*You don't remember what it was?*
Easton	*No, I don't remember.*
Det. Mains	*Um, something small? Heavy?*
Easton	*It was small and heavy. I—I mean, I'm imagining, anyways. You know what I mean. He was bashing her pretty good.*
Det. Mains	*Was he hitting her in the back of the head, front of the head? What could you see from where you were?*
Easton	*All I could see is his arms swinging.*
Det. Mains	*Was blood flying?*
Easton	*No.*
Det. Mains	*No?*
Easton	*No.*
Det. Mains	*When he was washing the car out, was there blood, though, that you could see?*
Easton	*There's like—there was some blood down on the side of the car, yeah.*

Det. Mains	Okay. When you guys pulled her out, how did you know, or how did he know that she was dead?
Easton	I didn't know. And I didn't know if he knew or not.
Det. Mains	Could she have been alive when you guys placed her in the hole and just been unconscious?
Easton	I don't know.
Det. Mains	Okay. Did he say, "Hey, we need to check her?"
Easton	No.
Det. Mains	Okay.
Trooper Aiello	Do you remember what she was wearing?
Easton	No.
Trooper Aiello	Did Greg ever tell you, ahead of time, prior to getting Dawn in the car, what he had in mind?
Easton	No. I had no idea.
Trooper Aiello	When it began in the car, did you try and stop him?
Easton	Did I try and stop him? I was like, Greg, you can't be doing this. You gotta stop. He was like, "No, she's got my baby and I'm not gonna have that. I'm not going to be pregnant with this lady."
Trooper Aiello	What did Dawn say?
Easton	She was just hollering for her life. "Help me! Stop! Stop! Don't hit me no more!"
Trooper Aiello	Why did she get in the car with you guys? What was the intention?
Easton	We were supposed to take her to Williamsport and drop her off.

Trooper Aiello	Do you remember if she left any of her property at the Academy Apartments?
Easton	No, I don't. I don't remember
Trooper Aiello	We believe that she did in the form of at least a backpack. Do you remember any idea what might have happened to that backpack?
Easton	No, I honestly don't.
Trooper Aiello	How about a diary or a journal? A notebook?
Easton	No.
Det. Mains	How about the clothing that you guys had on that night? What happened with it?
Easton	Oh, I don't even know.
Det. Mains	Did you get rid of it?
Easton	No.
Det. Mains	Did you have blood on you?
Easton	No, I had no blood on me at all that I can remember.
Det. Mains	Just dirt?
Easton	Just dirt.
Det. Mains	How about scratches?
Easton	No.
Trooper Aiello	'Cause we had people come forward to say you came back, you, as well as Greg, had some decent scratches on you.
Easton	No.
Trooper Aiello	You don't remember or you don't—you say you didn't have any?
Easton	I'd have to say I didn't have any.
Det. Mains	So then, let me get this right. If he's hitting her, are you sure that you guys were still driving while he was doing this, or could he have been pulled over to the side of the road?

Easton	It happened so quick. I mean, it was like— you know what I mean? It just happened so quick, then he was off the road.
Trooper Aiello	How long were you guys gone from the time you two left the Academy—three of you, left the Academy Apartments—to the time you and Greg returned? How long were you gone?
Easton	Probably a half-hour.
Trooper Aiello	So it took a half-hour to drive?
Easton	Maybe. Maybe.
Trooper Aiello	I'm talking everything. From the time the three of you left, two of you came back, how long—could you say—how long did it take to dig the grave?
Easton	Like a couple hours.
Trooper Aiello	So you were gone at least a couple hours, plus travel time?
Easton	Yeah.
Trooper Aiello	Three hours, five hours?
Easton	Three hours, four-and-a-half hours, maybe.
Trooper Aiello	Okay. Do you remember what time you left or what time you got back?
Easton	No.
Trooper Aiello	Were you drinking? Were you intoxicated?
Easton	I was drunk.
Trooper Aiello	From the time it began?
Easton	Yeah. I was drunk before I even got in his car.
Trooper Aiello	How about Greg? Was he drunk?
Easton	I don't know if he was or not.
Trooper Aiello	Was he a drinker back then?
Easton	He was a drinker back then, yes. But I don't

	know if he was drunk or not.
Trooper Aiello	*Is there any reason that your DNA should be on Dawn Miller's remains?*
Easton	*I sure hope not. I mean I don't—I was in—digging the holes. You know what I mean?*
Det. Mains	*Did you physically touch her at any time?*
Easton	*Did I physically touch her?*
Det. Mains	*Yes.*
Easton	*I think I might have helped him drag her.*
Det. Mains	*Okay.*
Easton	*Like, you know—I might have helped him drag her.*
Trooper Aiello	*You've indicated that you didn't say anything because you were afraid of Greg?*
Easton	*Yeah. Because he was in the Army and I didn't know what he was capable of doing.*
Trooper Aiello	*Did he threaten you?*
Easton	*No, he never threatened me. But I didn't want to take that chance of him threatening me and then have to go through all that, you know.*
Trooper Aiello	*Is that—did you guys drift apart after this?*
Easton	*Yeah.*
Trooper Aiello	*Is that why you drifted apart?*
Easton	*That's why I drifted apart from him, yeah. Why he drifted apart from me, I don't know.*
Trooper Aiello	*Let's fast forward to 2008 when you and Greg were interviewed back in April. Did Greg say anything to you—I think it was April 21st this year or afterward. Did he get with you and try to talk with you and say anything about this?*
Easton	*Nope. He talked to me and he said just, just don't say nothing and stick to the plan.*

Trooper Aiello	What's the plan?
Easton	I'm like, what's the plan Greg? And he's like, just don't say nothing. He says, "Talk to Bruce Manchester and he'll clear us," and you know, and I was like, "Greg, I'm not talking to him." I said, "I'm doing my thing and you do your thing." And here I am.
Det. Mains	So the story with the flat tire was all bullshit.
Easton	That was all bullshit.
Det. Mains	Okay. You never made it to Williamsport?
Easton	No.
Det. Mains	Um, as far as you can remember, as far as you made it was Howard?
Easton	Was Howard.
Det. Mains	Was that close to where they live now?
Easton	I think so, yeah.
Trooper Aiello	How long had Dawn and Greg been going out or dating? Do you know?
Easton	I'd say maybe, I don't know, a month. Maybe two.
Trooper Aiello	Did you ever talk with her? I mean, have any conversations?
Easton	Not very mu—not very often. No.
Trooper Aiello	Did you get the impression from her that she wanted to set up housekeeping with Greg?
Easton	No. I didn't.
Trooper Aiello	He said that he believed she was pregnant. Did she ever say to you or any other people at the Academy that she was pregnant?
Easton	If she did, I didn't know.
Trooper Aiello	She never told you?
Easton	She never told me.

Det. Mains	Did Greg ever say anything about anybody else that he could have done anything like that to?
Easton	No.
Det. Mains	Never said anything?
Easton	No.
Det. Mains	Do you know of any suspicions of him hurting anybody else?
Easton	The only one I know of is my Uncle Jeff's daughter. I don't even know her name.
Det. Mains	Brittany?
Easton	Brittany.
Det. Mains	And that was just the assault? Sexual assault.
Easton	That's the only thing I know about.
Det. Mains	Okay.
Easton	And then with him stunning Kali with—you know, in the neck.
Trooper Aiello	That was this month, 2008.
Easton	Yeah.
Trooper Aiello	Okay. (Easton), is there anything else you want to get out on the table? I'm going to—
Easton	I just gave you everything, buddy.
Trooper Aiello	Well, I appreciate that. I thank you and, look, I'm going to zing you here, just so we're on the same page. I'm not going to hold anything back. You did bullshit us in the beginning.
Easton	I know.
Trooper Aiello	Is there anything else that you want to get on the table? This is the bottom, end of the road truth?
Easton	I just gave you the truth.
Trooper Aiello	Okay. And there's no reason why your DNA

	would come up on her?
Easton	*Not that I'm aware of. I mean, I don't know how it would. Other than helping him drag her or whatever.*
Trooper Aiello	*Okay. If you were to drive around—if we were to drive you around or you were to drive around on your own, do you think you could pick out the spot where he pulled over and you guys buried her?*
Easton	*I probably could.*
Trooper Aiello	*Okay. Can we give that a try today?*
Easton	*Let's do it.*
Det. Mains	*Okay. End it.*
Trooper Aiello	*End of audio at 1628 hours.*

Easton then led us to the Howard Reservoir, where he stated Dawn is buried. This is the same location that Williams led police in January 2008, where Emel confirmed parking with Dawn and where, on the one-year anniversary of Dawn's disappearance, Emel went to threaten suicide, according to some.

My excitement could hardly be contained. As we were driving to the area, I knew where he was taken us. Too many coincidental happenings were occurring around this area.

Once we pulled into the area, we began to start recording Easton again.

The time is 1701 hours. It's Monday, October 27th, 2008. Trooper Aiello and Detective Mains, Mr. (John Easton).

Trooper Aiello	*Okay, Mr. (Easton). Do you understand you're being audio recorded again?*
Easton	*Yes.*
Trooper Aiello	*Okay. Do you understand that you still are under no obligation to talk with us? Do you understand that?*
Easton	*Yeah, I understand that.*

Trooper Aiello	All right, we're out at a location along Route—State Route 26 outside of Howard. It's in the cut in the hillside, the gap near the old Howard Reservoir. Uh, there's a one-lane bridge on State Route 26 and we took a dirt road off to the side of that one lane bridge. You're indicating areas up here where you believe that Dawn was buried. Is that correct?
Easton	That's correct.
Trooper Aiello	Can you just describe what you recall about how you got here on that night back in '92?
Easton	All I can remember is coming out that road and Greg just kind of whipped it up into the woods, which appeared to be a road. And it was like an upgrade hill and so this is—that's how I got here.
Trooper Aiello	Okay. You were on the hard-top, Route 26?
Easton	Yeah.
Trooper Aiello	And he turned off to the right?
Easton	Yeah.
Trooper Aiello	Before the one-lane bridge or after?
Easton	It would be before.
Trooper Aiello	And you said that road, dirt road, went up or downhill?
Easton	It went uphill.
Trooper Aiello	Is it smooth, bumpy?
Easton	It was bumpy.
Trooper Aiello	How far off the hard-top do you think he drove before he stopped the car?
Easton	I'd say 50, 60, 70 yards.
Trooper Aiello	Okay. Then what? When the car stopped, what happened?
Easton	He pulled her out of the car and said, "Come

	on, you're helping me. Let's get this out—let's get this underground so we don't—it's taken care of."
Trooper Aiello	What direction did he go from the car?
Easton	He went straight ahead and he went in front of his car.
Det. Mains	To which side?
Easton	To the left side.
Trooper Aiello	So if the car's facing uphill on a dirt road and, for example, like the direction the headlights might have been shining, he went that direction towards where the headlights would have been shining?
Easton	Correct.
Trooper Aiello	Were the headlights on?
Easton	No.
Trooper Aiello	So he went straight up from the front of the car and then to the left?
Easton	Yeah.
Trooper Aiello	Was that to the left uphill or downhill?
Easton	It was uphill on like, a flat spot.
Trooper Aiello	Up on the road. Now, when you get to that flat spot, was that on the right or left of the road you were on?
Easton	I don't understand what you're saying.
Trooper Aiello	If the car's here on the dirt road, facing up this hill and he goes up the hill on the road with the body, which direction then would he have stopped with the body? To the left or the right?
Easton	He went to the left.
Det. Mains	About how far from the car?
Easton	I'd say 20 feet.

Det. Mains	*So you drug her approximately 20 feet?*
Easton	Yeah.
Trooper Aiello	*He drug her, you drug, or you both did?*
Easton	I helped him.
Trooper Aiello	*Okay. And—*
Det. Mains	*She wasn't carried?*
Easton	No.
Det. Mains	*She was drug?*
Easton	She was drug.
Det. Mains	*By arms or legs?*
Easton	By her arms.
Det. Mains	*Okay.*
Trooper Aiello	*Was she very bloody?*
Easton	She was pretty bloody.
Trooper Aiello	*Was she bloody in the car?*
Easton	Yes.
Trooper Aiello	*A little, a lot?*
Easton	It wasn't—didn't appear to be all that much.
Trooper Aiello	*Okay. When you get to that flat spot you described, what happened then?*
Easton	Greg said, "Start digging."
Trooper Aiello	*What did you use to dig?*
Easton	Stones.
Trooper Aiello	*And your hands?*
Easton	And our hands.
Trooper Aiello	*How deep?*
Easton	I'd say four foot. Maybe three foot.
Trooper Aiello	*Deep.*
Easton	Yeah.

Trooper Aiello	*Four-foot deep?*
Easton	*Three foot, maybe.*
Trooper Aiello	*Three-foot deep?*
Easton	*It was deep. It was like, up to my knees, maybe.*
Trooper Aiello	*Up to your knees is about maybe 18 inches.*
Easton	*Okay.*
Trooper Aiello	*So was it deeper than your knees or about knee-depth?*
Easton	*Little bit—somewhere in here. About 18 inches. That sounds about right.*
Trooper Aiello	*Okay. That's about knee-height. From the heel of your foot to your knee. About 18 or so inches.*
Easton	*Yeah, that sounds about right.*
Trooper Aiello	*Okay. How long did it take you guys to dig?*
Easton	*A couple hours.*
Trooper Aiello	*Did she move during that time, to your knowledge?*
Easton	*I don't know.*
Trooper Aiello	*Did she say anything?*
Easton	*No.*
Trooper Aiello	*Make any noises?*
Easton	*No.*
Trooper Aiello	*Do you remember how she was dressed?*
Easton	*No.*
Det. Mains	*Was she naked?*
Easton	*No.*
Det. Mains	*She had clothes on?*
Easton	*She had clothing on.*
Det. Mains	*And she went in the hole with clothes on?*

Easton	*Yes.*
Trooper Aiello	*All the dirt that came out of the hole went back on top of her?*
Easton	*Yes.*
Trooper Aiello	*Did it leave a—if you remember, did it leave a mound?*
Easton	*Yes.*
Trooper Aiello	*Did Easton—I'm sorry, did Greg say anything to you at that time while you guys were here?*
Easton	*I don't believe he did, other than, "Let's just get out of here."*
Trooper Aiello	*This area where we're standing, as just described, do you believe this is the spot, this is the general area?*
Easton	*I believe this is the general area, yes.*
Det. Mains	*And that circle that I had you draw up there, how certain are you that that's where Dawn Miller's buried?*
Easton	*I'm 100 percent certain that's where she was at.*
Trooper Aiello	*And just so we're on the same page here, there's a metal gate on this particular dirt road, you're indicating beyond that gate 20, 25, 30 feet?*
Easton	*Yes.*
Trooper Aiello	*Okay. End of audio at 1706.*

Good enough for me to put him in handcuffs right then and there, right? I called the Centre County District Attorney and he said, "No."

So, let's talk about Easton and how he initially stated he had no involvement with the murder whatsoever. He had gotten away with it for almost two decades, of course he is going to deny and stick to the original story. That changed when we got the warrant for his DNA. His false blockade began to crumble.

Now his story changes to him only witnessing it. I knew this was the answer I was going to get from him before I sat in the back seat of the car with him. That is why I asked if his DNA could be on Dawn's remains. Easton again changed his story and stated he helped drag Dawn's body from the vehicle and that he helped Emel bury her. I knew he was going to give this answer as well.

When a suspect is confronted with an escape route, they will always take that route. I gave Easton an escape route to explain why we were going to find his DNA on Dawn's body. In my opinion, it would be because he actively participated in her murder and nothing short of Dawn coming back to life telling me differently will persuade me otherwise.

But suspects will always minimize their actions and involvement. So, instead of admitting his active participation, Easton takes the escape route to say, "Ok, I might have helped drag her."

He stated both he and Emel dragged Dawn by her arms from the vehicle and buried her in a particular wooded area using only stones and their hands to dig the grave. Easton stated they buried her in a grave approximately 18 inches deep, covered her with the dirt that came out of the hole and that digging the grave took several hours.

Easton went on to say that after burying Dawn, he and Emel drove to a car wash near the Academy Apartments. It is here that Easton observed Emel wash Dawn's blood from the inside front passenger area and from the object used to kill Dawn (although Easton states he does not know what the object was).

I asked Easton if he had nightmares about what he had done to Dawn, to which he replied, "You have no idea. She haunted me in my dreams." "Excellent," I thought to myself. I hope Dawn continues to haunt him every single day of his miserable life.

In October 2008, Bellefonte attorney Brian Manchester called Trooper Aiello and stated he was representing Easton. "I understand my client led you to a body yesterday," Manchester said.

In January 2009, Manchester stated in open court in Centre County that Easton led investigators to Dawn's body and that Easton was not involved but knows who did murder her. Easton led me to an area he believed the body was. To me, if he told this to his attorney, he was telling the truth. Dawn was there at one time.

Despite extensive investigation and excavation in the Howard Reservoir area, the remains of Dawn have not yet been located.

This investigation revealed that Dawn has had no contact with anyone since last being seen with Emel and Easton in October 1992. Dawn did not have an active bank account or credit cards in her name at the time of her disappearance. Dawn's Social Security number has never been used to open a bank account, credit card account or even been used for a credit check since she was last seen with Emel and Easton. The reason for this is very, very simple: Emel and Easton killed Dawn.

Dawn's family stated that she always kept in contact with them and would never go more than a day without at least calling them. Dawn has not had any contact with her family or anyone else after last being seen with Emel and Easton on or about Oct. 24, 1992. Her clothing and personal belongings at her Williamsport residence have never been claimed. The reason for this is very, very simple: Emel and Easton killed Dawn Miller.

In any case, investigators must search for clues in statements. Whether the statements are ambiguous or specific, they can obviously be used against someone. Statements can often be misconstrued or taken out of context. Defense attorneys relish these types of statements. Yet, an investigator must use them in order to get a better picture of what happened. Here is an example of statements that, in my opinion, leads me to believe they murdered Dawn Miller.

"That's OK, I've made women come up missing before." – Emel to Noll (1993–1994)

"I can make you disappear like another women." – Emel to Noll (1993–1994)

"Maybe a trucker or black guy nabbed her." – Emel to Gardner the night Dawn disappeared

"(Easton) had blood, I mean red paint, on his pants not me." – Emel to Officer Mains (April 21, 2008)

"If Dawn is pregnant, it isn't my kid." – Emel to Williams (October

1992)

"She's not coming back." – Emel to Williams while throwing away Dawn's belongings (October 1992)

"You want to die like her?" – Easton to Williams after Williams accused him of killing Dawn (2001)

"We are going to drop her off the Earth." – Easton or Emel (October 1992)

"She's gone like history." – Easton or Emel (October 1992)

"We'll roll her up in a rug." – Easton to Emel, overheard by Williams (October 1992)

"She ran off with a truck driver." – Emel to Williams, referring to what happened to Dawn

"Do you remember the spot?" – Emel to Easton, overheard by Williams as they hiked on trail near Howard reservoir/spillway (November 1992)

"I'll fucking kill you. I did it once, I can do it again." – Easton to Williams while Easton had him by the throat fighting him (years after Dawn's disappearance)

"She probably ran away to start a new life." – Easton to Agent Sorage, referring to what he believes happened to Dawn (April 24, 2008)

"If anybody did anything to her, it would have been Greg." – Easton to Agent Sorage when asked, "Who do you think did this?" (April 24, 2008)

"The only person would have been Greg." – Easton to Agent Sorage when asked who had the best opportunity to hurt Dawn (April 24, 2008)

"Probably go to jail." – Easton to Agent Sorage when asked what should happen to the person who did this (April 24, 2008)

"Get help." – Easton to Agent Sorage when asked what should happen to the second person involved in the disappearance (April 24, 2008)

"No, not at all." – Easton to Agent Sorage when asked if the person who did this should get a second chance (April 24, 2008)

"Yes, I do." – Easton to Agent Sorage when asked if the second person involved should get a second chance (April 24, 2008)

Just as victimology is extremely important in finding out the suspect, suspectology is equally important. It is not a given that just because someone has killed, they will have a violent history. A lot of the times, it will depend on what the crime scene looks like and how the victims are murdered. Crime scene assessment is a crucial component to solving the murder.

I want to know everything about my suspects. I begin with their criminal history and background.

Easton was a heavy drinker and drug abuser who became violent when under the influence. Past behavior is not always an indicator of future behavior, but it gives an investigator insight. It gives you a view of the leader and follower. Who is dominant and who is submissive. It allows you to piece the story together at the end. On this particular case, it allowed me to determine that Easton, although younger, was the dominant male. It also allowed me to view Easton as the aggressor. Here are some incidents of violent behavior in Easton's past:

Jan. 24, 1992 – Easton is involved in a domestic disturbance with Gardner at 616 Campbell St. in Williamsport. He is intoxicated, pulled her hair, choked her and slammed her head into a wall. Easton is armed with a knife and cuts the phone cord.

Jan. 29, 1992 – Easton is involved in a disturbance in Williamsport. This incident involves Easton wanting to fight someone he did not know inside a laundromat.

Dec. 5, 1993 – Easton is a suspect in a rape in Bellefonte. Charges were never filed.

Jan. 1, 1996 – Easton is subject in a fight in Bellefonte.

June 19, 1999 – Easton is arrested for fighting in Bellefonte. He hits another individual in the face with a hammer.

July 22, 1999 – Easton is arrested by Pennsylvania State Police for statutory rape, indecent assault and corruption of minors. He pleads guilty to the rape and corruption charges.

Aug. 16, 1999 – Easton is a subject in a disorderly conduct in Bellefonte. He attempts to fight another individual.

Aug. 21, 1999 – Easton is involved in a domestic disturbance with wife Jamie Emel in Bellefonte.

Oct. 24, 1999 – Easton is involved in a fight in Bellefonte.

June 28, 2002 – Easton assaults Williams. He has Williams by the throat and whispers into his ear, "You want to die like her?" Williams does not press charges against him, even though he is left cut and bloodied.

Aug. 12, 2007 – Easton is involved in a domestic disturbance in State College.

Bonnie Rager – Was hit and choked by Easton on many occasions.

Tim Duck – Observed Easton fight and abuse alcohol and drugs.

Jamie Emel – Was hit and choked on numerous occasions by Easton. Her husband's "rage was uncontrollable," she stated.

Michael Williams – Got into fights with Easton when he confronted him about Dawn's disappearance.

Joseph Miller – Observed Easton choke Bonnie Rager with a cord.

Norman Schreffler – Was hit in the face with a hammer by Easton.

Matthew Rupert – After following Dawn to Jacksonville quarry, Emel became verbally abusive.

Tim Rupert – Observed Greg punch many holes in their apartment walls when angry.

Jodi Noll – Observed Emel stab a picture of Jennetta Johnson with a knife.

Jennetta Johnson – Emel said some weird things to her and observed him stab a picture of her and drip red candle wax onto the blade and into a bucket. Describes him as psychotic and is "definitely capable of hurting someone."

All of these individuals play a key role in the investigation. They all can offer insight, stories and allow the investigator to see things in a broader scope. So, what happened to Dawn? It is my opinion that Emel and Easton planned and executed Dawn's murder because they mistakenly believed she was pregnant by Emel. I believe Emel had no intention of having Dawn as a girlfriend, let alone the mother of his child. I think Dawn liked Emel and wanted to keep him as a boyfriend. When she felt Emel distancing himself from her and eventually breaking up with her, Dawn made up the story that she was pregnant in a fateful attempt to get Emel to stay with her. That little lie ultimately and unfortunately cost Dawn her life.

When all three got in that car, it was by no accident that Easton sat in the back seat. While driving from Bellefonte, they had no intention of taking Dawn to Williamsport. They were going to a familiar place, not far from the Emel homestead and a place Emel had been thousands of times: the Howard Reservoir. He had been there previously with Dawn and most likely had sex with her at that location in the weeks prior to the night she was murdered.

Once there, or close to there, Easton reached up and put Dawn in a chokehold with his left arm and began cutting off her air supply. She attempted to fight him off and scratched his arm, a wound that was seen later by Dawn's brother, Joseph. Emel almost simultaneously began to beat Dawn with an unknown object from the car while Easton had hold of her.

Dawn fought back, causing the scratch on Emel's face and the scratches on Easton's left arm, the same arm he had squeezed around her neck.

The entire violent episode took no more than five minutes, before they were dragging her into the woods. Here, Emel or Easton hit her with a tree branch. They do this either to ensure her death or because she wasn't dead yet, and was only unconscious, and they thought she was dead.

She is buried in a shallow grave exactly where Easton led me 17 years later and where a cadaver dog alerted.

However, I think that the following day, after they regained their thoughts and composure, they agreed to move the body or at the very least, Emel decided to move the body. They did not take in account that the Howard Reservoir is a very populated hiking area and the body would certainly be discovered.

So, the body was moved, which is the reason Emel and Easton would not allow Gardner to put groceries in the trunk of the car a few days after the murder.

They decided to move her, most likely to the Jacksonville quarry, as it is hundreds of acres of unoccupied land with no visitors. A body won't be discovered in that quarry. There was no risk for him to relocate the body from the Howard Reservoir to the quarry. It is about ¼ from each other in a rural area with little chance of being seen moving the body.

I have walked the Jacksonville quarry countless hours, looking for Dawn. I excavated the entire side of a mountain at Howard Reservoir looking for Dawn. I have failed in finding her. Sometimes your best isn't good enough. Sometimes fate keeps secrets from us all. I believe Dawn's remains will be found eventually. That is a belief I hold deep inside me.

I thought I found her once. I saw a vertebra under a log that had a wire hanger wrapped around it. I kept moving leaves and debris and finding more bones—big bones. I'll never forget when my sergeant, who was with me, looked down at me and said, "I think you just found Dawn Miller." I fell down over the embankment in my rush and excitement to call the state police. They called everyone and they were all converging on the quarry to see the remains. After finding the jawbone, it was evident these were not human remains. I tried to convince myself they were. I even held the jawbone up to my own jaw while looking at Tim Miller, my supervisor, and said, "Look, it could fit." I saw in his eyes I was so desperate to find Dawn that he looked sad for me. It was just a large deer with no head that someone had dragged there decades ago and left.

Regardless whether she is found, the bottom line is she was murdered by two individuals who treated her like a piece of garbage. As Easton told me while he smoked a cigarette outside the Mount Nittany hospital after his confession, "That chick haunted my dreams." Guess what? I hope she haunts your every waking and sleeping hour for the rest of your natural-born life and beyond. That is what you deserve. That's for Dawn.

Two separate district attorneys have declined to prosecute Easton for this murder, for various and mostly ludicrous reasons. Yet, they are the attorneys and I am just a cop.

One reason I was given was that they believed we did not

sufficiently prove Dawn was dead. "If you could find a large amount of Dawn's blood where a person would be incapable of surviving with that amount of blood loss, we could prove she was dead." That is what the Centre County district attorney said to me. I laugh at this. Sometimes, legal justifications override common sense. This email from the Centre County district attorney sums it up:

Hi, Ken:

We still have the corpus delicti (no body) issue, but I would be willing to fight it if the evidence could win the case if we won that portion and got by it. There are multiple challenges here, including even being able to prove it is an unlawful killing. See my last email about that.

Again, if the jury only hears he said "Greg did it, I woke up and helped bury her," the statute has run on that charge (gross abuse of corpse) and we don't even get to a jury. I will not blow my one and only chance on a trial on him because jeopardy will attach if we make it to a jury trial and he beats it. You don't want that either.

He has to participate in the murder, we have to prove specifically how he helped kill her, we cannot make a jury guess how because we have to prove he did something for instance would impair a vital body part, not just slapped her etc., (because that is assault etc.,) and we have to prove he wanted her dead. She (Teri Emel) says he got out and helped "kill her," and then Greg finished her, we would need specifics as to what he did. Let's make some time to meet with her together and then brainstorm further.

Dawn Miller is dead and I proved that. Her remains have not yet been recovered, but all you have to do is spend 15 minutes with Sandy Northern, Dawn's mother. You look into her eyes and feel her pain. Those eyes will tell you that Dawn is no longer alive. Those eyes will tell you that your legal excuses are just that, excuses.

Dawn Miller is dead and if a district attorney or judge doesn't believe that, they should go sell burgers somewhere, because they are not qualified to hold such trustworthy positions within our judicial system. The second reason I was given was that the confession we obtained from Easton was "bad" and would be suppressed before trial. The district attorney believed that because I made a statement to Easton—"I can't believe you are going to take the rap for your dead uncle."—that elicited a response from Easton, the confession would be suppressed; therefore, our case against him was not winnable at trial.

I'm not an attorney and don't ever want to be one. I am a detective who investigates and solves crime. I believe I am educated enough with the law that I do things by the books. I have never lost a suppression hearing and have only lost one trial in more than a decade of arresting bad guys. I know for a fact Trooper Aiello is proficient with the law and he felt, as do I, the confession was good.

However, I don't make it a habit to second-guess a district attorney who prosecutes cases for a living. Just as I would not want them to second-guess my investigation method and tactics.

In the summer of 2015, the Centre County District Attorney's Office revealed it would convene a grand jury for some cold cases. I read about this in the newspaper. I sent an email asking that Dawn Miller's case be brought before the jury. The following was the response I received:

Hi Ken,

We have some cases in mind to start, but it can last 18 months. I will certainly keep her case in mind as an idea when we get through the cases we planned out. I know you had floated that idea before. Who did you think was uncooperative and refused to speak to you? Please feel free to remind me. Thanks!

So I decided to remind the district attorney as to the facts in the case:

My thoughts are this. (Easton) actively participated in the murder of Dawn Miller. 100% no question, yet he still walks free. As you know, a grand jury can listen to all the facts and recommend charges as well as getting people to talk.

I know you have stated in the past that the confession (Easton) gave me and Trooper Aiello is "no good," although I disagree. However, even if that confession is suppressed, he confessed to his ex-wife that he "helped" and helped bury her. If the full confession he gave me is no good, there is still the confession to the ex-wife.

As you are aware, a "No body" case was presented to the Grand Jury regarding Clinton County missing person Katherine Dolan Heckel last year and they recommended charging a co-worker with her death. PSP made the arrest after 20 years so it can be done.

This snippet of evidence, I believe, supports the arrest (of Easton) for the murder of Dawn Marie Miller in October 1992:

- *Left the Academy Apartments with Dawn Miller and Emel on 10/24/92. Left at approximately 7:00 Pm - 8:00 Pm and would not allow Bonnie to travel with them even though she had asked. This trip would take approximately two hours.*

- *Returned at approximately 11:30 PM and even as late as 2:00 AM and (Easton) immediately goes to bathroom and washes his hands. (From Bonnie Gardner)*

- *Observed with blood spatter on his leg, hands and arm also has a scratch on his arm. (observed by Mike Williams and Bonnie Gardner)*

- *Whispers to Greg and they go into the bedroom and shut the door behind them. They seem to be being very secretive. (Observed by Bonnie Gardner)*

- *After emerging from bedroom they throw away Dawn's backpack. (Bonnie Gardner)*

- *The following day Greg and (Easton) are observed throwing away Dawn's belongings into a community dumpster. Greg is heard saying, "She's not coming back." (Mike Williams)*

- *(Easton) is confronted by Joseph Miller (Dawn's brother) as to what happened to Dawn. He was evasive with his answers saying just saying that they dropped her off. Joseph confronts (Easton) about scratches he observes on (Easton's) neck and arm. He tells Joseph that he "fell." (Joseph Miller)*

- *They take Mike Williams to wooded area near Howard Pa and Greg asks (Easton) if "he remembers the spot." (Easton) vomits at this area and they are "creeping" Mike out by saying "weird" stuff.*

- *During polygraph interview he seems to implicate Greg*

and alludes to himself as just being there. He believes that whomever did this should go to jail but the second person involved should "get help" and deserves a second chance.

- He fails polygraph test in 2008.

- He is asked what happened to Dawn he states, "I think she ran away and started a new life."

- He confesses to Trooper Dave Aiello and Detective Kenneth Mains to witnessing Greg kill Dawn and had no additional involvement. He later states that DNA may be found on Dawn's remains because he helped drag her from the vehicle after Greg killed her and helped bury her.

- He tells Teri Emel that he did have blood on him when he returned to the Academy Apartments after Greg killed Dawn. He told people it was red paint and then threw away the clothing.

- Teri later confronted him and asked him if he killed Dawn. He responded by saying "I helped." He told Teri that Greg killed Dawn and he helped bury Dawn in the woods using their hands.

- Teri again confronted (Easton) and told him that she did not know whether she could be with someone that could take someone's life. He responded by saying, "I only helped." When Teri inquired about details, he stated the following: "We were in a car. I was asleep in the back. I woke up and saw Greg outside the car in a wooded area beating Dawn. Greg was yelling for my help. I got out of the car and helped kill her." Greg then "finished her off."

I fully understand that we do not have any physical evidence but we have the strongest circumstantial case I have ever seen. In addition, we have a bevy of witnesses that can implicate (Easton) for this murder as you can see from above.

In addition as we talked before, a gross abuse of corpse charge is not out of the question. The statute of limitations on that charge is not the standard when coupled with homicide.

I am fully aware that you have the discretion as to who or what is charged and I respect that. I just think this case should be charged, whether by you on the facts we already have or by an investigative

Grand Jury who hears these facts along with anything else that comes up during the sessions.

I strongly believe we have a prosecutable case that will result in a murder conviction of (Easton). Dawn Miller cannot be forgotten through the passage of time and her tragic death cannot become a folklore or myth like so many other Centre County disappearances. People have to remember she was a living breathing human being whose life was tragically taken from her by two individuals who thought they were above the law. As you know one of them met their maker....but the other smirks at us every day.

I work cold cases every day, that's what I do. I am good at it and I will work tirelessly to get this case the justice it deserves. As you can see, I have worked with and led the best investigators in the world on cold cases and I think you and I could bring closure and resolution to this one as well. There is no substitute for passion. I have that for these unsolved cases and can help on any others you have....(Gricar, Song, Condon, Offett, Shadle, Bailey, Ardsma, etc)

I know you have a lot on your plate right now...I also know that immersing yourself in your work and a specific case can help alleviate some of that angst.... Dawn Miller can be that case.

Well, there's my pitch.....one thing I have learned in my 15 years of law enforcement....you never know unless you ask......So I am asking you to revisit this case in some form or fashion. Thank you for your time and consideration.

Respectfully,

Kenneth L. Mains

Detective

The response I got was in my opinion, a bit sarcastic and done to placate me.

Ken,

Thanks. Rest assured, we care about Dawn Marie Miller and are aware of these facts. We certainly appreciate your enthusiasm on this one. I have no issue with a no body case or a circumstantial case. Circumstantial cases are my favorite.

I know the facts, what I would like to hear about are your thoughts regarding witnesses who wouldn't talk to you when you tried to interview them or who you think we could possibly bring to the grand jury that dodged you before. That is the issue I am interested in. Grand Jurys are helpful in that regard. They don't make evidentiary issues better or worse for existing facts. They are useful for potentially discovering new evidence if we thought there was some, in cases where we could not get that evidence in "ordinary" investigative ways. Let me know your thoughts on that angle. Thanks.

Obviously, my tone becomes a bit angrier because I feel the district attorney was being sarcastic and undermining me. So I responded on Aug. 11, 2015:

No individual person has dodged me regarding this case. Every person relayed the same consistent information... that Greg AND (Easton) murdered Dawn Miller and I have proven that.

I understand you know the facts, I was just "refreshing your memory" with those facts. Not sure if you recall but the last credible information I had in 2011 was that Dawn was buried in the Greg's basement (House vacant during murder timeframe) which came from a credible witness. I forwarded this information to you. You requested PSP do a knock and talk which I relayed to them. It was never done (not your fault as I know you do not run PSP) yet frustrating nonetheless.

My enthusiasm is for justice, not just this case. That is what the public expects from me, it is my job. I do not make it a habit to second-guess the prosecution after I solve a case, but sometimes it's inevitable. Apparently we will agree to disagree on this case ever moving forward in the system.

According to your reasoning of why this particular Grand Jury is being utilized (reluctant witnesses) then I guess this case isn't relevant for those purposes.

Thank you for taking the time to respond to my emails.

Kenneth L. Mains

Detective

I never received another response and Dawn continues to be

forgotten—but not by me.

I will say that the reason not to prosecute is done based on if they believe they can win. No one likes to lose and some don't like to gamble, either. I understand because we only get one chance to convict; if we lose, he forever walks. However, I think—at least in this case—we have enough evidence to charge Easton with co-conspiracy to commit murder or gross abuse of corpse, which has no statute of limitations when coupled with a homicide.

With that said, I will say I am still very irritated to this day that a murderer walks the same streets as my family, free to kill again.

Nothing—and I mean nothing—is more heart-wrenching than telling Sandra Northern that I not only did I fail to locate her daughter, but I cannot arrest the remaining suspect who took her life.

This is a letter she sent me on Wednesday, Sept. 24, 2008:

> *Ken, Thank you so much for the update. Also, thank you for all your hard work in this case. I know you have gone above and beyond to try and find Dawn and I can't tell you how much that means to me that after all these years somebody really cares enough to try and find out what happened to her.*
>
> *I truly do hope that her body is found and that whoever did this to her is punished. That would at least ease some of the pain that I feel at the loss of my daughter. Also, it would bring justice for Dawn, who was a beautiful young girl who never had a chance to live her life. Thanks again for all your hard work in this case.*
>
> *Sandy*

The hug that I received from Dawn's mother the end of that conversation is something that will stick with me forever. Her caring, warmth and genuine empathy for me as a "failed" investigator are something I will always remember. As was this letter from Dawn's aunt:

> *Hi,*
>
> *You do not know me, but my name is Carol Miller, and I am the aunt of Dawn. My sister is Sandy, Dawn's mother. She forwarded this email as we keep in touch about what is going*

on.

First of all congratulations on your reward and promotion. I read the article in the paper on Saturday night. It certainly brought many tears to my eyes. I guess seeing in writing that it was considered a homicide just really made it all the more real.

Dawn and my daughter Kim were about the same age, and spent a lot of time together, especially in their teen years and younger. I loved Dawn very much, and although she had a difficult life, and got mixed up with the wrong crowd, that sweet girl was a God send to her mom, always watching the kids and helping her Mom out. She had to live through some real tough times, but I knew in my heart no matter how angry she got, she would never take off and leave her brothers and sisters. I knew that, yet there was a part of me that kept hoping some day we would find her. I even went on and paid one of those find people places, to see if anything would turn up.

I guess there is a part of me that is so angry by the Wmspt. Police Department for their lack of investigation in this case. All they could say is she was over 21 and they really couldn't do anything. Both Sandy and I knew Dawn would never leave the kids. She was like a mother to Shawn and was extremely close to Kristie. She wouldn't leave her clothes and check at her friend's house and not get them. I believe the police ignored evidence that was right there. I think changes need to be made somehow to treat cases individual, not just assume things, and not pay attention to things family and friends try to say. I wonder if the police department knew what it was like to look every time you go somewhere, to see if the person walking or riding a bike may be the loved one you are missing. Do they know the countless hours you go searching, crying, feeling hopeless, and then trying to regain hope. Do they know how it feels to know that a precious young girl was robbed of her life? Do they know the nightmare that so many people who loved her have had to live? How much did they care that they spent so little time and effort to find her? This is a crime in itself and should not be tolerated.

My sister thinks very highly of you, as we all do. For 15 years her case was put to rest, and yet you come in and on a lot of your own time, cared enough to solve this. I am aware of the man who hung himself. There are so many questions I guess we all have. I hope someday maybe they can be answered. I hope and pray that she did not suffer much. I do not know the details of her death, but I pray it was quick. I do not know if it were premeditated or if it were done out of anger. I just pray it was quick. I hate to think of her suffering.

A man who committed a murder was allowed to live his life all these years, because our police department made that possible for both of them to do so. Then I ask myself what kind of life could you live always wondering if someone would find out, knowing you robbed someone of a life. He was a coward to hang himself. I do not know the details, only what I have been told. I try not to be vindictive, not to hate, but only to hate what people do. My mom taught me that. When I was little my sister Sandy liked to aggravate me. So she made me so angry I told her I hated her. My mom was furious and said never say you hate someone, that you hate what they did, but never hate someone. Hate eats you alive, as does holding on to anger and resentments. Yet at a time like this it is difficult to not be angry and resentful. I guess only time will help that.

I very much would like to help my sister with a memorial service after all this is over. I think all of us need that closure. None of us have a lot of money, but we are going to all chip in and do what we need to do to honor my niece. And most of all to put her to rest, even if we can't find her remains. I do not even know where he said she was killed. Someday I hope we can know that. And I wonder why no remains can be found if he knew where they buried her. At any rate, we need to finally put all the years of wondering, hoping, crying, and searching, to rest.

I am going to have an oil painting done for my sister of Dawn when she was a little girl in pigtails, so beautiful before she was old enough to experience the hardships of this world. I want my sister to be able to look at that, and think of those days, and remember her with love. In that picture I am going to have her brothers and sisters in it when they were younger.

I want her to look at ALL her children together, and because of her strong faith in God, she will also believe that she will be with Dawn again in heaven.

Thank You so much for all you have done to bring some closure to all of this, for doing what should have been done long ago. Thank You for caring so much that you would dedicate so much of your own time to solve this case. As much as it hurts to know she is really gone in such a terrible way, at least we can all go on without false hopes, and somehow move past this.

Sandy is a wonderful lady and my heart goes out to her. But she is so strong, more than she knows. But I guess we are both hurt and angry that her life meant so little to the police that they could not do a proper investigation, and jump to conclusions that she just took off. I hope somehow something good can come of this so that another family doesn't have to go through something like this.

Thank You for reading this and for all you have done. If you ever have questions or need anything please don't hesitate to email me or call. Thank you so very much.

Sincerely,

Carol Miller

Carol Miller had it right. She hit the nail on the head at every aspect of her letter. I keep it because it shows the ripple effect of cold cases. How they reach beyond the immediate players and families. People (mostly law enforcement) have to remember that we are supposed to go above and beyond. We are supposed to care about the victim, no matter if that victim is Ray Gricar (missing district attorney) or Dawn Miller. *Nobody* deserves to be forgotten.

Everyone in life has something to give, a gift to offer this world. Dawn supplied many of you with great memories and love. She supplied me with a gift as well. Dawn gave me the ability, the hope and the passion to never let another victim be forgotten— that was her gift and because of Dawn, she will affect many, many lives because I will continue to fight for every Dawn Miller out there. That is what is right and that is what I do! Thanks, Dawn, thanks for giving me that gift! I will never forget you.

Dawn Marie Miller

Newspaper Article 1992

Mains and the nephew eye to eye 2007

*Mains, undercover with ponytail, searching
for Dawn Miller's remains 2008*

JENNIFER HILL

*"Ken Mains has been the inspiration and driving force
behind the founding of The American Investigative
Society of Cold Cases. You should be given a medal
for what you are doing. Organizations like this emerge
because of the energy, inspiration and organizing skills
of experts like Ken Mains—willing to give so much
of themselves while keeping their own egos all but
invisible. I guess I just defined true leadership."*

Dr. John Liebert, MDCM

This brutal crime took place before I was born. Yet the case still creates waves in Lycoming County more than 40 years later. This is the first case in which I met resentment from every side. I got grief from the old cops who investigated the murder, the victims' family who just wanted it to go away and, of course, the accused and his minions. This was the first case in which I truly felt unappreciated for my efforts. I felt I had an obligation to everyone involved to get to the truth. Most of all, I owed it to the victim. Kim Hubbard was convicted of this murder and served 10 years. When he got out of prison, he began his campaign to proclaim his innocence. So, when the convicted began proclaiming his innocence, little did he know he opened up the floodgates. Those letters he sent to judges were given to the district attorney, who gave them to me and said, "Solve this." I did!

On Oct. 22, 2013, I was requested by Chief County Det. William Weber and District Attorney Linhardt to follow up on an email that was sent to all of the sitting judges of Lycoming County:

Framed for murder in Lycoming County in Williamsport, PA.

States own evidence reveals courtroom deception by DA, coroner, and Pennsylvania State police 40 years ago.

Visit: KimHubbardstory.com

All 1287 pages of transcripts are on this website. All evidence photos are on this website, even the postmortem report or medical records that the prosecutor did not enter into evidence are on this website. See what he was trying to hide. Read and decide for yourself was what they did to Kim Hubbard and his family right or wrong.

Kim Hubbard

On Nov. 1, 2013, I did meet with Hubbard at the Humdinger restaurant in South Williamsport, Pa., where he proclaimed his innocence and emphatically stated, "I did not kill that girl." I looked him dead and the eyes and inched closer to his face and said, "I will find out." He leaned back and stated, "I like you." He went on to assert the Pennsylvania State Police framed him and evidence was planted to ensure his conviction. He also would say that all the evidence in the case was destroyed; therefore, nothing forensically could be done to prove his innocence.

After requesting and receiving the police report from the Pennsylvania State Police, I began my review of the case. Not long after my review, I was sitting in my office when I overheard some people in the waiting room talking about ghosts. I paid little attention to it, but as a cop, you listen to everything. I then heard one of the people mention seeing orbs or ghost activity in the basement of their office. Again, I overheard, but didn't pay any attention to it as I was typing a report. They said that there was a box down there and someone seen orbs around it. Then I overheard a statement that took this case in a whole new direction for me. "Yeah, it was the Hubbard box." I immediately slid my chair out of my cubicle and went to the discussion. I thrust myself into the conversation by asking, "What did you say?" They repeated and I said, "What box and what is in it?" The employee stated that there was a box in their basement that said "Hubbard" on it but they did not know what is in it. I said, "Take me now."

Apparently, the Lycoming County 911 Center had a large box with the name Hubbard in its basement. I figured it was more paperwork—possibly from appeals—but nonetheless, I wanted to read it. I did locate the box in the basement. To my surprise, it was a very large wooden box and the top was screwed shut. The box was about the size of a chest freezer and was sitting alone in a basement with cobwebs affixed to the edges. After I removed the top, to my surprise, I did locate various items that were labeled and identified as evidence used at Hubbard's trial. It was a monumental find and I could not believe how lucky I was to find it. There were tires, plaster castings, letters from Hubbard, dirt samples, what would become a famous blue "33" jersey from the victim, shoes and white hard hat. I knew I had hit the mother lode. This evidence was supposed to be destroyed, but here it was. Fate.

Any testing of the evidence would have to wait, as I was still reading and reviewing the case documents. Always first things first. Never test evidence before reviewing the case. Never get ahead of your investigations and always work the case backwards from possible appeals and trials.

I had to put myself back in 1973 when Hubbard was just 20 years old. I had to taste the crisp October air and understand the culture of that year. Most importantly, I had to view the case through an unbiased set of eyes beginning with the victim, 12-year-old Jennifer "Jenny" Hill.

On Oct. 19, 1973, Jenny was spending the day with her friend, Ruthie Hubbard, age 12. Jenny had spent the previous night at the Hubbard residence, which was not uncommon. Ruthie lived at 1030 Central Ave. in South Williamsport with her brother, Kim; father, Joe; and mother, Doris.

At approximately 3:45 p.m., Norma Hill (Jenny's mother) called the Hubbards' home and told Jenny that it was time to come home. Jenny did not want to leave, according to her best friend, Ruthie, as she wanted to attend the high school football game. However, Jenny left the Hubbards' home shortly after the call to walk to her home at 353 Hastings St., less than a mile away. Jenny never made it home.

It would have taken about 17 minutes for Jenny to walk home. She had done it numerous times before. It was daylight; there was nothing to fear. At 6 p.m., the Hills called the South Williamsport Police Department to report Jenny missing. Where was Jenny?

The first thing I had to do when reinvestigating this case was go to the scene. I had to see the houses involved. I had to walk the route, breathe the air and feel the pavement beneath my feet. I had to do everything Jenny did in 1973. Then, I constructed a timeline with known facts from interviews.

Jenny's Timeline

Oct. 19, 1973

11:30 a.m.–12:05 p.m.: Jenny is at the Humdinger restaurant eating lunch. She then plays football and kickball with a group of similarly aged kids. During this game, she rips the crotch of her pants. The pants are darker blue with red heart patches. This will become important later and deepen the mystery further.

3:30–4:10 p.m.: Jenny receives a call from her mother at the Hubbards' home telling her to come home. Jenny leaves the house wearing the dark blue jeans with red heart patches and a blue jacket, with her shirttail pulled over the back crotch area to cover the rip.

4:15 p.m.: Jackie Hill, Jenny's teenaged sister, called the Hubbards' home and talks to Ruthie to see if Jenny left yet because she still had not made it home.

4:30–5 p.m.: Jack Hill, Jenny's father, calls the Hubbards' home and talks to Kim Hubbard to see where Jenny is. Hubbard asks his mother and is told that Jenny left "about an hour ago."

Sightings of Jenny

There were confirmed sightings of Jenny after she left the Hubbard residence and began her walk home.

Gary Whiteman (who grew up to be a Williamsport police officer and is now a district judge), then age 10, had played kickball and football earlier in the day with Jenny. He saw Jenny walking eastbound on Central Avenue passing Winthrop Street, walking away from the Hubbard home toward her home between 3:30 and 4 p.m.

Mary Mundrick saw Jenny walking eastbound on Central Avenue near Kane Street around 3:45 p.m. She stated Hill was alone carrying a Glick shoe bag.

Joe Mendez, who was driving through the area with his wife, saw Jenny at the corner of Market Street and West Central Avenue around 3:50 to 3:55 p.m. She was wearing a blue football jersey with the number 33, which stuck out to him because that was his number when he played football. No mention of the bag she was carrying. His wife could not substantiate his sighting.

Betty Nevel and her daughter saw Jenny at 4:30 p.m. (later said it was closer to 4 p.m.) in front of her home at 503 Howard St. This sighting becomes extremely important to the case.

Discovery of the Body

Jenny's disappearance did not go unnoticed in the community. Search parties were organized. On Oct. 23, 145 junior and senior boys from South Williamsport High School volunteered to search the woods in an effort to find her.

Two days later, two men pounded on the door of the Hubbards' home and accused Kim Hubbard of being involved in Jenny's disappearance. The police were called and handled the incident, but it's unknown exactly why the two men were blaming him for the disappearance.

On Oct. 28, 1973, nine days after Jenny disappeared, shortly before 4 p.m., a search party discovered her body in a cornfield just a few miles from her home. Her pants and underwear were pulled down to her ankles, her shirt pulled up over one breast and a jacket covered her body with one arm inside the sleeve of this jacket. The pants on her body are *not* the pants she was wearing when she left the Hubbards' home. The Glick bag she was seen carrying was located near her body. Inside were the dark blue jeans with the hearts and ripped crotch that she was wearing when she began her walk home nine days earlier.

At the scene, investigators discovered tire prints and shoe impressions. When her body was removed, two shoe impressions were observed under her body. It had begun to rain heavily and attempts to preserve the evidence were made. Eventually, plaster casts of the impressions were made.

An autopsy would show Jenny was strangled, probably on the day she went missing. Though the disarray of her clothes on her body suggests she might have been sexually assaulted, no semen was found and she died a virgin.

What happened to Jennifer Hill? Where was she for those nine days? Who would want her dead? Through good, old-fashioned police work by the Pennsylvania State Police, we would find out.

Police started with the last place Jenny came from, the Hubbard home. The Hubbard home fell under the jurisdiction of the South Williamsport Police. However, the area that the body was discovered was State Police jurisdiction. Eventually, their questions were directed at a young derelict who was described as a tough, wild and vulgar South Williamsport native named Kim Hubbard.

Hubbard became a suspect, I believe, after he could not provide an alibi for a certain timeframe and his answers to certain questions changed. I don't think it helped Hubbard that he was known to be a bully and troublemaker. He also was one of the last males to see Jenny alive. Hubbard was 20 years old and had served 14 months in the Army before being honorably discharged for hardship reasons. Hubbard then returned to finish his education and was in his senior year in high school.

Most people who claim Kim Hubbard is innocent, do not know that Joe Hubbard told police on Nov. 3 that his son "had been acting unusual ever since Jenny went missing, more so after she was found in the cornfield." Even Joe Hubbard could see that his son's explanations were thin, including when he was asked how his car got muddy. "Kim told me he got that mud on his car when he was parking with his girlfriend Colleen down at the bottom of Allen Street," Joe said. "The area there is all cinder." Joe also said his wife covered up for their son constantly. "Kim has been acting strange since this happened. He acts like a scared mouse. I will speak out in court about this," Joe said. "My son, Kim, is not right."

On Nov. 16, 1973, at 11:13 p.m., Hubbard was served with a warrant and arrested for Jenny's murder. Hubbard was arrested at the same restaurant we would meet at 38 years later.

The Accused: Kim Hubbard

To understand the dynamics of this crime and the aftermath of what Hubbard's actions and motives were, you have to understand Kim Hubbard. When speaking with him, he wants to be in control. Hubbard will stop and listen during the conversation, but he is not listening to what you say. Instead, he is formulating a thought in order to interject his next topic. Hubbard was prone to violence and troopers during surveillance after the murder saw him punching his sister and pulling her hair. Others saw him slapping his girlfriend and choking her. He was described as a fighter who usually swung first.

Hubbard quit school after the ninth grade and joined the Army. After being discharged, he returned to high school as a much older student. Hubbard maintains his innocence, which is reinforced by the people around him. His glare and voice tone are that of someone who is trying to intimidate and essentially bully. His elaborate webpage goes in very great detail to proclaim his innocence. However, if you break it down and not look at it in general terms, there is only the reasonable conclusion that he is guilty. All Hubbard does is focus in on inconsistencies in testimonies, photographs that are inverted but show the same thing and other non-essential elements of the crime. His conjecture and theories have zero merit and I have disproved many of them.

Hubbard served his time for this crime, although his sentence was much too lenient if he did in fact commit this crime, in my opinion. He has moved right back to the same community where he was arrested and where the murder took place. Some will see this as an act of an innocent man, wrongly convicted. However, if you know Kim Hubbard, that is not the case. Hubbard is an in-your-face type of guy. He wants to dominate and be in control. When he looks at you and tells you that he is innocent, he believes it and he states it with enough force and determination that you believe it. He moved back to the same area out of spite, continuing the charade of innocence. He likes the notoriety.

Hubbard is a type-A personality and his paranoia is not brought on from being wrongly convicted, it is from knowing he is guilty and he understands there are people who unequivocally know this, which scares him. Some examples of Hubbard's mentality can be seen in the following emails he sent me.

On Oct. 22, 2013, I received this email from Hubbard:

> *Mr. mains, good morning Sir. My name is Kim Hubbard. You must read all my webpage carefully, take your time. All the evidence that you need or need to see is in fact on this webpage. Even the postmortem report that was never admitted into evidence is here. It clearly shows what they did to me. I've been told by people they never seen a whole case put on an Internet webpage like this before. I only emailed five people in the courthouse, they were all the judges. They are all good people. But they need to know what happened, they weren't around back then. When you're done reading the webpage and still have a question for me. I am here.*

After reviewing the case, I understood how a boot print that was under the victim's body was the most compelling evidence against him. I met with Hubbard on Nov. 18, 2013, at the Humdinger restaurant. I asked Hubbard to explain how his boot impression was discovered underneath the victim's body. "Is it possible," I asked, "that it could be someone else's boot print and you were not framed"? Hubbard replied, "No, that is not possible. That is my boot print, but it was planted."

Hubbard contends that police and others planted it there in a grand conspiracy. It was at this time I began to see through Hubbard's charade. Yet, as a professional investigator, I would do a thorough and accurate review of the case regardless of what my initial impressions were. After meeting Hubbard for a second time again at the very restaurant where he was arrested, I received the following email from him:

Mr. Mains,

The more I think about our conversation that we had at the Humdinger, the more that I think this case is much bigger than you. I mean no disrespect. I can tell by your questions and answers (we're) not on the same page, or even in the same book. I wasn't the only one the police were looking at, but you already know that, transcripts 407 clearly state they were showing pictures of a young man with dark hair around age 30 driving a light colored Pontiac. As for Trooper Houser, taking the scrapings off Jennifer's fingernails, he didn't do that Dr. Catherman did. As far as the scrapings that were taken from underneath Jennifer's fingernails, they were never tested, but you already know that. The reason there were never tested is the same reason that they never tested the red stuff on my white helmet, because if they would have, it would've showed the red stuff was jelly from Strhoman's bakery. That's what you should be testing. The reason they never tested the scrapings was simple. They already knew what was under them, and so do you, it's in transcripts. But, you should have them tested anyhow, just to prove to yourself. It's Jennifer's own skin. I know that you know they did a thorough search of me from the waist up at the state police barracks. There were no scratches on me. But I know you already know that. I know you're smarter than what you're letting on. Trying to tell me that Jennifer laid on a concrete floor for four days, doesn't make it. You know Jennifer's body was refrigerated. There is no doubt about that. But I know you know that too. Trusting the DA's office is hard. Especially when you tell me you can see no difference between photos seven and eight, but, you know photo eight was inverted. Mr. Mains, I've already been through enough shit in my life. I don't need anymore.

I've already did the time for this crime, Mr. Mains. If you are trying to help me, you need to focus on the pictures, Dr. Miller's testimony, and all the lies the state police told. There is no way you can do this by yourself. All the evidence that you need to prove me innocent, if that is truly your intent, and exonerate me, it is already on my webpage. I stand by it.

Kim Hubbard

Initially, Hubbard was happy that I was looking into the case. However, once I told him that I was not doing it to exonerate him (which is what he thought) and I was doing it for the truth, his demeanor shifted and he became standoffish. After that meeting with Hubbard he stopped contacting me. I next met with Hubbard to let him know I had found evidence, in particular, Jenny's clothing, which could be tested for DNA. Hubbard stated that he has documents that proved I was lying because those items were destroyed. He began to shake and spilled his coffee. I asked him for his DNA. He refused, saying he had to talk to his attorney. I repeated that if he were innocent, he should provide a DNA sample. He again refused. Let's look at why the commonwealth arrested and a jury convicted Hubbard of this murder to begin with.

The Commonwealth's Position in 1973

Hubbard picked Jenny Hill up in his car in front of Betty Nevel's home at 503 Howard St., on Oct. 19, 1973, at 4:30 p.m. Hubbard drove her to a remote area called Sylvan Dell area in which he was familiar with and had gone parking there with his girlfriend. There, Hubbard strangled Jenny and dragged her body into a cornfield. Hubbard returned home, where he took the call from Jenny's father between 4:45 p.m. and 5 p.m.

Evidence Against Hubbard

After requesting the case file and photographs from the State Police and reviewing them, I initially came to the conclusion that Hubbard was "more than likely" responsible for this murder. I based this on the following evidence:

- Expert testimony from a shoe impression criminalist confirmed that Hubbard's boots matched the prints found underneath Jenny's body in the cornfield. The pictures at the end of the chapter show the casts from the field and Hubbard's boots with the corresponding matches. The same expert matched tire prints from the cornfield to Hubbard's car.

Hubbard's Innocence Claims

Hubbard has always maintained his innocence. He took the stand in his own defense and was still convicted by a jury of his peers for the second-degree murder of Jenny Hill. His demeanor on the stand was that of a cocky young man who wanted people to believe his lies. Just because you begin every answer with "Sir" doesn't mean you are respectful. Hubbard was sentenced to 10 to 20 years in a state prison for this murder.

As I stated before, Hubbard served 10 years and was released. In an effort to rehabilitate his reputation, Hubbard created his website and wrote letters to the judges, which prompted this case review. He believes that the state police and the District Attorney's Office framed him. His assertions:

- Jenny's body was discovered sometime between Oct. 19–21, 1973, and refrigerated at the Williamsport Hospital until it was removed by state police and placed back in the cornfield where it was found on Oct. 28.

- The tire print and boot evidence was planted by police.

- He had a different tire on his car on Oct. 28, 1973, and the tire expert testified that it made the tire impressions in the cornfield. This is impossible because he hadn't even had the tire until after the plaster casts were taken from the field where the body was discovered.

- Stated that according to the commonwealth's timeline, he would not have enough time to commit the murder.

- Jenny's body was not decomposed enough to be in the cornfield for nine days.

- Photographs were altered and there are actually two different body locations. The original and where police placed her body back into the cornfield.

- The rip in Jenny's crotch area of her pants had started to be repaired by a sewing machine and white thread. This shows that she made it home and died as a result of domestic violence.

Hubbard's Claims Debunked

I will take each individual claim asserted by Hubbard and explain the facts and how I came to my findings.

Claim:

Jenny's body was discovered sometime between Oct. 19–21, 1973, and refrigerated at the Williamsport Hospital until it was removed by state police and placed back in the cornfield where it was found on Oct. 28.

Fact:

This would have to be a conspiracy between the person who discovered the body, the coroner, the pathologist and members of the state police. This is a ridiculous assertion, plain and simple. There is simply no way the body was discovered, removed and refrigerated and then placed back out in the same cornfield days later. Quite frankly, it is a waste of my time to even entertain this notion, as it is completely false and ridiculous.

Claim:

The tire print and boot evidence was planted.

Fact:

I met with Hubbard on Nov. 18, 2013, at the Humdinger restaurant. I asked Hubbard to explain to me how his boot impression was discovered underneath the victim's body. I asked, "Is it possible that it could be someone else's boot print and you were not framed?" Hubbard replied, "No, that is not possible. That is my boot print." I think he states this because he cannot refute it. It was also one of the biggest reasons he was convicted.

He contends that police and others planted it there in a conspiracy. When people start claiming evidence was planted you can bet your bottom dollar that nine times out of 10, you are talking to a guilty person. And you can make that 10 out of 10 times the person is guilty if I am involved in the case because my integrity is above reproach. Hubbard later made this claim about me, as you will read. This claim comes from a desperate man who has run out of lies to explain the overwhelming evidence against him.

I asked George Schiro, an expert in tread wear to look at the castings from the body dump/crime scene and Hubbard's boots. This was not the Pennsylvania State Police who Hubbard claimed framed him; this was an independent, unbiased expert who has zero affiliation with the case. Schiro has more than 25 years of experience as a forensic scientist and crime scene investigator. He has examined evidence in more than 3,200 criminal and civil cases. He has also consulted on cases in 24 states, for the United States Army and Air Force, and the United Kingdom. He has also testified as an expert witness in more than 160 trials in 30 Louisiana parish courts; Pope County, Ark.; San Bernardino County, Calif.; Escambia and Lee counties, Fla.; Washington County, Miss.; St. Louis County, Mo.; Clark County, Nev.; Bronx County, N.Y.; Harris County, Tex.; Cabell County, W.V.; and federal court (Louisiana Middle and Nebraska districts); and two Louisiana city courts. His specialties are: crime scene investigation, crime scene reconstruction, general forensic science, DNA analysis, serology, bloodstain pattern analysis, shooting reconstruction, shoeprint identification, hair examination, latent print development and fracture match analysis.

> *"I completed my examination of the boot and cast. In my opinion, it's <u>highly likely</u> that the left boot is the source of one of the impressions represented by cast L-5 (Hubbard's boots). I stopped short of saying it's the source of the impression because there are some minor measurement discrepancies (no greater than 1.31 mm) between the features in the cast and the features in the boot. These discrepancies could be the result of the age of the cast and the boot. There are also features found on the boot that are not found on the cast, although this could be due to the soil filling in those areas on the boot and not getting transferred to the impression. Some of the features on the cast that Mr. Krebs (trial expert) identified are in areas that I would be hesitant to call as features. That's not to say they aren't actual features, they are just in places that make them difficult to discern. They certainly correspond to the same placement as features on the boot. There are two significant random markings on both the boot and cast, one of which was previously identified by Mr. Krebs and one that I discovered. These random marks along with the majority of*

overlapping measurements between the cast and the boot, and the qualitative features of the boot and cast form the basis of my opinion."

So, a second expert confirmed that Hubbard's boot print was located in the mud, in the cornfield, under Jenny's body. In addition, the plaster casters of the boot prints were obtained on the day the body was found, Oct. 28, 1973. Hubbard's boots were obtained from him on Oct. 31, 1973. How could the boot prints be planted when police did not even have the boots in their custody until three days later? Because it was not planted.

Claim:

He had a different tire on his car on Oct. 28, 1973, and the tire expert testified that it made the tire impressions in the cornfield. This is impossible because he hadn't even had the tire until after the plaster casts were taken from the field where the body was discovered.

Fact:

The tire impression expert testified that this tire could have made the impression, not that it "was" made. This is another play on words by Hubbard and his defenders.

Claim:

According to the commonwealth's timeline, he would not have enough time to commit the murder.

Fact:

Since no times are absolute in Hubbard's timeline and other witnesses' times fluctuate, this is hard to determine. I will say that in my opinion, it would have been difficult for Hubbard to pick up Jenny, murder her and dump her in the cornfield during the allotted timeframe—not impossible, but difficult. Of all of Hubbard's assertions, this is the only one that has a hint of credibility. Again, although all the times he produced and witnesses have produced are not exact, it is impossible to determine either way. However, a timeline can be constructed that demonstrates that he had enough time to do this crime. On Oct. 31, Nov. 1 and Nov. 3, investigators formally questioned a 20-year-old high school senior, Hubbard.

The following are his movements for the day Jenny went missing, according to Hubbard:

1–1:15 p.m.: Awoke and went to the store to buy cigarettes, then went home.

1:45 p.m.: Rented a buffer to polish floors in his home. Police later confirmed this with a receipt and follow-up interview with the store clerk.

3:15 p.m.: At the Humdinger eating and was there about 25 minutes. Then went home and worked on his car for about an hour. Next, he went to a car wash and was there about 25 minutes. Next, he went back to the Humdinger for a drink.

4:45 p.m.: Back home, where he received a call from Jenny's father looking for her.

Claim:

Jenny's body was not decomposed enough to be in the cornfield for nine days. The condition of the body appeared to be fresh, not a body that had been in the field for nine days during varying weather temperatures. Jenny's body was found earlier, removed and refrigerated for a period of time. Then the body was placed back in the cornfield so Hubbard could be framed.

Fact:

At first glance, an amateur may also agree with Hubbard. However, I am not an amateur, nor is Dr. Werner Spitz.

I reached out to the one of the foremost forensic pathologists in the world to get a definitive answer on this. Dr. Spitz has practiced forensic pathology for more than 50 years. He works as a consultant, forensic pathology and toxicology professor of pathology at Wayne State University School of Medicine and adjunct professor of toxicology at University of Windsor, Ontario, Canada. Dr. Spitz previously worked as the chief medical examiner of Wayne County (Detroit), Mich. (1972–1988); forensic pathologist then chief medical examiner for Macomb County, Mich. (1972–2004); deputy chief medical examiner for the State of Maryland; associate professor at University of Maryland School of Medicine, Johns Hopkins University and Department of Legal Medicine at the University School of Medicine, West Berlin, Germany. He is certified by the American Board of Pathology in anatomic and forensic pathology and received medical training at the Geneva University Medical School in Switzerland and the Hebrew University Hadassa Medical School in Jerusalem, Israel. Dr. Spitz is the author of 96 scientific publications and author and editor of the textbook "Spitz and Fisher's Medicolegal Investigation of Death," first published in 1972, now in its fourth edition. He has served on various committees investigating the assassination of President John F. Kennedy and Martin Luther King, including the U.S. House of Representatives Committee on Assassinations. He has served as an expert and testified in all level of courts across the United States and Canada and in numerous high-visibility cases including the Mary Jo Kopechne/Ted Kennedy/Chappaquiddick case, the Preppy Murder in New York, for the Goldman family in its wrongful death lawsuit against O.J. Simpson, the Jenny Jones trial, the Crown v Truscott case in Toronto, Owen Hart's high-wire fall during a WWF event, the Philip Spector case in California and the Casey Anthony trial in Florida. He consulted with the Boulder, Colo., police regarding the JonBenét Ramsey case. He has lectured and given expert testimony worldwide and has performed or supervised approximately 60,000 autopsies.

These are Dr. Spitz's findings in the Hubbard case:

"I reviewed the autopsy report that you sent regarding 12 year old, Jennifer Hill and the photographs on the website. The autopsy showed evidence of early decomposition which could explain absence of sperm cells and acid phosphatase. Acid phosphatase is an enzyme which is likely to disappear with increasing postmortem period when decomposition is in progress. The same is true of sperm cells. It is quite obvious that this is a sexual crime.

As to the time between disappearance and the finding of the body, it is my opinion 9 days is consistent. The body shows evidence of green discoloration in the right lower abdominal wall and the eyes are soft and sunken.

I used to think that identification of the last meal in stomach contents would suggest an approximately 2 hours postmortem, but this is variable depending on a host of other factors. In this case, the stomach contents were slimy to watery which is likely due to digestion. If the bread was not immersed in gastric juices, it would not be subjected to the digestive process; otherwise carbohydrates start the digestive process in the mouth.

The environmental temperature of 33.9 to 63 degrees and rain would lend support to my estimate, considering that bodies kept in a refrigerator would usually be kept at 40 degrees and would be comparable to what this body showed. I knew Dr. Catherman who did this autopsy as a competent forensic pathologist. The black and white photographs showing the body do not contradict my opinion."

Claim:

Photographs were altered and there are actually two different body locations. The original and where police placed her body back into the cornfield.

Fact:

I cannot see what photographs were allegedly altered or display two separate locations. I do see that one photograph's image is flipped or reversed and I don't know the reasoning behind this. However, it doesn't mean there are two different locations. Because the testimony of some at trial differed, Hubbard contends people are lying and the body was in two different locations. I cannot find any evidence to support this.

Claim:

The rip in Jenny's crotch area of her pants had started to be repaired by a sewing machine and white thread. This shows that she made it home and died as a result of domestic violence.

Fact:

I did locate, photograph and inspect the rip in Jenny's pants almost 40 years later. My conclusion is that the white thread is, in fact, original stitching from the pants and not made by someone trying to repair the jeans. See photographs at the end of this chapter that I took of the rip that show the white thread continuing up the seam where you can observe the same white thread under the jeans material.

The Letter

One day in 2013, the District Attorney's Office received a mysterious letter from someone named Danielle M. Conley. I received this letter after being assigned to follow up a claim made by Hubbard that he was innocent. Hubbard had sent an email to Lycoming County judges and directed them to his website www. kimhubbardstory.com. That website appalled me and I continue to get angry thinking about it. A picture of Jenny, partially clothed, on the autopsy table is shown. Why? At the end of this chapter, you can read the answer to that. This letter was intended to exonerate Hubbard of this murder. In fact, some of Hubbard's supporters will likely use this letter after reading this book to solidify their beliefs. I, too, believed it had some merit after reading it. Yet, just like every other investigation, you must dig deeper and deduce possibilities until you get probabilities. Once you break down the letter, the truth will show itself.

According to this mysterious letter, Conley, now a middle-aged woman, had gone to a psychologist to deal with some emotional issues stemming from her childhood. Conley was a next-door neighbor of Jenny Hill and a family friend. Conley stated she witnessed her father, Daniel Gerber, murder Jenny in their home on Hastings Street.

Conley was 5 years old at the time of Jenny's murder. She went into great detail about the events she allegedly saw on the night of Oct. 19, 1973. Conley stated that her father was sexually abusing her and confided this to Jenny. Conley believes this is why her father murdered Jenny.

Conley stated her father stored Jenny's body in their new home that was being constructed at 530 Hill St., until her father and his brother-in-law moved her body to the cornfield.

Conley described her father strangling Jenny with his hands and how Conley tried to wedge her fingers between her father's hands and Jenny's neck. Conley stated that she left scratch marks on Jenny's neck.

Conley described Jenny falling to the floor and a puddle forming underneath her body (presumably urine). "I remember my dad deciding to remove her pants. I remember thinking, 'How is she going to get home without pants?' I believe I even asked my dad this question and he responded that he would get her something to wear." (Jenny was found with a different pair of pants than what she was last seen wearing. She had an extra set of clothing in her Glick bag from just spending the night at the Hubbard residence.)

Conley states the reason Jenny stopped in to her home that evening was to return a blue South Williamsport letterman type of jacket that Jenny had borrowed from Conley's mother. This type of jacket was found with Jenny's body. (I confirmed that this jacket did belong to Conley's mother.)

So far, this letter matched some of the evidence. It sounded plausible. The condition of the body could be consistent with being stored in a garage-type area to slow the decomposition process. I believed that this letter, if real, could very well change the Lycoming County justice system and, more importantly, prove Hubbard's innocence.

I followed up the letter by calling Conley and exchanging some emails with her. Obviously, I wanted to know more. Why is she just now coming forward? Had she told anyone else about this in the past 40 years? My mind was racing with questions and possible answers. If this information could exonerate an innocent man, I wanted to act on the information as soon as possible. The following are excerpts from email correspondence I had with Conley after I had asked her to supply additional information; I wanted to dig deeper into what she allegedly saw. This is the information she shared with me in her own words:

> *"It's been some time since I've read the document (original letter) I sent though there were some things I had pondered since then. I wanted to make sure I got these right. I just did a mental review the best I could. Some of these things may be repeats of what is already in the original statement.*
>
> *- The day that she came to door: It seemed dark/gloomy outside as if the sun was down or not out. I wouldn't say dark like night though.*
>
> *- I keep thinking during encounter it was suggested by her that she had more belongings left on front porch as if in a bag.*
>
> *- I keep thinking she was wearing earrings and one came off.*
>
> *- Her wearing a light color shirt comes to mind - I already know that this was a jersey style shirt, but I think there were*

numbers on the front - two numbers coming to mind, couldn't say what though.

- The color blue, light blue like a powder blue and keep thinking this was underwear color

- Her head was positioned towards left side of kitchen towards basement door, feet were left side towards the driveway side of house (when she was lying on floor)

- Kept seeing kitchen doorway being partially blocked from the basement door (when the door was opened)

- I remember the general path taken when she entered the house and remember general place in rooms where we stood, I remember basic location the chair was located when she was seated, and where I stood on the other side of the wall.

- Her older sister and I rode with my dad in a large van or truck like vehicle the day the Hill kids (excluding Jenny) came to our house on Hill Street. I believe this was during the time we were moving. I said something to her older sister pertaining to my dad hurting Jenny after we got out of the vehicle...we were in driveway of the house on Hill Street.

- I remember she urinated after she was on floor lying down not moving when that happened. I was present a period of time when her pants were pulled down to remove them after she urinated. I recall this, but a good deal of that process is vague. At some point I saw her underwear, this is vague, it's like catching a glimpse, but a light color...powder blue is what I keep seeing when I review it.

- My grandparents, Otis and Helen Allen, lived on second Avenue. My parents drove a station wagon at that time, may have had another car too....not sure. I remember one that had a panel on each side with wood look, like paneling that was brown and the rest of the car was light like white or light blue. Don't remember color car my uncle drove...The car that I saw looked like a sedan type. I think you had another question, but I accidently must have deleted that so could you send me that other question unless I got them all...thought there was four.

- You had a question about the jacket. I just remembered. It

was my mom's school jacket from South Williamsport....I think it had her year, 1958, that she graduated on it. My mom let her borrow this and Jenny came by to return it. There was a football game for South Side that she attended. I have cousins that might know, but we are not in contact.

- I just want to point out that my uncle is not responsible for her death. I have been searching for pictures-I thought there was one that had a portion of the jacket in it. There's a group of photos I haven't located here, I'll keep searching. I think the jacket was mostly blue, but did have white in it too. these are south sides school colors. I think the there was a flap that opened across the back that was white like a hood when unzipped. The jacket disappeared when Jenny did. My mom believed that when Jenny was found, the jacket was found with her. I don't know why or how my mother got that idea unless it is what she was told. I heard this different times as I was growing up and even before my mother died. That Jenny was found with the jacket. My mom even told me that it was in the possession of the police station and if I wanted it, I could have it. Of course I did not care to have it.

- I believe 100% that I witnessed this, and things happened the way I described in my statement. I believe 100% that she stopped at our house that day only to return that jacket, got invited in, things transpired from what should have been a quick drop off, to an escalated confrontation that resulted in her never to leave alive. I understand how this would change things for a lot of people and I understand the necessity of asking that question. I spent a lot of time looking at it up, down, crossways, and every other which way and asked that same thing. Was this from a dream? The answer that I came up with and dealt with on my own and in therapy, is no. There are too many details for me that fit and make sense to me about the way things happened. Just the scratches on her neck alone....remembering verbal interactions with my dad over it and my upset over it. Remembering the way I felt in my body as things were happening. I thank you for putting time into this. It's easy for me to push it down and suppress it all, as I had to do for many years, yet at this point I feel like it's

hanging with me and over my head, and I'm the only one that knows what really happened. I honestly believe 100% that this is what happened to her.

- As far as the area of the house where I think Jenny was kept, it is actually not a room in the house. It is accessible only from the outside. I guess it could be called a storage area, built into the house, next to the garage. It is directly below the enclosed back porch and next to the back of driveway. (This could have supported the lack of decomposition in the body) I took pictures of it when I had my time to go through the house when we were cleaning it out. May be a picture of it in an album as well, but it would be in with the same group with that car that I'm looking for. I will look for these things as I search through pictures. "

Of course, this letter and email exchange with Conley is a game changer. It has some merit and I wanted to know more. This is the first time the existence of this letter is being made public. I don't believe Hubbard or his supporters ever knew about this letter. In fact, it gives them even greater ammunition to shout his innocence. I thought the letter could certainly exonerate Hubbard, therefore I worked this lead.

After I started interviewing people and bringing up this very tragic topic again, I got some bad looks from people. A newspaper article came out during this time and the reporter asked me what old cases I had on my desk currently and I answered, "Jennifer Hill case." The reporter printed that I thought Hubbard was innocent; my office received a flood of calls. Those calls were not of the praising variety. They were from past investigators or relatives of past investigators or characters in this story. People were very mad that I was looking into this case again. Very mad. Yet I felt I owed it to Hubbard if he was wrongly accused and convicted. One thing I know for sure, most of those people who called and bad-mouthed me for looking at the case again did not know of the existence of this letter. I am sure that some people would have read this letter and thrown it in the trash. That is not professional and we owe it to the community. I owed it to everyone involved and regardless of the bad looks I was getting, I was gonna follow it up.

So, after I spoke with Conley, I contacted her family members, who all stated that Danielle is the "black sheep" of the family and is known to be a "crazy." She doesn't attend family functions and moved away from the rest of the family. Conley's sister stated that the rape allegations that Danielle brought up against her father are untrue as is this claim that he murdered Jenny Hill. Conley's brother, Eric, told me that "this seems like a waste of taxpayer money 'cause Danielle is nuts." Regardless, as a professional, I did follow up. Again, I believed there was enough detail in that letter that warranted a further investigation.

I looked into the background of Dan Gerber and the family. I eventually obtained DNA samples from Conley's brother as her father had since passed. If DNA is found on Jennifer's clothing, I could compare Gerber's son's DNA to anything found on the evidence. Eric Gerber did meet me without reservations and provide me with his DNA.

I did interview Jackie Hill-Emerick, Jenny's older sister. When I knocked on the door and told her who I was and what I was doing, I could see the shock in her eyes. She asked if this was a joke. I could see all those years of emotion coming back to her. I could also get a sense of "Please just leave me alone. I want to go on with my life." Yet, I felt Jenny Hill's family was entitled to know we received this letter. I let Hill-Emerick read the long letter from Conley and watched her eyes and body movement. I could immediately tell she was not happy that this traumatic and horrible experience was coming back into her life. I understood.

Hill-Emerick and Conley's families grew up together and Hill-Emerick wished to speak with Conley over the phone. Writing a letter is less intimate than speaking to a family member. I did not know if this would change Conley's position or not. However, I thought it was a great idea. Hill-Emerick and Conley did speak and she stated Conley relayed the same information that was in the letter, verbally to her. To say Hill-Emerick was skeptical of Conley's claims would be an understatement. Hill-Emerick, even after reading the letter, believes Hubbard murdered her sister and she let me know that. Hill-Emerick and her husband did not want me to involve her mother and father, who were elderly now. They did not want them to read this graphic letter. I respected their wishes and never told them. Hill-Emerick said Hubbard continues to bully her parents by going out of his way to say hi to them when he sees them in the grocery store. They knew about Hubbard's website and the allegations he continued to come up with. I could tell that Hill-Emerick and her husband did not want me to pursue this angle any further. However, it is my responsibility as a professional investigator to follow up all leads, no matter other's thoughts and opinions. If Hubbard is innocent and someone else, including Gerber, were guilty of this crime, I would find out.

2014 Expert Psychologist Review of Letter

I wanted an expert opinion on the letter and, more specifically, the recollections of a 5---year-old more than 40 years later. So I spoke with a reputable psychologist, Dr. Jenette Mack-Allen. Dr. Mack-Allen earned her master's degree and doctorate of clinical psychology (PsyD) from Widener University, with concentrated coursework in forensic and organizational psychology. At Widener, she co-authored several publications on an integrative model for forensic mental health assessment, as well as completing research in the area of emotional intelligence. After graduation, she completed a forensic residency at Northern Virginia Mental Health Institute in Falls Church, Va., where she later became the facility's forensic coordinator. In this capacity, Dr. Mack-Allen was tasked with chairing the Internal Forensic Review Board that oversaw the granting of privileges to Not Guilty by Reason of Insanity (NGRI) acquittees as part of the State of Virginia's graduated release process. In addition to completing violence risk assessments, she also provided expert testimony at release hearings, and served as a liaison to the state's Forensic Review Panel.

Upon relocating to Delaware, she accepted a position as mental health director at the James T. Vaughn Correctional Center. Clinically, she was charged with developing mental health programming for mentally ill inmates, managing suicidal inmates in the prison setting and creating behavior plans for inmates who were creating challenges for custody staff. As a trauma specialist, she works with survivors of military sexual assault and those given combat PTSD diagnoses. I had her analyze the letter from Conley and its authenticity. This is an excerpt of what she said:

"This is an extremely detailed play by play for a 5-year

old child to make. Traumatic memory is laid down piece meal, especially in young kids. To have the story this coherent tells me she's had some sort of therapy to help her organize and process this memory. Essentially, that's what I do and have them write a trauma narrative. Her letter reads exactly like the narrative one of my folks would write, especially the parts where she focuses on feelings, and changes in her father's demeanor. A child can't articulate those things, but an adult can, especially an adult that was repeatedly abused. As a kid she would have been very perceptive to the slightest change in mood or demeanor from her Dad because it might mean she was going to be harmed, and she knew Jenny was in trouble even at age 5.

A defense attorney might argue that she made it up to punish her Dad for abusing her. I would find it very unlikely given the level of detail. Traumatic memory is very detailed once it is processed. I'm always surprised by the depth of that detail... down to being able say for example, "I looked at the clock. It was 5:20." It also makes sense that the details of the events that happen after the murder are still jumbled time wise. They are not traumatic in the same way, so they were not as vivid. I'd put less stock in them because in an effort to make sense of what happened, survivors will connect dots that don't necessarily connect.

Elaborate stories like this have been known to be completely fabricated because the client was led. However, she mentions the word "suppressed: and she mentions "processing" this event. My only real fear is she dealing with "recovered memory" therapist. She would have every reason in the world to want to believe this about her father. A disreputable therapist could lead her to that conclusion. I might ask a little more about other people's reactions to her telling them her Dad hurt Jenny. I'd find it strange that anyone would let that go. She may be wishing she said it, and so she stretched the memory to include it. But if she did, I'd want to talk to the people she said this to. I'd want to know when she first recalled the memory, what were the circumstances? Usually these memories don't come back all at once."

So, now the letter from Conley seems to have some additional merit. This 5-year-old girl could have this repressed memory. One area of criminal investigations that does not require interpretation is forensic evidence. Evidence. Evidence. Evidence. It was time to look at the evidence.

DNA Forensic Testing 2014

DNA wasn't around in 1973 when this crime occurred. Any semen or blood samples were just typed based on blood type. In late 2013, I was able to locate physical evidence in this case that was in the basement of the County's 911 Center. It appeared to be evidence that was used at trial and therefore not returned to state police custody, hence never destroyed. It included tires, boots, plaster castings, helmet, clothing, letters, etc. Evidence not submitted as trial exhibits was destroyed by the Pennsylvania State Police, per protocol after conviction and the appeal process was exhausted. It was just pure luck this evidence remained. Hubbard claims this evidence doesn't exist and I have made it up. He believes I planted evidence in my review of the case and I have fabricated having the evidence. At the end of this chapter, for the first time made public, are photographs of the evidence box I found in the old courthouse basement 40 years later. It is an eerie feeling handling the evidence, knowing it played such an integral part of Lycoming County history and impacting people lives, forever changing and altering their own destiny. Again, as I hold it (with rubber gloves I might add) I am transported to 1973.

I sent Jenny Hill's clothing to the Pennsylvania State Police Laboratory, which was no easy task. The laboratory personnel initially did not want to do the testing because the case was over. Hubbard had been convicted, sentenced and did his time. In their mind, the case was closed. I was summoned to a meeting with the lab supervisors from the Pennsylvania State Police as to what I wanted tested and why. After I was able to convince them as to what and why, they cautiously agreed to test certain pieces of evidence. For me, if there is a chance someone is innocent, regardless of conviction or sentencing, you need to follow up on the investigation. In this case, it meant testing the evidence I found. Hubbard's assertions and the letter from Conley was enough for me to want to look in to the case further.

On Jan. 22, 2014, I did take various pieces of evidence to the Pennsylvania State Crime Laboratory for DNA analysis. The following are some of the results from the serology department.

The blue no. 33 jersey: Jenny was wearing this when last seen alive and it was on her body at time of discovery. The mud from the cornfield still caked on the left sleeve decades later.

Panties: Jenny's panties that she was wearing at time of discovery. Blood was found in a red stain on the front and a brown stain in the inside crotch panel. This blood was Jenny's. It is unknown the cause of this blood, possibly part of the menstrual cycle. Urine was found in the inside buttocks and crotch area, but no seminal material was found. Dirt-like brown and grass-like green stains were found on the back waistband, undoubtedly from being dragged in the cornfield.

Light-colored jeans and belt: The light colored jeans with belt she was wearing at the time of discovery. Urine was found in the crotch area, consistent with the urine stains found on the panties. Dirt-like brown and grass-like green stains were found on the inside back area. Again, these were probably from being dragged to her final resting spot. No seminal material was found.

Dark jeans: The dark jeans with red patches Jenny was last seen wearing when she left the Hubbard residence on Oct. 19, 1973. These jeans were located in the Glick bag next to her body. No seminal fluid, blood or urine was found in them.

Second pair of panties: These were found in the Glick bag next to her body. No seminal material or urine was found.

The following is what was found after DNA analysis:

DNA from two people was found under Jennifer's fingernails, the front waistband of the panties and waistband of the light blue pants she wore when her body was found. This means Jenny's DNA was located on all of these items in addition to someone else's that the lab was unable to determine, as it was at too low of a level to interpret. The right side of the orange underwear found in her Glick bag had DNA that matched Jenny only.

After I got the serology and DNA results back, I was confronted with the fact that low-level male DNA was present on Jenny's clothing and in particular, the waistband of her jeans and fingernail scrapings. However, the lab was not able to tell me whose DNA it was.

People do not understand that there are policies regarding DNA and interpretation of the DNA. For example, the lab found two individuals' DNA on the waistband of the pants Jenny was wearing when her body was discovered. However, the lab has a policy that unless the DNA meets a certain threshold, it will say it is uninterpretable. So you have Jenny's DNA and some unknown person's mixed with it. This doesn't move the ball for you as an investigator. You must be able to decipher this. I knew that a company called Cybergenetics would be assisting me if this happened. So, with this knowledge, I needed to send the DNA data to Cybergenetics but I needed to send them the suspect's DNA to compare it to. There were two suspects in my mind at the moment, Hubbard and now Dan Gerber. Hubbard refused to provide me with his DNA, saying he thought I would plant it.

I certainly could not understand why Hubbard wouldn't be jumping up and down and celebrating that I found evidence in this case *and* obtained male DNA from Jenny's clothing. I know if I were innocent, I would be giving every DNA sample I could. Yet he refused. I even went so far as offering to accompany me to the lab to deliver his DNA, so he knew there could be no tampering. He again refused. I remember telling him I had evidence in the case to test and needed his DNA. He was taking a drink of coffee and became so nervous, his hand began to shake to spill the coffee. He cut our talk short, saying he needed to talk to his attorney.

There is only one reason he refused over and over again. I asked Hubbard on three occasions to provide his DNA and he refused. At this point, I was just gonna close the case. Hubbard was the whole reason the case was given to me to look at to begin with. Now, he wouldn't cooperate, so why should I continue on? Jennifer Hill, that is why. She deserved my utmost dedication and perseverance to see this case through.

In November 2014, I received a telephone call from a professor from Duquesne University who said he had interest in the case and was in contact with Hubbard. He wanted to help, as he felt Hubbard to be innocent. I did have an hour-long conversation with the good professor about Hubbard and my intentions of finding out the truth once and for all. I explained to him that there was no help needed in particular, that Hubbard had refused to provide his DNA for testing, therefore halting the investigation of the case. He stated he understood and would talk to Hubbard about submitting his DNA.

As I stated earlier, I did obtain Eric Gerber's DNA for the purpose of comparing it to the DNA obtained from Jennifer's clothing and fingernails. Eric Gerber is Dan Gerber's biological son and Danielle Conley's brother. On Jan. 12, 2015, I received the results from the state crime lab. The report indicated that Eric Gerber's DNA (or a relative of his) was *not* a match to any interpretable DNA obtained in this case.

I decided to get Hubbard's DNA one way or another in order to confirm or omit his guilt. Many in law enforcement have asked me what did this matter at this point? He cannot be convicted for the same crime again. Yet, he ran his mouth to an entire community about how he was convicted by police and prosecutors who planted evidence. Why does he get to spew his rhetoric and make the police look bad without any recourse if he is guilty? Why does he get to degrade Jenny Hill without recourse if he is in fact guilty? I decided to finish the game Hubbard started.

I went back to the evidence I found in the basement of the old courthouse and found two letters Hubbard wrote from when he was in jail. One was to his mother and the other one to his girlfriend at the time, Colleen Whitenight. I sent both letters to the Pennsylvania State Police crime lab to obtain Hubbard's DNA. The first letter did not yield any interpretable DNA. To say I was disappointed is an understatement. However, the second envelope did yield male DNA. So, now the real game began. I sent the DNA evidence from Jenny's clothing and Hubbard's DNA from the old envelope to Cybergentics to compare to the DNA found on Jennifer's clothing and underneath her fingernails. What was found put this case to bed and slammed the door on a convicted murderer, hopefully forever.

Cybergentics and TrueAllele

TrueAllele® Casework is an automated computerized DNA

interpretation system that rapidly infers genetic profiles from all types of DNA evidence samples. TrueAllele's validated probabilistic genotyping provides accurate identification information and matches for crime scene evidence and reference samples. So, basically it takes low-level or mixed DNA results and enhances those to produce probabilities with correlating statistics.

The inventor of this revolutionary system is Dr. Mark Perlin. Mark and I shared dinner once in Pittsburgh and chatted about DNA. One remark he made during our conversation I always remember was when he said to me, "I want CODIS." Of course, he was talking about the FBI National Database for storing and comparing DNA. Mark has two PhDs and is one of the smartest men I have ever met, so I would not dismiss his statement as being made in jest.

Mark is a member of my cold case organization dedicated to truth and justice for victims of cold cases. I use his pioneering company to interpret low-level DNA and advocate it to everyone that I can. Mark is a brilliant person and I believe his TrueAllele system will revolutionize DNA interpretation and solve many cold cases.

The following was his part of his interpretation of the DNA in the Jennifer Hill homicide:

> *Cybergenetics has completed its initial TrueAllele® computer analysis of the DNA mixture items in your Jennifer Hill homicide case. Here is an informal summary of the statistical results.*
>
> *The victim's DNA (Jennifer Hill) was found on multiple items. In particular, her DNA was found on the pants waistband.*
>
> *The waistband produced a second genotype, different from that of the victim. This second genotype is informative, having an expected match statistic (to the true contributor's full profile) of over a billion, and comparable exclusionary power. However, a full profile was not available for the accused Kim Lee Hubbard. Instead, we were provided with an envelope file that showed low-level mixed data at a few genetic loci, from which we inferred a genotype to use as a reference.*
>
> *Hubbard's DNA (as inferred from the envelope) was found on the pants waistband.*

There you have it, folks. Hubbard's DNA, taken from a 40-year-old envelope, was found on Jenny Hill's waistband of the pants, pulled down to her ankles, that she wore at the time of her death. Let me repeat this. Hubbard's DNA, which I was able to get from an envelope he licked and sent from jail in 1973, was found on the waistband of the pants she was wearing when her body was found. Mystery solved. Case closed, again. The Pennsylvania State Police were right 40 years ago when troopers arrested Hubbard with outstanding police work.

Hubbard did not want to give his DNA that morning in the Humdinger restaurant because he knew he was guilty of murder. Period. End of story.

Final Opinion

After a painstaking two-year review of this case, I am of the opinion that beyond a reasonable doubt, Hubbard murdered Jennifer Hill on Oct. 19, 1973, and the Pennsylvania State Police did an *incredible* investigation that led to the arrest and conviction of a 20-year-old South Williamsport resident, Kim Hubbard. There was absolutely no cover-up, conspiracy or planting of evidence to frame Hubbard.

Although Conley's letter seemed to have some merit, or at least the possibility that her father committed the crime, suspectology on Dan Gerber failed to show any indication of violence or sexual abuse. This alone obviously doesn't exclude him, as there have been thousands of people who have murdered without having any indication of violence or sexual abuse. Yet, I had to break down certain details of her letter and either validate or eliminate the detail. Jenny arriving at the Gerber home was certainly along her travel path as the Gerbers lived next to the Hills. The sightings of Jenny certainly could line up. To me, there are only two sightings of Jenny during her walk home that come into question. The Nevel sighting, which is odd as it is off of the path Jenny would take to be walking home, unless she was meeting someone who didn't want to be seen with her. In addition, the Mendez sighting that puts Jenny closer to home and presumably giving plausibility to the fact Jenny went to the Gerber residence to return the letterman jacket. So, who to believe, Mendez or Nevel?

Hubbard will tell you that Nevel was paid a reward for her information. According to the trial transcript, she may have been paid a reward, but that doesn't change the facts:

> *Q. Did you come here to testify to receive a newspaper reward for testimony?*

> *A. No, I didn't have any idea any reward would have anything to do with it. I didn't find her. The only reward I knew when they found her body looking for her.*

So to me, this woman wasn't making this up. The reward was for the finding of Jenny's body. She just reported what she observed. In addition, her 11-year-old daughter also observed Jenny getting into a car. She knew Jenny from school, so there was no mistaking it. Now you have two separate people observing Jenny getting into a car. I deem this credible.

Was the Mendez sighting bogus? I have been told Mendez was a friend of Hubbard's, which is why he stated he saw her and that is why Mendez's wife failed to confirm the sighting of Jenny. Apparently, the jury believed Nevel's testimony over Mendez's.

Breaking down the letter from Conley and comparing it to the forensic evidence needs to be done to determine if the letter is authentic. I believe forensic evidence decades later proved the letter to be a figment of someone's creative imagination.

When Conley stated she observed Jenny urinate herself after being strangled and that she relayed this concern to her father— *"I remember my dad deciding to remove her pants. I remember thinking how is she going to get home without pants. I believe I even asked my dad this question and he responded that he would get her something to wear."*—it appears that this has merit because Jenny was found to be wearing different clothing then she was last seen in. This was a detail in the letter I took as something that could explain why Jenny was found wearing different pants.

However, forensic testing in 2014 showed that urine was present on the underwear and jeans that were found <u>on her body</u> the day she was discovered deceased. The jeans and underwear that she had on when she was last seen did not have any urine stains. This would completely contradict Conley's supposed observation of the urination and changing of clothing.

-The day that she came to door: It seemed dark/gloomy outside as if the sun was down or not out. I wouldn't say dark like night though. This was not true, as the weather on Oct. 19, 1973, had an average of 41 degrees with no precipitation or snow. The sun set at 6:20 p.m. and dark descended at 7:52 p.m. on that day, so it was not dark. This, however, does not discredit her memory, as I do not know whether the sun was shining or it was cloudy.

-The color blue, light blue like a powder blue and keep thinking this was underwear color. This was not true, either, but you have to remember this is a memory from a 5-year-old girl. So you can't discredit her on this failed memory alone.

-Her older sister and I rode with my dad in a large van or truck like vehicle the day the Hill kids (excluding Jenny) came to our house on Hill Street. I believe this was during the time we were moving. I said something to her older sister pertaining to my dad hurting Jenny after we got out of the vehicle...we were in driveway of the house on Hill Street. I spoke to Jenny's older sister and she does not recollect this and Hill-Emerick felt this is something she would definitely remember.

No single event caused me to believe in Hubbard's guilt, but more of the totality of a number of events to include behavioral characteristics, crime scene assessments and interpretations, suspectology, victimology and last forensic technology. Look at all the evidence that points to Hubbard's guilt:

1. His proclivity toward younger females, especially days leading up to the murder, is a huge factor and cannot be overstated. This is an extremely important aspect to this case and the proximity to this murder cannot go unnoticed. On Oct. 13, Hubbard asked Brenda Merrick, age 13, if she would ride around in his car with him. This occurred between 1 and 1:30 p.m., so it was in daylight hours, as it was with Jenny. That same day, Hubbard asked Suzanne Mitchell, age 14, if she wanted to go for a ride in his car with him. During the summer of 1973, Hubbard asked Kim Ungard, age 14, to "blow him" at the Humdinger restaurant. Also that summer, Hubbard made sexual advances on three occasions toward Tammy Ungard, age 16. On at least one of the occasions, she

had to struggle to get away from him. And also over the summer, he tried to pick up Sue Perry, age 14, on six occasions in his car. On one occasion, he pushed her head into his crotch area.

2. The tire prints at the crime scene/dump site matching his vehicle. These prints were on fresh mud and could not have been there previous to the homicide.

3. His preserved boot print found under the body. No other boot made that print; it was Hubbard's boot, even by his own admission to me. I believe that is why he was hesitant to give up his boots to police. According to Hubbard's own testimony at trial where he spars with the district attorney:

Q. Wasn't it true we asked you, after you gave your statement at the end, if you had a pair boots?

A. Sir, you specifically asked for a pair of boots.

Q. And isn't it true that you first produced a pair of sneakers?

A. That is incorrect, sir.

Q. Then you produced a pair of slippers that your father said—or loafers which were your father's.

A. Sir, I gave you the boots plus every pair of shoes I owned.

Q. Didn't you next produce a pair of loafers?

A. That is incorrect, sir.

Q. Didn't your father say "they are my loafers"?

A. My father gave them to you.

Q. Didn't you go upstairs and get a pair of boots after your father said you had a pair of boots!

A. Incorrect, sir, were laying right there in the front room in plain view.

Sgt. Peterson also testified at trial regarding this incident:

A. In talking to Kim Hubbard, the defendant, we asked him if he would voluntarily submit his shoes or footwear for examination and he stated that he would.

Q. What happened then?

A. He went and got the shoes that were requested.

Q. What shoes were they?

A. Well, he brought, talking about a pair of boots.

Q. What did he bring first, what was the first object he brought?

A. As I recall, I believe it was a pair of sneakers.

Q. Then what?

A. Then what? Then a pair of loafers.

Q. What happened about the loafers?

A. Well, then in discussing the loafers were, we learned that the loafers belonged to Mr. Hubbard (Kim's father).

Hubbard was trying to distance himself from those boots for a reason. Although he is denying this, why would the district attorney and a state police trooper lie about the events? Look, who is more credible: the state police and the district attorney or Hubbard?

1. His demeanor when I told him we still had Jennifer Hill's clothing, which he assumed was destroyed. He began to shake and spilled the coffee that he was getting ready to drink.

2. His refusal to provide his DNA in order to compare to DNA found in 2014 on Jenny's clothing and body.

3. Hubbard's willingness to push me aside after telling him I was not doing this case to exonerate him, but to find out the truth.

4. Hubbard's ability to push focus on "word play" and not actual physical evidence. An example would be instead of focusing on male DNA found on the clothing Jenny had on when murdered, he pushes the focus to witnesses describing which row of the cornfield she was located. Because one person testified or stated it was row two and, in fact, it was row three, I didn't do this murder. This is just sleight of hand by Hubbard to take away from the facts.

5. When I asked Hubbard, "Is it possible that it could be someone else's boot print that was located under Jennifer's body?", he stated unequivocally and as a matter of fact, "No, that's my print." He qualifies this answer by stating, "but it was planted."

6. His almost demanding and excited tone when he asked me to send him a picture of Jenny's jeans to prove I still had them. His creepy tone was more of kid who wanted to relive the crime, not someone who wanted proof that evidence still existed after 40 years to could exonerate him.

7. A single piece of broken fingernail located in Hubbard's car. Jenny had a broken fingernail when her body was discovered.

8. Modern-day forensics put Hubbard's DNA on the pants Jenny had on when her body was discovered. More importantly, the location on those jeans (waistband) rules out "accidental DNA," in my opinion.

9. No alibi.

10. Washed his car during the timeframe Jenny was last seen.

11. Inconsistent statements as to where he was and what he was doing between when Jenny left the Hubbard house and he answered the phone call from Jack Hill.

12. Nevel and her daughter saw Jenny getting into his car and she was very detailed about certain things. Look at this except from the trial about observing Jenny getting into the car:

A. She was looking around.

Q. Would you sort of show the jury exactly what you mean by "looking around"?

A. Well, she was looking towards the street and in my back yard and just looking around.

Q. Then what happened?

A. Well, then the car pulled up and she took a <u>little skip</u> before *she started to run, and she went across the back of the car and into the opposite the driver's side.*

It is my opinion that that detail—"little skip"—is significant. That is coming from someone who saw it happen. You can contend that Jenny did not get into Hubbard's car, but Nevel absolutely saw Jenny get into a car. When you are making something up, you would not include this detail. She saw Jenny skip and then run and get into a car. There are two things we can learn from this observation: Number one, Jenny knew the person and number two, she was very comfortable getting in the car.

What happened that caused the death of Jenny Hill?

We may never know the answer to this, unless Hubbard speaks about it himself. However, this will most likely never happen because he would have to swallow his ego and admit guilt. Hubbard is not the type of person to do that. He is a classic narcissist who only cares about himself. He was a bully growing up and he is a bully now. Yet, I wasn't about to let him bully me—even though he has tried. He will go to his grave shouting his innocence, no matter the outcome or mountain of evidence against him.

It is not inconceivable that Hubbard had the strict intent on picking up Jenny who was walking home. He may have told Jenny to meet him and he would take her to the football game she so badly wanted to go to. His intent would have been sexual in nature because he had an attraction to younger teenage girls. In just weeks and even days leading up to this murder, Hubbard had offered rides to several young girls. One was documented to be at 1:30 in the afternoon, daylight hours as well. This attraction to younger girls had a lot to do with Hubbard wanting to be in control.

Norma Hill, Jenny's mother, called the Hubbard residence and told Jenny to come home around 3:45 p.m. Doris Hubbard stated that Jenny left her home around 4 p.m. However, initial reports state Jenny left five minutes after that call. Doris got a call again from Norma at 4:20, asking if Jenny had left yet. At around 4:30, Jackie (Jenny's sister) called. Then the last call was by Jack Hill (Jenny's father) to the Hubbard residence between 4:45 and 5 p.m.

Jenny most likely left the Hubbard residence around 3:50 p.m.

It would take 13 minutes to walk to her home, which would put Jenny at home from 4 to 4:30 p.m., just as Betty Nevel stated. This sighting of Jenny seems "odd" or out of the normal path that she would follow to get home. However, it does not take away the fact that Nevel stated she observed Jenny getting into a green car with a white "round object" in the back window, wearing a blue jersey with the number 33 and carrying a Glick bag and jacket. Hubbard claims that he didn't have this helmet on Oct. 19, 1973, so it would be impossible for Nevel to recall seeing this. The commonwealth proved this to be a lie at trial.

Her recollection was that Jenny was looking around for something and immediately walked to the car when it pulled up and got in the front passenger side. These details are compelling and credible in my opinion.

We will never know why Jenny ventured in this direction. Maybe she was mad at her parents for not letting her go to the football game that night and she was rebelling by taking her time getting home. Maybe she had a prearranged time to meet Hubbard on that street after she left his home. Hubbard stated that at 3:45 p.m., he left his home in order to wash his car at the Fifth Ave Car Wash. I find it coincidental that he leaves to wash his car at the exact same moment Jenny is leaving to walk home. If that were the case, why didn't Hubbard offer her a ride home from the house? The answer is simple: He had something other than just giving someone a ride home on his mind.

Hubbard stated he was gone about 25 minutes before returning home. This means he was without an alibi during the time that Jenny was seen getting into a car and presumably, the last time she was seen alive. Perhaps Hubbard simply stumbled upon Jenny when he was driving around and agreed to take her home but instead offered to take her for a ride like he had done with other girls. Remember, Jenny had spent the night at Hubbard's home on numerous occasions. Possibly some sort of relationship blossomed between Jenny and Hubbard that no one knew about. I am not talking about a boyfriend/girlfriend relationship. By all accounts, Hubbard was dating one of the prettiest girls in Williamsport. But I am talking about a flirty relationship. A power relationship. A relationship in which Jenny looked up to Hubbard and thought he was "cool." A relationship in which she trusted Hubbard. A relationship in which Hubbard used this to his advantage. We will never know.

What we do know is that he returned home between 4:45 and 5 p.m., in time to take the call from Jenny's father. This gives him a minimum of 15 minutes and a maximum of about 35 minutes of opportunity to kill/dump and return home. Is this possible? In my opinion, yes, it very possible and likely, because it happened.

From the location where Hubbard picked up Jenny (Nevel's house) to the cornfield where the body was located is 3.2 miles and a 6.5-minute drive averaging 35 mph. It would take Hubbard a maximum of 13 minutes to drive to the cornfield and back home and another 10 to 15 minutes to kill and dispose of Jenny to be home in time to take the phone call from Mr. Hill who was looking for Jenny. So, not only is possible to do, it is obviously probable that it was done. It is a tight window—not impossible as Hubbard and his supporters claim. You have to remember that when someone is in a panic, everything is done faster. Just because the timeframe is tight doesn't take away that it could happen and doesn't take away the fact that evidence shows he committed the act.

He was comfortable in this area because he had gone parking there before with his girlfriend, Whitenight, although he denied this in interviews. It is also a great place to be concealed during daylight hours.

I think it was either Hubbard's plan to watch her change her pants, have Jenny perform oral sex on him or both. Those are the two most likely scenarios, in my opinion. Perhaps they were there at the cornfields to just make-out or he tried to convince Jenny to perform oral sex on him as he had requested other young girls to do previously. Just a week before Jenny's murder he had an encounter with a young teen girl described at the trial:

> They were on the Sylvan Dell Road (where Jennifer was found); they went up to the Look Out and back to her house. During the time he kept putting his arm around her. At one point, he pulled her head down towards his crotch. *He asked her if she ever undressed in front of a boy* and the (indication) that he wanted sexual activities with her.

This pre-homicide behavior is extremely important and cannot be overlooked. This is possibly exactly what happened with Jenny, possibly undressing to change her pants in front of Hubbard.

Perhaps Hubbard promised to take her to the football game or home and suggested she change her ripped pants first. Perhaps she removed her ripped pants and underwear to prepare for intercourse and Jenny changed her mind or stopped Hubbard because it was going too far. However, I do not believe intercourse was the plan.

She was just changing her pants, which is why her shirt and bra were left on and only the pants being removed. This is also why her shoes and socks were found on her body, as they did not need to be removed because both pairs of bell-bottom pants could slide over the shoes very easily. We know these jeans were above her pubic area when she was murdered because they were urine soaked (confirmed by forensic testing, 2014). This most likely occurred when she was strangled.

When Jenny did not accept or stopped Hubbard's advances, he became enraged and violent. Hubbard strangled her, most likely in his vehicle. During the struggle, Hill broke a fingernail that was found in his vehicle by police. He did not rape Jenny; although this was a "sexually motivated" crime it was more about control. He did not plan on rape or murder; it was out of rage that he killed. If this were strictly a sexual/fantasy murder, Hubbard would have finished the fantasy or sexual act. He did not, as confirmed by the absence of semen and Hill's hymen still being intact.

Perhaps he was trying to get Jenny to perform oral sex on him after she changed her pants. Remember, Hubbard was trying to get other girls to do this only days before. Maybe Jenny stated she was going to tell someone and Hubbard—because of his need to maintain a reputation—didn't want this information out, snapped and strangled Jenny. When Jenny's body was found, the blue letterman jacket had only one of her arms partially inserted into the jacket sleeve and laid on top of her body. This is consistent with the jacket being on Jenny during a struggle, although most eyewitness accounts state she was carrying the jacket. She managed to free one arm while fighting off Hubbard, but not the other. Or she was in the process of getting redressed from changing her pants and decided to put the jacket on when she was attacked.

Hubbard then dragged her body a short distance to conceal her body in the rows of corn. His sexual appetite was not fulfilled, but he is panicked due to what he just had done. He had not intended on murdering Hill, of this I am sure. Hubbard leaves several boot prints in the mud. Yet it is the boot print in the mud under Jenny's body when he drags her to her final resting spot that is preserved from the elements and contains enough identification points to identify Hubbard as the murder. It was Jenny's body that shielded and preserved that print for the state police to find. Essentially, it was Jenny herself who convicted Hubbard in her own murder. It was Jenny's final act on this earth that ended up sealing the fate of her murderer.

Hubbard threw the Glick bag in the field next to her, along with the blue pajama top that had spilled out of the bag when she took the other pair of jeans out to change into. Hubbard pulled down Jenny's pants and underwear to her ankles, leaving his DNA on the waistband to be discovered 40 years later. Remember, those pants were not pulled down prior to her being strangled because forensic testing found they were urine soaked. That means they had to have been pulled up when she was strangled. They were pulled down after she was dead. This is Hubbard's one last act of control and dominance over Jenny. It was not done to degrade her, which often times is the case, it was done more to show he is the boss and he decides when the act is over. His one last act of dominance, which fits his personality.

Hubbard returned home around 4:45 to 5 p.m., when he received a call from Jack Hill asking where Jenny was. Hubbard, with no remorse, stated she had left an hour ago. That is Kim Hubbard—murderer of Jennifer Hill.

I will not say conclusively this is what happened, because only Jenny and Hubbard know for sure, however based on the evidence presented to me, both behavioral and forensic, I believe this is a likely scenario.

Here is a timeline of significant events that I was able to determine through police reports, interviews and other sources.

10/28/73 around 1:15 p.m. – Joe Hubbard (Hubbard's father) voluntarily appears at police department and is interviewed.

10/28/73 around 4 p.m. – Search party finds Jenny's body in a cornfield.

10/28/73 – State police take plaster castings of footprints and tire impressions from the body dump location. One of the footprints was located directly under the victim's body, which preserved the print from the weather.

10/29/73 around 9 a.m. – Hubbard purchases a new summer tread tire. It was installed on the left front wheel of Hubbard's green Oldsmobile.

10/29/73 around 10:30 a.m. – Jack Hill positively identifies his daughter's body.

10/29/73, 5:50 p.m. – Autopsy was done by Robert L. Catherman, M.D., forensic pathologist. His findings were that Jenny died of manual strangulation and there is "nothing inconsistent" with Jenny dying on Oct. 19, 1973. He also concluded that there was no semen present and the victim's hymen was intact, which would rule out vaginal penetration and the victim died a virgin.

10/29/73 – State police take additional plaster castings of footprints and tire impressions from the body dump location.

10/30/73 – Ruthie Hubbard, Hubbard's sister, called state police and stated Jenny should have two bars of soap as they were going to do some pranking for Halloween.

10/31/73 – Geoffrey Nevel goes to the police department and stated he believes his wife, Betty, saw the victim getting into a car.

10/31/73 – Trooper Gomb receives spare tire from Mr. Frost who had changed Hubbard's tire on the 29th.

10/31/17 at 10:45 a.m. – Hubbard family is interviewed at their home by state police and District Attorney Allen Ertel.

10/31/73 – Hubbard is interviewed at South Williamsport Police Station. He signs a voluntary consent to search his vehicle.

10/31/73 – Hubbard's car is released to Pennsylvania State Police and three tires are removed. Right front, right rear and left rear. Mud is observed under each tire well and on the driver side front floor mat.

10/31/73 – Consent to search Hubbard's home was obtained by

state police. At 1:15 p.m., Sgt. Peterson collects Hubbard's boots from his home.

11/1/73 – A partial fingernail is found on the front seat area of Hubbard's car.

11/1/73 – Footprint and tire impressions sent to the Pennsylvania State Police Crime Lab for analysis.

11/1/17 at 9:07 a.m. – Hubbard appears at state police barracks and submits to polygraph. Polygraph examiner opined deception was indicated.

11/1/73 – Carol Dunn receives a call from Hubbard. He states, "You're talking to the murderer. Haven't you heard?"

11/2/73 – Betty Nevel is interviewed. She stated she saw Jenny at 4:30 p.m. (later stated it was closer to 4 p.m.) in front of her home at 503 Howard St. Nevel stated Jenny was getting into a car. She stated she was wearing a blue jersey with the number 33 and a Glick bag. Nevel's daughter, Beth, stated it looked as if Jenny was looking around as though she was looking for the vehicle to pick her up.

11/2/73 – Surveillance is being conducted on Hubbard. At 0030 Hrs. Hubbard approaches the police vehicle, taps on the window and asks the cops if they would like a cup of coffee.

11/3/73 at 1:30 p.m. – Doris Hubbard, Hubbard's mother, called the South Williamsport Police Department and asked for the district attorney. When the DA answered the call, it was Hubbard on the line. Hubbard asked to speak to the DA personally, but Ertel declined. At 1:57, Hubbard showed up at the police station with his mother. He stated he wanted to clear up his activities for Oct. 19. He was asked if he had ever been in the cornfield where the body was found. Hubbard stated, "No."

11/3/73 at 12:30 p.m., – Joe Hubbard is interviewed at the hospital, stating his son "had been acting unusual ever since Jenny went missing."

11/3/73 at 10:30 p.m. – During surveillance, a shirtless Hubbard is observed pacing. He then is observed striking his sister and pulling her hair.

11/7/73 – Hubbard takes possession from police his car, a 1967

Oldsmobile sedan.

11/10/73 – Betty Nevel is hypnotized by Dr. Larue Pepperman to recall any additional information she may have. Nevel was unable to provide any additional information.

11/13/73 – Nevel is hypnotized again. She recalled in detail a young girl carrying a blue jacket with white stripes. She recalled the car being a full-sized car and a white object, round, on the rear window ledge. She stated she believed she observed the same vehicle (Hubbard's car) at the South Williamsport Borough Building Garage.

11/16/73 – Arrest warrant obtained for Hubbard for murder at 12:13 p.m. Hubbard arrested at the Humdinger restaurant. Car was impounded again.

11/20/73 – Evidence submitted in this case, including victim's clothing and hair samples, are analyzed by the state crime lab.

11/27/73 – Construction helmet is removed from vehicle.

12/7/73 – Preliminary hearing, all charges bound over.

12/28/73 – Shoe impression, tire impression results are completed and an opinion rendered.

2/12/74 – Tammy Ungard, age 16, is interviewed and says Hubbard made three sexual advances to her during summer of 1973, which required her to struggle to get away. Diane Fisher, Hubbard's friend, was interviewed and she stated that Hubbard told her that when he gets mad he just snaps and cannot remember what he is doing.

2/14/73 – Private investigator Michael Rotman (defense) examines plaster casters from 1130 a.m. to 1 p.m.

1/15/74 – Testimony given during grand jury hearing. Grand jury approved case to be presented to the Lycoming County courts.

1/22/74 – David Kinney is interviewed and tells police the defense attorney is making a big deal about the white helmet in Hubbard's car and that he couldn't be in possession of the helmet because Hubbard did not begin employment with Strohman Bakery until 10/24/73 so the helmet couldn't be there on 10/19/73. Kinney stated he worked with Hubbard at Eastern Wood Products and saw

Hubbard with as many as three helmets in his car at one time.

2/19/74 – Jury trial begins.

3/1/74 – Jury is excused at 10:15 a.m. to render a verdict. At 2:40 p.m., the jury returns verdict: guilty of second-degree murder.

7/16/74 3:40 p.m. – John Felix (public defender) and Joe and Doris Hubbard view evidence at PSP. Joe Hubbard drops Hubbard's boot on the floor and then cast #4 L-10, breaking it in four pieces. Viewing terminated at 4:30 p.m. It is unknown why they were allowed to handle physical evidence from this case. I can say that that practice would not be acceptable today. The parents of a convicted murderer handled and destroyed physical evidence in this case. Could it have been an accident or was it something more deliberate?

11/7/74 – Evidence in this case turned over to Lycoming County sheriffs after a petition for new trial was filed.

2/18/75 – Hubbard's car returned to Joe Hubbard.

3/14/75 – Joe Hubbard and Charles King appeared at PSP Maj. William Grooms' office and make their case that the District Attorney's Office, Pennsylvania State Police, Lycoming County judges and court had conspired to frame Hubbard. During three-hour meeting, they at no time presented any additional information to indicate the case should be reopened. Grooms stated in his report, "After terminating the interview, it is my considered opinion that Mr. Joe Hubbard, father of accused, and Charles King are literally obsessed with this matter and it could have an effect on their mental state in the future."

3/26/75 – Hubbard is sentenced by Judge Charles Greevy to pay a $1,000 fine; costs of $1,600; and a prison sentence of 10 to 20 years.

1/15/90 – Ken Osokow, district attorney first assistant, recommends that evidence should be retained until the expiration of the maximum sentence in 1994.

1/11/93 – Trooper Smith contacts ADA Osokow again and advises him evidence will be destroyed since Hubbard did his time and maxed his parole time. Osokow stated the evidence can be destroyed. *He also advises that the evidence that was maintained*

by the courts will be destroyed by the courts at its convenience.
Cpl. Hile and C.W. Smith destroy all evidence in the care of PSP Montoursville.

10/22/13 – I receive a letter from Det. Al Diaz from the DA's office written by Conley that states she observed her father murder Jennifer Hill and I am requested by Chief County Detective William Weber and District Attorney Eric Linhardt to follow up on the case.

10/23/13 – I request files from state police and begin my review.

11/1/13 - I did meet with Hubbard at the Humdinger restaurant, where he proclaimed his innocence and emphatically stated, "I did not kill that girl." He went on to assert the Pennsylvania State Police framed him and evidence was planted to ensure his conviction. He also would say that all of the evidence in the case was destroyed; therefore, nothing forensically could be done to prove his innocence.

11/18/13 – I met with Hubbard at the Humdinger. I asked Hubbard to explain to me how his boot impression was discovered underneath the victim's body. I asked, "Is it possible that it could be someone else's boot print and you were not framed?" Hubbard replied, "No, that is not possible. That is my boot print." He contends that police and others planted it there in a conspiracy.

1/26/15 – I receive an email from a professor and law student from Duquesne University who wanted to meet me and also "see" the evidence that they believed was destroyed. I did meet with them and physically showed them the evidence. They were in disbelief as they thought for some reason I was lying.

2/15/15 – The Williamsport Sun Gazette runs an article that misquotes me saying I believed Hubbard was innocent. I called them and the young reporter apologized and they ran a retraction the very next day.

6/26/15 – I locate and send a second envelope written by Hubbard while in jail and mailed to Colleen Whitenight in evidence. The first envelope failed to yield DNA. I send this second envelope to the state police to obtain Hubbard's DNA, since he refused to give me a sample.

9/1/15 – I request all DNA evidence be sent to TrueAllele.

12/1/15 – I obtain DNA results. The waistband produced a second genotype, different from that of the victim. This second genotype is informative, having an expected match statistic (to the true contributor's full profile) of more than a billion, and comparable exclusionary power. Hubbard's DNA (as inferred from the envelope) was found on the pants waistband.

12/10/15 – I send the following email to Hubbard after not being able to track him down to let him know the results of my investigation:

Mr. Hubbard –

I wanted to inform you that the District Attorney's Office and I, have officially closed this case. I have conclusively reached an opinion after a two year review of all the evidence and with the help of advanced forensics.

As I told you two years ago when I first met you at the Humdinger, I would find out if you did this crime or not. Last week I did receive conclusive DNA evidence that links you, Kim Hubbard, to the murder of Jennifer Hill.

*In addition, I would like to clarify something you have on your Facebook Page. Yes, it is true I was interviewed by Tory Irwin of the Sun Gazette newspaper in February. However, what she quoted me of saying was completely and utterly incorrect. I **NEVER** said it appears that you are innocent. In fact, I confronted her on this the very next day and she apologized and immediately ran a redaction that was run in the following day's paper (albeit not front page as I would have preferred).*

In fact what I did say was that Kim Hubbard refused to give his DNA and he proclaims his innocence. However, I was able to obtain your DNA despite your refusal and have compared it to evidence in this case which clearly satisfies any questions I had of your guilt.

Regardless of your acceptance of these facts or the facts presented at your trial or your refusal to admit to this murder, this case is officially closed and it is my opinion the right person was arrested, convicted, and sentenced (although in my opinion 10 years was not enough time) for this crime.

If you would like to discuss this matter any further, I am available at the District Attorney's Office.

Kenneth L. Mains

Detective

Hubbard's response:

Mr. Mains,

Let me begin by saying; this case was closed the day I was sentenced. I was framed by the District Attorney's Office and the evidence proves it. I did not kill Jennifer Hill. Therefore, there wouldn't be any DNA from me. If there is DNA, Mr. Mains, we know how it got there and so will everyone else.

I know why you're no longer a Williamsport Police officer, I know what you did. It was explained to me quite thoroughly. Seems you can't be trusted my friend. I am surprised the DA's office even hired you. This statement was made by a retired Williamsport Police officer. So you say what you want, it doesn't matter, the evidence is what it is and it proves Jennifer Hill's body was taken out of the field and put back in. It also proved they manufactured not only evidence but testimony. Oh yes, by the way, there is a record of how much money Betty Nevel received for her testimony.

I know why my name will never be cleared, because I know about the cover up and who was involved. Like I said, Mr. Mains, we're not on the same page.

Kim L. Hubbard

12/15/15 – I sent email to the attorney/professor who questioned police conduct and Hubbard's guilt.

Just wanted to let you know that I have officially closed the case of Jennifer Hill after a two year review. After assessments by renowned experts in the field to include Dr. Werner Spitz, George Schiro and myself; I am of the opinion that the correct person was arrested, convicted, jailed and sentenced for this unfortunate murder.

The totality of evidence along with Mr. Hubbard's refusal to provide DNA were only a part of my reason I came to my conclusion. The DNA results that I was able to obtain in 2015 were the turning point.

Although Mr. Hubbard refused on numerous occasions to provide me with DNA once he learned I had located the victim's clothing; I was able to obtain his DNA without his cooperation.

Mr. Hubbard's DNA was located on the victim's clothing in an area it should not be.

Now, with that said, there will be an implication once again that evidence was planted or other conspiracy theories brought forth by Mr. Hubbard or maybe even his supporters, but this cannot and will not take away from the facts.

My integrity is above reproach and anyone who knows me will tell you that I am all about the truth, regardless where that leads me. The truth here is that Kim Hubbard murdered Jennifer Hill and the Pennsylvania State Police did an outstanding job in determining who the offender was and arresting the correct person for the crime.

His conviction for this crime is just (although 10 years is far too light of a sentence in my opinion) and any other conspiracies set forth by Mr. Hubbard should be disregarded and viewed as it is, untruthful.

Thank you for reaching out to me in the past regarding this case and I wish you a very happy holiday season.

Their brief response:

Ken,

I appreciate you reaching out to me with regard to your findings. However, Professor Rago and I no longer have an outstanding interest or involvement with the matter.

It can be assumed by their response they were no longer believers of Hubbard's rhetoric, either.

So why does Hubbard keep that picture of a partially clothed Jennifer Hill on the webpage? To relive the moment he killed her and continue to degrade her, decades after her death, because that is his personality. He is a bully who has to be in control. I will never forget when I told him I found the evidence and the pictures I took of Jenny's ripped jeans. He almost was salivating wanting to see a picture of this. Almost as if he was reliving or wanted to relive further what he did. His voice changed and he almost begged to see. I refused, because I wasn't going to give him the satisfaction. It was very creepy.

Regardless of evidence and explanation of facts, Hubbard will always have his supporters. He got out of jail and moved back to the same small town he was arrested in. Anyone can look at the same evidence and interpret it two different ways. It happens all the time, every day. That is why the prosecution calls an expert and the defense counters with its own expert. Both view the same evidence and both have different conclusions as to what that evidence means.

So, I understand some people reading this will pick apart pieces of the evidence or Danielle Conley's letter and say there are doubts. Some people continue to say Hubbard's dad, Joe, was the real murderer of Jennifer Hill, despite him having a solid alibi. Hubbard's dad knew his son was responsible for this murder. Joe told police Kim had been "acting strange" after Jenny's disappearance and murder and that his explanations were thin when questioned about things like mud on his car. "My son, Kim, is not right," he said. As sure as I am that Joe Hubbard believes his son killed Jenny, I am positive Joe did not want to believe his son was responsible. This is why he later spent hours upon hours picking apart trial transcripts, pictures and testimony to convince himself that his son didn't do it. You can't blame the guy. He loved his son. He had already lost one son in an accident years earlier—he didn't want to lose another one. But just like Maj. Grooms said in 1975 after meeting with Joe Hubbard, "After terminating the interview, it is my considered opinion that Mr. Joseph Hubbard, father of accused, and Charles King are literally obsessed with this matter and it could have an effect on their mental state in the future."

The ranting and raving doesn't change the facts. You can sit in a jail cell for 10 years picking apart testimonies for inconsistencies, but it doesn't change the evidence. You can find inconsistencies in everything we do in life. But an investigator and the public have to always look at the totality of everything. The evidence is there and when you cannot pick that apart, you have to resort to the only explanation left: the evidence was planted, which is an utterly pitiful explanation that has zero merit.

Sometimes, people cannot fathom the truth, especially when it comes to someone they know committing a horrible act. They shake their head and disbelief and say, "Not Johnny, we ate lunch together in ninth grade," or "Not Johnny, because he helped me fix my car one time. He doesn't seem like he would do something like that." One thing the murder business has taught me is that you never know under certain a specific set of circumstances how someone will react—including Johnny. Just because you cannot envision it, doesn't mean it didn't happen. If you look at the facts—the facts, not conjecture—there is only one responsible party for the death of Jennifer Hill.

Hubbard believes—or wants you to believe because he knows the truth—that the tire impressions were planted. Hubbard wants you to believe that his boot impressions were planted. Hubbard wants you to believe that I planted his DNA 40 years later. Hubbard wants you to believe that Jennifer Hill's body was removed from the cornfield, refrigerated for a period of time and then placed back into the cornfield to be rediscovered. If anyone believes this preposterous theory, they need to have their head examined. This would take a conspiracy on a grand scale involving multiple agencies and multiple corrupt people. In addition, it is just plain ludicrous and a desperate attempt to explain away what really happened. I have better things to do with my time then to drum up a case that cannot be prosecuted again by planting DNA evidence. The state police in 1973 had neither the time nor inclination to plant Hubbard's tire tracks and boot impressions, especially since they didn't even have the evidence in their possession at the time. It is a joke and it quite frankly pisses me off. My integrity has never, and I repeat never, been questioned or in doubt. Just like those meticulous and dedicated state police and law enforcement personnel of South Williamsport that solved the case in 1973. The Pennsylvania State Police did one of the best investigations and meticulously followed leads and evidence to arrest the correct person. Those troopers: Barto, Fama, Gomb, Houser, Hynick, Keppick, Krebs, Miller, Peterson and Reitz among others should be applauded for their tremendous effort and investigation on this case. The former district attorney, Allen Ertel, should be congratulated for properly and successfully trying the murderer of Jennifer Hill. If I could I would personally shake all their hands for the diligent and thorough investigation cumulating in the arrest of Kim Hubbard.

Remember this, just because a person continually proclaims innocence and uses sleight of hand magic to make things appear as they are not, doesn't make them innocent. Smoke and mirrors do not make a magician's magic real; it's still an illusion. All the illusion is good for is entertaining people. Most know that it is just magic and is fake, but others hold on to the belief that the magic is real. Those same people believe in dragons and unicorns as well. There will always be those types of people in society. Those are the people who believe in Hubbard's claims. Their belief that the government conspired to frame him only makes them desperate. Yet, there are and will be people who will continue to believe Hubbard and his mockeries. They will believe his magic and illusions. They will believe his absurd claims of cover up regardless of fact.

Some people will say, "Leave Kim alone. He did his time if he did do this." That's right, he did do his time. Yet, Hubbard is the one who proclaims his innocence and created a website with misleading information. It is Hubbard who keeps this case alive. It is Hubbard who sent letters to the Judges proclaiming his innocence. His fatal flaw was that he did not have the foresight to know that those letters and follow up investigations would end up in the hands of a passionate and determined investigator who wouldn't give up until he found the truth. He didn't know that his case would end up in my hands—someone who doesn't believe in magic.

He could very easily just kept quiet and moved on with his life and most people wouldn't even know he was accused of murder. However, he chose not to. That's because he wants to be the center of attention; he wants people to believe his false claims in order to be pitied by misinformed individuals. Hubbard wants this case to continue on to make himself relevant in today's society, like he was in 1973 when he was getting headlines in the newspapers, when the kids were packing the courthouse to watch the trial.

However, through all of this, the most important person seems forgotten. Hubbard makes this entire unfortunate and tragic event about himself—when it should always be about young girl named Jennifer Hill. The Jennifer Hill that never got to grow up and get married. The Jennifer Hill who never got to experience true love. The Jennifer Hill who never had the chance to have children of her own. The Jennifer Hill who was loved by her mother and father. The Jennifer Hill who was adored by her sister. The Jennifer Hill who was just walking home in that blue no. 33 Jersey swinging that Glick bag by the strings with a bar of soap and candy wrapper in her pocket. The Jennifer Hill that was just a kid. That is who we should remember. That is who we should remember Jennifer Hill and feel sorry for—not the person who took her life!

If you look at the evidence and the facts like I have, using common sense, you will come to same conclusion the Pennsylvania State Police, district attorney and 12 jury members did in three hours in 1974—and that I did 40 years later—Kim Hubbard, beyond a reasonable doubt, murdered Jennifer Hill on Oct. 19, 1973, in South Williamsport, Pa.

530 Hill Street (Gerber Residence 1997)

1030 Central Avenue (Hubbard Residence)

Glick Bag Contents 2017

Cornfield where victim's body was found 1973

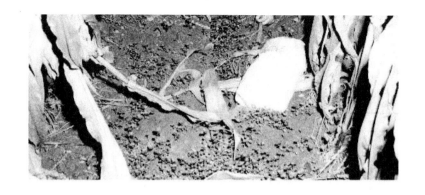

Glick Bag Jennifer was carrying, laid next to her body

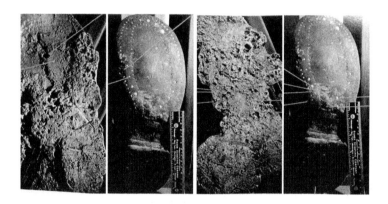

Hubbard Matching Boot Print Evidence. Arrows show the matching characteristics, between the evidence and the casts.

Found box of Hubbard evidence 2013

Gerber Home at 359 Hastings Street

Glick Bag 2017. Discoloration due to fingerprint dust

Jennifer's Jersey with mud 2017

ce Suspect Homicide;
utopsy to Be Performed

JENNIFER M. HILL

...topsy was scheduled late ...rnoon on the body of Jen... M. Hill, 12, of 353 Hastings ...outh Williamsport, which ...und just before 4 o'clock ...ay afternoon in a cornfield ...ylvan Dell Road, east of South ...amsport.

...e body was half nude when ...vered but there has been no ...cial determination yet as to ...her the girl was sexually ...aulted. Bruises were found on ...body, but police said it has not ...termined if they occurred ...re or after death.

...Atty. Allen E. Ertel said ...police have begun an intense ...out" the assumption ...the girl was murdered. "We're ...on the basis of a ...the DA said today.

...Earl R. Miller, county cor-...and Dr. Robert Catherman, ...city resident, a forensic ...from the Philadelphia ...were called to go over ...inch-by-inch to deter-...what happened.

...Oct. 19 ...grade student ...and Mrs. Jack E. ...since about ...after she left

who is heading the case, said after examining the place where the body was found that police have already been checking possible suspects but declined to say whether anyone was a prime suspect.

South Williamsport Police Chief Charles E. Smith identified the body as Jennifer Hill. Capt Francis X. Ross notified the parents. The girl's father went to Williamsport Hospital today and made positive identification of the body.

Area Sealed Off

After the body was discovered the area was sealed off completely for more than three hours while police investigators, Ertel and Dr. Miller went over the area around the body.

State police reopened Sylvan Dell Road after the body was removed and all evidence taken out, but stood guard over the cornfield through the night.

State police today continued their search of the area where the body was found but would not disclose if any additional clues were uncovered.

Following a combing of the area

in heavy rain this morning, in-vestigators met at South Williams-port Borough Hall to discuss the evidence so far.

State police took soil samples today from the area where the body

(Continued on Page 8, Col. 4)

Hill newspaper Articles

...1973 · 15c Single Copy ...c per week Home Delivered

utopsy Shows Girl
trangled to Death

...death of Jennifer May Hill, ...daughter of Mr. and Mrs. Jack ...Hill, of 353 Hastings Street, ...outh Williamsport, was termed ...urder by Dr. Earl R. Miller, coun-...coroner, last night.

...Dr. Miller reported the autopsy ...erformed at the Williamsport ...ospital showed the girl died of ...neral strangulation. He said ...here was no evidence that she was ...exually assaulted.

...Dr. Robert Catherman, of the

Philadelphia area, a forensic pathologist, performed the autopsy, beginning shortly before 5 p.m. yesterday. The announcement of the results of the autopsy was made about 10 p.m.

The girl's death, according to Dr. Catherman's report, could have oc-curred anytime between the time she was reported missing the af-ternoon of Friday, Oct. 19, until last Wednesday, Oct. 24.

Dr. Miller and police officials

reported there is no evidence to determine if death occurred in the cornfield off Sylvan Dell Road where her body was found at 3:40 p.m. Sunday or elsewhere.

Funeral Thursday

The funeral for the girl will be at 10 a.m. Thursday at Noll's, 1 East Central Avenue, South Williams-port. There will be no visitation.

State police explained that when the report indicated that Jennifer had been strangled, it meant possibly choked to death

Hill Residence 353 Hastings Street

The jeans Jennifer was last seen wearing

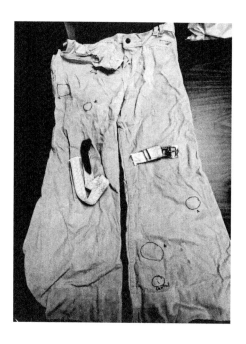

Jeans Jennifer was found wearing when her body was recovered, pulled down to her ankles.

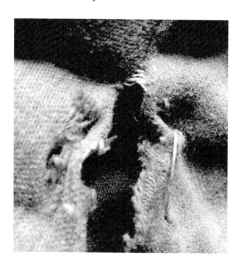

The rip in pants. You can clearly see the white stiching is part of the fabric and not from an attempt to repair.

Another view of the ripped jeans jennifer was wearing.

Letterman Jacket Jennifer was carrying and found on top of her body

Jennifer's Shoes 2017

oung Man Held In Girl's Murder

Kim Lee Hubbard, 20, of 1030 West Central Avenue, South Williamsport, was arrested by South Williamsport and state police late last night and charged with first degree murder in connection with the strangulation death of Jennifer M. Hill, 12, of South Williamsport.

Hubbard was arrested at 11:15 p.m. just after he drove into the parking lot of the Nu-... Drive-In Restaurant, 715 W. Southern Avenue, South Williamsport.

The Hill girl, a seventh grade student at the South Williamsport Junior High School, had spent the night before she was murdered at the home of Ruth Hubbard, classmate who is a younger sister of the accused man.

According to state police Sergeant Stephen J. Hynick, Hubbard's arrest came immediately after "additional information that we were looking for was finally developed."

Hubbard had just gotten out of his car at the rear of the restaurant and was walking toward the front of the building when police arrested him. He offered no resistance, Hynick said.

Hubbard's car was impounded by police, Hynick said.

The criminal complaint lodged against Hubbard, read in part that he "caused the death of Jennifer M. Hill" by "wilful, deliberate and premeditated killing, or while engaged in or as an accomplice the commission of, or an attempt to commit, or flight after committing, or attempting to commit rape, deviate sexual intercourse by force or threat or force of kidnaping..."

He was arraigned before District Justice James T. Nesbitt and committed to (Continued on Page 8, Col. 3)

KIM LEE HUBBARD
charged with murder

...se Claims Coder

Kim Hubbard 1973

Kim Hubbard 1997

Hubbard found guilty

bard's story. Ertel pointed to the letter Hubbard sent his girlfriend while he was in prison and the different stories Hubbard's mother, Mrs. Doris A. Hubbard told the police and the jury as examples of the "consistent lies" which occurred.

While Ertel read the letter from Hubbard to Colleen Whitenight, of the strangulation, but he suggested to the jury that the circumstantial evidence was enough to find Hubbard guilty.

He pointed out that only two parties knew exactly what happened that evening.

"One party to the explanation is dead and the other party isn't telling the truth." Ertel said.

Young Persons Wait In Hall for Verdict

Nearly 50 persons lined the hall outside Courtroom 1 in the Court House today awaiting a verdict in the murder trial of Kim Lee Hubbard, 20, of 1030 West Central Avenue, South Williamsport.

Most of those were young people from area high schools. Some were playing cards, others were nibbling on candy bars and several were in small groups visiting and discussing the trial.

Hubbard is accused in connection with the strangulation death last October of 12-year-old Jennifer M. Hill, daughter of Mr. and Mrs. Jack E. Hill of 353

Hastings Street, South Williamsport.

Judge Charles F. Greevy who presided at the trial, said the condition of Courtroom 1 "resembled a theater without the popcorn."

Because of legal evidence presented as part of the case, the courtroom was locked at the close of the trial each day. Several court officials said articles left in the courtroom included sandwiches, large wrappers and candy, which the officials removed.

The restrooms were reportedly left in bad condition during the period the trial was in session.

Brotherhood Awar

Teenagers flocked to see the trial of their classmate

Hubbards boots 2017

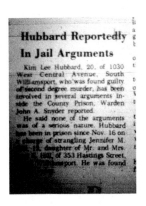

Hubbard Reportedly In Jail Arguments

Kim Lee Hubbard, 20, of 1030 West Central Avenue, South Williamsport, who was found guilty of second degree murder, has been involved in several arguments inside the County Prison, Warden John A. Snyder reported.

He said none of the arguments was of a serious nature. Hubbard has been in prison since Nov. 16 on a charge of strangling Jennifer M. [...] daughter of Mr. and Mrs. [...] of 353 Hastings Street, [...]port. He was found [...]

Hubbard in argument in jail

...ng Appeal on Murder Conviction

...bbard Transferred to State Prison

...Hubbard, 20, of 1030 Central Avenue, South ... was transferred from ...Prison to the State Correctional at Rockview ...reasons yesterday afternoon his conviction for ...e murder. ... was convicted of the ...death last October of ...ennifer M. Hill, ...f Mr. and Mrs. Jack E. ...Hastings Street, South ...asked to be taken to

, the names of the man and woman who served as alternates.

Before the trial began, Judge Greevy issued an order limiting the news media to reporting only what took place in the courtroom during the trial.

His order prohibited identification during the trial of the jurors or where they lived; questions asked prospective jurors, and information on where the jury was sequestered and its activities.

It took two days to select the jury

members from more than 70 persons questioned by the district attorney and Hubbard's lawyer.

The questions asked prospective jurors included the number of children they had and the children's ages.

They were asked by the lawyers if they had read or heard news accounts concerning the missing girl from Oct. 19 until Oct. 28, when her body was found in a cornfield in Armstrong Twp., or other news accounts of the case.

The district attorney question the prospective jurors ab... circumstantial evidence a... whether they would be able to sider it in reaching a decision the case.

The DA also asked the juro... they knew any member of the H... bard family or any of the witne... who might be called to testify...

Hubbard's lawyer questi... those brought in as prospec... jurors pertaining to rumors jurors pertaining to rumors

(Continued on Page 6, Col. 4)

Hubbard transferred to state prison

Jennifer Hill wearing same jersey she was murdered in.

Jennifer Hill's route with eye witness sightings

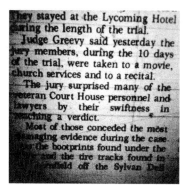

[They] stayed at the Lycoming Hotel [du]ring the length of the trial.

Judge Greevy said yesterday the [j]ury members, during the 10 days of the trial, were taken to a movie, church services and to a recital.

The jury surprised many of the veteran Court House personnel and lawyers by their swiftness in [rea]ching a verdict.

Most of those conceded the most [da]maging evidence during the case [was] the bootprints found under the [window and] the tire tracks found in [the field] off the Sylvan Dell

Jury was not out long

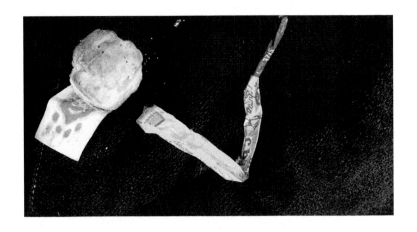

Contents of Hill's jacket 2017. If she was really set to return jacket would she still have soap in the pocket?

Hubbard tire matches imprints at the scene of the body recovery. Arrows show the matching characteristics, between the evidence and the casts.

Hubbard tire matches imprints at the scene of the body recovery. Arrows show the matching characteristics, between the evidence and the casts.

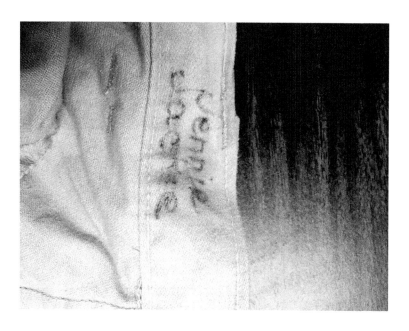

Waistband Jennifer Hills jeans on her body where Hubbard's DNA was found 40 years later

DEBORAH MARCHESE

"I can attest to Ken's unwavering commitment to doing the right thing in everything he does. I can say without hesitation or reservation that Ken Mains is a great detective, leader, partner, and friend. I highly recommend and support Ken, our mission at AISOCC, and his leadership towards helping bring justice to victims."

Dr. Laura Pettler

This is another case where I took a fair amount of abuse by the victim's family. It is amazing that even though you try to do the right thing, people will turn against you if you do not see things their way. I was asked to look into a fire that took the life of a young woman in 1985. I took up the endeavor even though I had no reason to do so other then I was asked by the victim's daughter, who believed her mother was murdered. I wasn't ordered to look at it by my supervisor or the district attorney. I felt it was the right thing to do so I did.

This was the first case in which I learned that no matter how much evidence you provide, some people will not be swayed. It also showed me that no matter how much you try to please someone— some people will hate. It is a sad existence to me when people can hate without even knowing or caring about the others feelings. I learned in the murder business that you had better have thick skin because you will always have people who what to tear you apart for no other reason than to make themselves look better.

Regardless, I work every case the same and my opinion on this case has not changed. If other information were to come available, my opinion might change. So far, that has not happened, so my findings and how I came to the conclusion has not wavered.

On May 27, 1985, at 12:48 a.m., Michael Yourish called the Lycoming County Communications Center and reported a fire in a mobile home next to his mobile home in the Chad Lee Trailer Park in Armstrong Township. Two fire departments from the borough of South Williamsport responded, arriving at around 12:55. Within a short period of time, the fire was brought under control. While extinguishing the fire, the firefighters discovered the body of Deborah Marchese in the living room. Fire Marshal James DeVore of the Pennsylvania State Police initiated an investigation. Yourish stated that around 9 p.m., he was outside his mobile home, saw Debbie and Randall Probst return to Debbie's mobile home and enter. Yourish reported that later that evening, between approximately 10 and 10:30 p.m., he was standing in his mobile home at the kitchen sink looking out the window toward Debbie's mobile home. At that time, he noticed Debbie and Probst in the rear master bedroom of the trailer fully clothed and lying on the bed. He noticed that Debbie had a cigarette in her mouth.

By about 12:45 a.m., Yourish was in bed. His mother-in-law, who said that she saw flames in the rear master bedroom of Debbie's mobile home, awakened him at 12:47 a.m. Yourish got out of bed, saw the flames and immediately called for help. After reporting the fire, he again looked out the window and saw that the flames had progressed from the rear master bedroom to the living room. Yourish left his mobile home and found Probst lying on the ground outside the door to the living room.

Probst was severely burned. Medical records from Geisinger Medical Center revealed that Probst suffered second-degree burns over 45% of his body. The burns were on his arms from his elbows up to his shoulders, face, chest, stomach, back of his head and back. According to Yourish, Probst was wearing jeans, but no shirt, shoes or socks. Firefighters entered the front door, which led into the living room, and the rear door, which entered into the master bedroom. The living room area and rear bedroom were engulfed in flames.

According to police reports, on May 26, Deborah Jean Marchese attended a family picnic with her 31-year-old boyfriend, Randall Probst. Debbie's friends said she had been dating Probst for about three months. Probst said he had been seeing her for about three weeks. Regardless of the amount of time they were together, on this day, they were together as a couple.

Between 6 and 8 p.m., according to witnesses, both Debbie and Probst were heavily intoxicated and decided to leave the picnic. Debbie's father kept her young daughter, Heather, because he believed she was too intoxicated drive with her.

From about 7 to 8 p.m., Debbie and Probst decided to stop at a bar in Montoursville and buy more beer.

According to a witness, they arrived at Debbie's trailer in Armstrong Township around 8:30 to 9 p.m.

From about 10–10:30 p.m., a neighbor saw Debbie lying in her bed with Probst on top of her. It is a trailer park, so the trailers are close together. The neighbor states that Debbie had a cigarette in the corner of her mouth. He observed Probst help Debbie off the bed.

At 12:42 a.m., a neighbor called 911 to report a fire at Debbie's residence.

At 12:52 a.m., ambulance 11 arrived and at 12:55 a.m., the first fire truck arrived and the trailer was fully engulfed. Rescue personnel respond within minutes. They found Probst outside with burns to his face, arms, chest and back. Probst is heard saying, "She's in there. She's in there." He is on his hands and knees appearing in shock or disoriented. A witness said he stopped Probst from trying to re-enter the trailer.

After the fire was extinguished, rescue personnel found Debbie's body inside the trailer. She was found in the living room, lying across an end table next to the couch she had been laying upon, perhaps a sign that she tried to escape the fire before being overcome by smoke and fire.

Probst was admitted to Williamsport Hospital, and then flown to Geisinger Medical Hospital with second-degree burns over 45 percent of his body. He had elevated carbon monoxide levels as well.

Victimology

As always, to understand this crime or any homicide for that matter, you have to know the victims. Victimology will help you understand what type of person the victim is and what the risk factors are for being victimized.

By all accounts, Debbie was a fun-loving, energetic person who enjoyed life. At 19, she had a daughter, Heather.

Debbie was known to drink and was a heavy smoker, according to family members. Debbie was average build, 5 foot 3 and weighing about 130 pounds.

It appears that her risk factor for being a victim was relatively low, but was increased by her drinking and association with Probst and Kenneth Stevenson.

Suspects

1. Randall Probst. Probst at the time was twice divorced and living with his girlfriend, Peggy Rhone, who was pregnant with his seventh child. None of his children lived with him. He had several siblings in Pennsylvania and his parents lived in the state as well. Probst had little contact with any family

members besides occasional contact with his sister.

Probst's social history was varied and full of conflict, according to most. He described a troubled childhood with estranged parents and learned to deal with conflict through violence at an early age. He had been arrested several times for assault and served time in prison. He admitted to counselors having a long history of alcohol abuse.

Probst worked as a cashier at a convenience store. He is a big man—6 foot 5, about 245 pounds. Probst, by all accounts, was a nice, easygoing person when sober. However, when he was intoxicated, Probst became violent, abusive verbally and extremely possessive.

Probst told a trauma counselor that he was injured while in the house trailer of a woman he was seeing at that time. He reported that he and this woman had been drinking, had fallen asleep and had trouble waking up when the fire erupted. His friend died in this fire and he was injured attempting to save her. During this admission, he was experiencing not only grief at his friend's death and guilt at failing to save her, but also guilt at what he perceived as cheating on his other girlfriend. Probst was able to express these ideas clearly and seemed to benefit somewhat from normalization, ventilation and discussion of long-range plans to deal with his grief. Probst intended to follow up with counseling as well as visiting the grave of his friend. According to the counselor, "I believe he romanticized a bit regarding the nature of his relationship with this woman, but his grief for her was real."

The social worker's assessment: "I experienced Mr. Probst as a troubled man who had many anxieties both related to this hospitalization and with his life situation in general. Several of his problems appeared to be of a long-standing nature and I encouraged his continued involvement with Community Mental Health Center in order to resolve some of these issues. My goals in this Hospitalization were to help Mr. Probst maintain his equilibrium during the hospitalization and facilitate his continuation of outpatient treatment. We discussed alcohol rehab program several times but he refused them. I see this man as needing very specific intervention from outside agencies in order to prevent his deterioration in coping ability."

At the time of the fire, his criminal history included duties to stop at an accident, unsworn falsification to law enforcement, disorderly conduct and harassment, criminal trespassing, theft and aggravated assault.

Probst seemed to be a self-serving individual, who only cared about his well-being, according to most people's accounts. He was also violent.

Probst confessed to five people on different occasions to setting the fire. In a taped phone call with his ex-girlfriend, Probst denied starting the fire, but continually asked her not to tell police what he told her. He repeated this request over a half-dozen times. In addition, he told at least one person who came forward, "The fire I was in where Debbie burned up? I did that." Sounds like a confession, right?

Three years after the fire, Probst was arrested for the attempted homicide of his girlfriend, Nicole "Nicki" Diemer. He was in jail when the conversation with Rhone was recorded. Probst had used a sharp object and slashed her body in numerous places. She was drained of nearly half of her blood before Probst called for help hours later. Probst had cleaned up most of the blood and tried to bandage her up, apparently, while in an intoxicated state.

According to Probst's ex-girlfriends and family members, he did not want women to break up with him. Breaking up infuriated him, especially if the girlfriend was leaving him for another guy. Although Probst was "seeing" Debbie, she was most likely going back to a former boyfriend, Kenneth Stevenson, and even had talked about it with friends a few days before the fire. Could this have been the catalyst for setting a fire or murder?

After being arrested for the attempted murder of his girlfriend, Probst was charged with setting the fire that killed Debbie Marchese three years earlier.

2.   Kenneth Stevenson. Stevenson had lived with Debbie as her boyfriend. He moved out in February 1985, but they continued to date. Stevenson seemed to truly love and care for Debbie, even though they had split up. They had been talking and, according to some, she wanted to get back together with Stevenson. Debbie did have an active restraining order out

on Stevenson. According to Stevenson, that did not prevent them from hanging out and continuing their relationship. Why Stevenson? Stevenson was at a bar on March 26, 1985, and had talked of possibly seeing Debbie there. On March 7, Debbie had obtained a PFA against him. He made an odd statement while being interviewed. Stevenson stated that he was lying in bed the night of the fire and heard the fire whistles, he thought, "Deborah's mobile home was on fire." An odd statement to make, for sure, but that doesn't make a person guilty.

Investigation

All investigators involved agreed the fire started on the bed. Stevenson would have had to have been inside the trailer while Debbie and Probst were both there. According to Probst, he was not. Stevenson also took and passed a polygraph.

During the investigation, an electrical expert excluded an electrical malfunction as the cause of the fire. Further, weather information excluded natural causes. Trooper DeVore, who was the acting state police fire marshal, determined that the fire began in the master bedroom on top of and near the head of the bed. Trooper DeVore observed that the mattress, which was a 6-inch foam rubber mattress, appeared almost fully consumed. Trooper DeVore further observed what appeared to be flow patterns on the floor and sides of the bed. Trooper DeVore's initial impression was that the fire was accidentally caused by smoking in bed, but continued the investigation to exclude other possible causes.

On May 28, Trooper DeVore interviewed Probst at Geisinger Medical Center. Probst was sedated, but was able to. Probst told Trooper DeVore that he had been dating Debbie for a short period of time. Probst had stated that upon returning to the mobile home, they were both intoxicated. Probst indicated that they were watching television and that Debbie was lying on the couch facing the television while he was lying on the floor alongside of the couch facing the television. Probst indicated that they fell asleep. Later, he awoke because he was having difficulty breathing. According to Probst when he awoke the living room was full of smoke and he could hear a crackling noise. He noticed a glow in the bedroom area reflecting off the hallway. Probst stated that he attempted to wake up Debbie but was unable to do so. During this time the heat was burning his hair and his face seemed to be on fire. Probst went to the front door and the front door was hot. The door seemed to be locked but he forced the door open. Probst stated that he fell to the ground and yelled for help. Probst stated that both he and Debbie were smoking while watching television but could not recall whether they were smoking in the bedroom.

Trooper DeVore sent 12 samples of cloth from the master bedroom to the Pennsylvania State Police crime laboratory in Wyoming, Pa.:

Carpet taken from the east wall of the master bedroom near the headboard of the bed.

Carpet taken from the west wall of the master bedroom.

Carpet taken from the foot of the bed.

Covering from the box springs.

Covering taken from the foam rubber mattress.

Covering from the underside of the box springs.

Section of a white blanket believed to be on the bed.

The purpose of forwarding these samples to the laboratory was to determine, if possible, whether an accelerant was used and what may have caused what appeared to be a pour pattern on the floor. The crime lab uses a gas chromatograph to separate components of a substance to help identify it. A carrier gas is used to carry a sample of a gas from a piece of evidence through a column. A column consists of many circular tubes, packed with a liquid substance. As the sample of gas is swept through the column, the molecular components are retained in the column for different periods of time. Thus, all components pass through the column at varying speeds. Upon emerging from the column, the components immediately enter a detector. The detector registers a series of signals that appear as a succession of peaks that are recorded on a graph. The time lapse between the injection of the sample and the emergence of the peak provides a strong clue to its identity.

For unequivocal identification, at least two columns are required and a standard reference substance is chromatographed under identical operating conditions. These days, there are additional and more sophisticated instruments to identify the components, but they were not available at this laboratory in 1985. According to the director of the crime lab, the results of the gas chromatogram are to be used only as a supplement to confirm, if possible, investigators' conclusions based on physical evidence.

A forensic scientist at the Pennsylvania State Police Laboratory tested the 12 samples forwarded to the laboratory and advised Trooper DeVore that the readings on the graph indicated that an accelerant may be present, but he believed the readings may have been caused by foam rubber from the mattress. The scientist requested samples of the foam rubber from the home, which Trooper DeVore obtained from the master bedroom mattress and a chair in the living room.

Subsequent to the additional laboratory tests, in July 1985, the criminologist reported that a volatile substance was detected in some of the items and that the substances therein were similar to a reading of the foam rubber taken from the master bedroom. A volatile substance includes any type of carbon and may include carbon from materials such as wood, foam rubber, etc. <u>This does not mean that there was a finding of an accelerant</u>. Based upon this information and his investigation, Trooper DeVore concluded that the pour patterns were due to the decomposition of the foam rubber (which can resemble pour patterns as it burns) and listed the fire as accidental in nature. Trooper DeVore closed the investigation "As the most probable cause as smoking in bed." Trooper DeVore further noted, however, that if any information were learned to the contrary in the future, the investigation would be reopened. The evidence, which was returned to Trooper DeVore, was subsequently destroyed.

In March 1988, Probst was arrested for the assault and attempted murder of his girlfriend, Diemer. During the investigation of the assault by the Williamsport Bureau of Police, it was discovered that Probst had allegedly confessed when he was extremely drunk to setting the fire that killed Marchese. Probst made these statements when he was extremely intoxicated. The statements did not describe in any detail how the fire was allegedly set, but were general statements wherein he said he set the fire. In May 1988, the commonwealth conducted a consensual intercept using one of Probst's former girlfriends. The police recorded a conversation between Peggy and Probst. Peggy made contact with him while he was being held in the holding cell of the sheriff's office. Below are excerpts from the call.

PR: Can I talk to Randy Probst

UM: Yeah, watch. Just a second.

PR: Hi.

RP: You still here?

PR: I had to wait till your lawyer left.

RP: You're so sweet,

PR: Yeah, he had to go see about a job.

RP: How did you get back in here.

RP: What am I going to do? You wouldn't believe the rumors going around.

PR: You're not going to tell anybody else about that fire? You had to.

RP: No, I didn't. Why?

PR: 'Cause he (the investigator) came and talked to me yesterday, right?

RP: At your house?

PR: Yeah, right, so I acted like I didn't know anything, I didn't say that, we never talked about it or anything, right? He said since this thing with Nicki has happened he says several people have come forward with information. I said, "Well what do you mean by information?" So he wouldn't tell me nothing, right?

PR: You don't take, you don't take no lie detector test, you just tell them we never talked about it, and that's it. There is no way, you, you didn't have nothing to do with the fire, you, you don't know nothing.

RP: There's no way that I could possibly have started that fire and stay in there and get burned half to death.

PR: I'm just saying are you sure you never told anybody else.

RP: Positive.

PR: No, but, what, whatever happened?

RP: I offered to take a lie detector test then, and they won't let me take one.

PR: Okay, what would happen if I were to say I don't want to ...

RP: I didn't do it. Peggy, listen, never in my life start that place on fire. Holy shit, what do you think, you just say, "Hey, look, you people make me nervous just because I've never been around the law before," 'cause I've never been trouble, you know, you're because you're, you're not a witness to the fire, you're not nothing to the fire. You was my girlfriend when it happened. So they're going to try to scare you, say that, say that you can just give us one thing just to go on. You don't have to say a word. I'm—my right hand up to God—you don't have to say a word, you can say, I refuse, there's no sense in this, "Why would you bring up something like this now?" I need help.

PR: All right.

RP: You can't, you can't never tell them what I said I, I made up so many crazy stories when I was drunk.

PR: Yes, but I'm just saying, I'm the one person you trust, you at least gotta—

RP: Yeah.

PR: Tell me the truth if you want me to help.

RP: What do you want to know?

PR: Well...

RP: I never started the fire. I didn't do this to Nicki. I'm innocent. All the way, all the way. I'm going to have to try to hire myself a, a good—all's that was drunk talk, with my right hand to God, that's all that was drunk talk. That's it. Look, it's something to flipped out things that I said to you when I was drunk. I had a girl—I had a girl one night believing that I was a crane salesman from Brazil. You can't say—

PR: Okay, I won't say anything unless—

RP: I didn't do it. I didn't do it. I never—that, that would be a little bit stupid, wouldn't it?

PR: What?

RP: I almost died, do you remember? I almost died.

PR: Okay?

RP: Yeah.

PR: Not, I mean, I don't even treat you like a criminal or nothing. I'm just saying do you remember? I mean you just said that you—

RP: Okay.

PR: ... hadn't intended to fall asleep after it started.

RP: I can't remember even telling you that.

PR: That's what you said that time you got—

RP: No.

PR: ... burnt, because you didn't intend—

RP: No.

PR: ... to fall a—

RP: How would've—I, you mean that I lit the place, then lay down and went to sleep?

PR: You just said because you were drunk and that you didn't intend to fall asleep.

RP: Oh my •••

PR: I just—you got to make sure you—

RP: On my right hand up to God, I never did it. I'm telling the truth. I'm telling the truth. My right hand up to God.

RP: I'm begging you. I'm begging you, you don't ever say nothing about that night I said that.

PR: I won't.

RP: That was drunk talk. That's all that was— (inaudible)

RP: You got to be smart (inaudible) I'm not telling you what was said, but I am really worried about this trial and all.

PR: Okay, don't—

RP: She told her mom that, she told her mom that that I was, I was in love with her and I wanted to marry her. I didn't even know nothing about it. She thought—I—she wasn't my girlfriend. God bless her, but I didn't love her.

PR: (inaudible) saying I would never, never ...

RP: I'm telling you the truth.

PR: You didn't (inaudible) are you sure when you went drinking that you didn't tell anybody else—

RP: No.

PR: ... not even your mom's family or nothing?

RP: No, nope. Never, never. Never, ever, ever, never, ever. Nope, nobody. I'm sure about everything. It just seems to me like everybody that even looks at me now thinks that I'm lying. I'm going to get paranoid like everybody thinks I'm lying. You don't know how serious this is.

RP: You've got to say that. And I didn't under any, under any doubt start that fire and I didn't do this to Nicki.

RP: You can't, you can't tell them that I ever said anything about the fire. We just never talked about the fire. They're not going to do diddly. Only thing they, they know, they just want to talk to you, to, ah, to see what kind of person I am. I said when I was drunk in bed, one night when I was drunk out of my mind and then I told you the next day that I never did it.

PR: I know, but you used to tell me when you were drunk that's when you was telling the truth.

RP: Oh don't ever, don't ever tell them what you know. My God, I'm begging you please don't ever tell them nothing like that.

PR: No I won't. I just don't know what to say. You know me.

RP: We never talked about it.

PR: I'm not a going to lie.

RP: We never even—you don't have to lie. We just never talked about it.

PR: All right.

RP: I, ah, we never talked about it. You don't have to—you don't have to lie 'cause we never talked about it.

PR: Right.

RP: You have to—

PR: I know, well I'm not saying, you know I'll be all right,

RP: Don't ever tell them that I said that. That was because, that was you and me when we was in bed and nobody in the world ever has to know that.

PR: Mmm.

RP: Then you don't have to do nothing. You, you can just say, we never talked about it because of the kids, it was forgotten.

PR: Right.

RP: You can't tell them that I said, this was in our bedroom between you and me.

PR: I know.

PR: I didn't know what to say to them.

RP: You'll never know that I made that statement about the fire, never.

RP: Never, that should be buried in your head. That was between you and me in our bedroom.

RP: There's a lot of things you and I talked about that I have never repeated to no one.

PR: I know.

RP: That was part of our life. The four years that we lived together.

RP: Hell, that night, I was out for like, two or three days at a time. I remember what you're talking about. I was laying on my belly on the bed and I said, I said you know that fire, and you I said I'm the one that, that did that, no way did I, my right hand up to God on, on little Serina's life. I never, I couldn't have started that fire. I don't know how I'd have got this burnt.

PR: I know, but you say you fell asleep.

RP: I did. What are you, what are dreaming up that I started the fire and then I fell asleep and this is how I got burned?

PR: No. That what—

RP: Oh, God.

PR: I'm not going to say nothing. I'm just saying that's what you and she knew too much, wanted too much. You said that—

RP: You can't about the fire and I'd be dead. That's going to be buried. That's going to have to be buried.

PR: Okay.

RP: Please reassure me that you won't say that, that one statement I made, oh my God.

PR: I won't say anything.

RP: As far as the fire, that's going to be buried, that can't up in this at all.

PR: Okay.

RP: I'm begging you please, please, please tell me you won't say one word?

PR: I won't say anything. I promise.

RP: Honey, you don't have to tell them nothing. You can say, "I don't know what you ask me about the fire because I was nowhere around when that fire happened."

PR: Okay.

RP: Don't ever get nervous because of what we're going, we're going to find out one way or another, just say, "Well, I have no comment on it 'cause I was nowhere around when that fire started."

As you can see by the transcripts, Probst was extremely worried about a statement he made to Peggy one time while they were in bed. He repeats to her about not saying it to the police. He begs her. He pleads with her. But the question becomes, is he doing this because he is guilty of starting the fire or because he truthfully made the statement, but it was a lie? He denies starting the fire but admits to saying he did.

During that consensual intercept, Probst admitted that he had made the statement, but denied that it was true, indicating that he had told that person the following day after the statement it was only drunk talk. Peggy confirmed this statement. Trooper DeVore was then asked to review his investigation and exclude from his consideration statements of witnesses, relying solely on the physical evidence and the laboratory results. Trooper DeVore concluded in June 1988 that the fire was a slow, smoldering type of fire that could have been caused by smoking in bed or intentionally setting some type of material such as paper in the bed clothing, allowing a slow fire to build up.

Subsequently, Trooper DeVore reviewed the case with an independent expert retained by the commonwealth. At a preliminary hearing, Trooper DeVore excluded a cigarette as the cause of the fire based upon two factors. First, the bedsprings from the box springs had not annealed. Sometimes, when a cigarette burns through the mattress, the heat generated as it slowly builds intensity through the mattress causes springs to collapse. The bedsprings had not collapsed. Second, sometimes the heat generated is so intense that the bed will collapse and a hole will be burned completely through the floor underneath the bed. This had not occurred. Trooper DeVore did testify, however, that the heavy smoke and carbon buildup was consistent with a cigarette fire and that it would take about an hour and 45 minutes to 2½ hours if a cigarette was on the bed and insulated by bed clothing or other material to burst into flame. Trooper DeVore excluded the possibility of an accelerant based upon his investigation and concluded that it was not a fast, rapid fire that one would expect with an accelerant. The district magistrate found that there was probable cause to proceed and Probst was bound over for court.

During the investigation, the commonwealth consulted numerous experts: two foam rubber experts (one a urethane foam rubber expert and one a latex foam rubber expert), two independent arson investigators (one from an independent investigative team and one an instructor at the National Fire Academy in Emmetsburg, Md.), five forensic scientists (one from an independent laboratory retained by the commonwealth), a forensic pathologist, forensic psychiatrist and psychologist.

The commonwealth's experts reviewed, either jointly or separately, all aspects of the case. The foam rubber expert requested that urethane foam rubber and latex foam rubber be burned with and without gasoline and tested in the gas chromatograph used in 1985. Urethane foam rubber and latex foam rubber both were to be tested because it was not known what type of foam rubber the mattress was constructed of in 1985. In addition, the specific variation of foam rubber was not known. (Different latex and urethane foam rubbers may differ chemically.)

Further, the same operator was requested to perform the test. The gas chromatograph used in 1985 was no longer in operational condition and in the process of being discarded by the Pennsylvania State Police. At the request of the Lycoming County District Attorney's Office, the Pennsylvania State Police was able to repair the gas chromatograph, which included the installation of a new column. The gas chromatograph was rebuilt by mid-July, 1990, and additional tests were performed on Aug. 1, 1990, and observed by an expert from an independent laboratory.

The gas chromatographs from burned latex and urethane foam rubber were then compared with the gas chromatographs from 1985. The independent laboratory reported that the samples from 1985 appeared to be consistent with a fuel such as Coleman propane fuel, gasoline, gasohol, etc. Further, some appeared to have peaks consistent with fuel oil. In addition, the forensic chemist performing the tests concluded that the latex foam rubber burned with gas was consistent with items from the bed. The results of burning urethane foam rubber were not consistent.

The director of the laboratory disagreed with the conclusion regarding the interpretation of the peaks in the gas chromatogram. The director indicated that the peaks did not show a sufficient discernible pattern, thus without corroborative physical evidence, a conclusion could not be reached. The commonwealth also consulted a forensic scientist from state police headquarters in Harrisburg. That scientist indicated that the gas chromatograms were inconclusive due to the fact that there were too many variables. First, the 1985 test were run on a gas chromatogram with a different column than the 1990 test, different attenuations were used (adjustments of the graph machine during operation; different sample sizes may have been used, etc.). The commonwealth consulted a forensic scientist at the Pennsylvania State Police's Bethlehem laboratory. That forensic scientist indicated that he had burned foam rubber without gasoline and tested that substance on the gas chromatograph and the gas chromatograph showed similarities to gasoline. He further indicated that he could not render an opinion that the 1985 gas chromatograms were consistent with gasoline.

On Aug. 7, 1990, the investigators met with one of the independent arson experts and Trooper DeVore at State Police headquarters in Harrisburg to review the entire investigation and prepare expert reports for trial. The independent expert had indicated that he consulted the Commonwealth's expert from the National Fire Academy before the meeting. The expert determined the evidence did not support a conclusion that the gas chromatographs indicated the presence of an accelerant. First, the expert indicated that a flashover occurred. A flashover occurs when gases are being produced by a slow, smoldering fire and at some point, the heat is sufficient to ignite a gas-filled room. When the gas-filled room ignites, the entire room ignites at one point. Second, the evidence indicated that there was a lack of low burn around the legs of the bed. If there is an accelerant, the legs of the bed should have been damaged. Third, the V-shaped pattern from the bed indicated that accelerant was not spread about. Fourth, there was no low burning under furniture. Fifth, an explosion did not occur. If an accelerant was spread in a bedroom in a mobile home and subsequently ignited, an explosion would have occurred. Sixth, the windows to the bedroom showed a dark carbon buildup, which is consistent with a slow-burning fire. Seventh, foam rubber while burning and melting can yield a pour pattern. Eighth, Probst did not suffer any injuries to his hands or feet, which would have occurred if an accelerant were used. The expert was further of the opinion that the fire was consistent with smoking in bed. This was based upon the statement of Michael Yourish, that the springs of the bed would not necessarily anneal and that a cigarette on bedsheets could smolder until igniting and then set the foam rubber on fire. Also, that Probst's original statement was consistent and his injuries were consistent. The expert indicated that the fire could only have been started by a cigarette on the bed clothing or by another type of material such as paper that was ignited and placed on the bed. In his opinion, however, by a preponderance of the evidence between those alternatives, the fire was caused by a cigarette.

After reviewing the case, I agreed. Yet, let's make a case for arson first.

The Case for Arson

State police investigators concluded that the fire started on the bed. They took samples of the bed and carpet around the bed. These samples were sent to the Pennsylvania State Police Crime Lab. A lab technician got an indication that an accelerant (gasoline) was in the samples.

To be sure of his readings, the technician wanted a control sample. The investigator took a piece of foam rubber from the fire-damaged mattress and a living room chair. The technician again got an indication that an accelerant was present.

It was the technician's opinion that the foam rubber was giving him readings that an accelerant was present, though one was not. In other words, there was no accelerant.

When Probst was arrested for the fire in 1989, four years later, a preliminary hearing was held. State Trooper DeVore, whom I know and respect very much, testified that he believed the fire was intentionally set. He based this opinion on the fact that he observed what appeared to be accelerate pattern on the floor by the bed.

However, in DeVore's initial report, he made no mention of this pattern. His initial conclusion was that the fire was more than likely started by a discarded cigarette. During the preliminary hearing against Probst, he stated the fire started on the bed and, more specifically, toward the center to the headboard side. In addition, he believed he saw an accelerant pattern on the floor as if "someone poured an accelerant on the floor." Yet the final determination according to the trooper at the preliminary hearing was that no accelerant was used. Although there was some indication that there was originally, final lab reports no accelerant was used. An electrical expert ruled out faulty wiring as the cause of the fire.

According to a witness, a gas can was seen behind the trailer on the night of the fire. No one else mentioned this can.

Now we have deduced the possibilities of how the fire started from three to two. It was either arson or accident.

Case Against Arson

According to all of the investigators and experts who consulted on this case, the fire was a smoldering type of fire that would take from an hour and 45 minutes to 2½ hours to ignite into an open flame. An example of this type of fire would be a lit cigarette being dropped on the bed.

According to Devore, an open flame fire would ignite immediately and engulf the whole bedroom in flames within 10 to 20 minutes. An example of an open flame fire would be someone taking a lighter and burning the sheets on the bed.

Devore seemed to be contradicting himself by saying he believes it was a smoldering type of fire, yet he believes it was set by an open flame.

So, if Probst started the fire by lighting the bedding with an open flame, he would have had to immediately go out in the living room and fall asleep in order to get the types of injuries that he sustained. This is not likely and makes no sense. Why, after setting the fire, would he fall asleep within 10 to 20 minutes of setting the fire and make himself susceptible to injury or death? If he set the fire on the bed as the fire investigators claim he did and then passed out on the floor in the living room, he would have had to do so within 10 to 20 minutes of setting the fire. That is how fast, according to investigators, it would take for the fire to engulf the bed and bedroom. However, you cannot blame Devore for this. He was basing his decision off of the fact he believed an accelerant being used.

Probst was found outside the trailer wearing only his jeans. If he had set the fire and was planning an escape, he would have been fully dressed—at least he would have had put his shoes on, in my opinion. However, if intoxicated, his judgment would be altered.

Probst spent three weeks in the hospital with second-degree burns over 45 percent of his body. This is a very painful injury and his injuries are consistent with what he was wearing at the time: jeans.

Is it possible his injuries were caused by accidently setting himself on fire while lighting the fire? Not likely, because if an accelerant were dumped on the floor around the bed and Probst lit the fire, his feet would have been burned along with his upper body.

I was able to review the entire police report, which I obtained from the Pennsylvania State Police. I was also able to obtain Probst's attempted homicide case relating to his attack on Diemer from the Williamsport Bureau of Police. This report was used to gauge any particular patterns or similarities used by Probst regarding criminal activity.

I also was able to obtain the autopsy report and photographs of the fire and autopsy from the Public Defender's Office. Luckily, these key pieces of evidence still existed and they assisted me in making my final determination as to whether this was arson or an accidental fire.

The original investigator did an outstanding job collecting evidence and investigating this case. He did make one mistake that makes investigating this case further extremely difficult. After he determined that the case was probably accidental, he made the following annotation in his report on July 16, 1985:

"… fire is listed accidental in nature. Evidence from property records 7908 A, 7908 B, 7908 C, 7908 D, 7908 E may be disposed and destroyed as this investigation is closed."

"At this time, the investigation will be closed as the most probable cause is smoking in bed. However, if in the future any information is learned to the contrary, this investigation will be reopened."

It appears that new information did come to light in 1988; however, the evidence had already been destroyed.

According to the Pennsylvania State Police on Oct. 5, 2011, the only evidence that remains in this case is a control sample of a satin sheet.

So, even if I believed that this was arson, which I don't, there is no physical evidence to test or corroborate that finding. Further testing on evidence collected at the scene is now impossible.

However, that does not take away interviews, expert opinions and other investigative techniques to determine if this was arson or accidental in nature.

Was the commonwealth correct in dropping the charges against Probst? Why drop the charges? The commonwealth has the burden of proving the *corpus delecti,* or body of a crime, which may not be established by statements of the defendant. The *corpus delecti* must be established before the statements are considered. Specifically, in regard to alleged arson murders, the *corpus delecti* must consist of the proof of a death resulting from a fire or incendiary origin.

In this case, the commonwealth was unable to establish a *corpus delecti*. The results of the gas chromatographs must be considered inconclusive. This is based upon the difference of opinions between the experts, a review of the entire investigation, the fact that an accelerant was not identified in 1985, and the numerous variables identified by the experts. The opinion of the experts then would be that, more likely than not, the fire would have initiated by smoking in bed.

Although not directly relevant to the determination of whether the commonwealth can present evidence of *corpus delecti*, the witnesses who were interviewed by the commonwealth indicated that Probst had a history of making statements about killing someone and other activities. The commonwealth consulted Dr. Kenneth Kool, a forensic psychiatrist, who previously examined Probst. Dr. Kool indicated that Probst's limited mental capacity and psychological makeup is that of an individual who would fabricate such statements.

Let's be clear why Probst was arrested—because of his statements. The evidence did not support an arrest. However, the statements he made, his violent assault on Diemer and the *possibility* that an accelerant was used were enough. That is called probable cause. Was this enough to win a conviction at trial? Absolutely not. I believe if you look at the totality of all the evidence, he is innocent and the commonwealth made the correct decision to withdrawal the charges against him.

My Expert Opinion as to What Happened

Debbie and Probst returned to Debbie's trailer around 8:30 p.m.

on May 26, 1985. They continued to drink beer that they bought from the Montoursville store. Debbie was very intoxicated, as indicated by her father and her blood alcohol content. This is a fact that cannot be disputed.

At approximately 10 p.m., Debbie and Probst are lying on the bed and Debbie is observed with a cigarette in her mouth. After they finish on the bed, where it is possible they engaged in some sort of voluntary physical contact, they return to the living room with Probst only wearing jeans. The cigarette either fell out of her mouth during the interaction between two intoxicated people or was placed on the bed voluntary because of her inebriated state. Debbie's blood alcohol content was 0.18 percent. The legal driving limit in Pennsylvania is .08 percent.

Debbie fell asleep on the couch and Probst on the floor next to the couch. Around 12:40 a.m., a substantial fire begins to engulf the bedroom and trailer. This would corroborate the fire expert's opinion that it would take an hour and 45 minutes to 2½ hours for a smoldering fire to combust into open flames.

Probst is awakened when the smoke makes it difficult to breathe. He attempts to wake Debbie, who was still asleep on the couch. It is not known how much effort he put in to waking her up before fleeing the trailer. Debbie, being asleep and heavily intoxicated, did not awake in time.

Once outside, it appears that Probst may have tried to re-enter the trailer to get Debbie, but was thwarted in his efforts by the intense heat, smoke being generated by the fire and a neighbor.

Probst was continually asking paramedics "What is going on?" and "What happened?" This is consistent with someone being extremely intoxicated and just waking up from a drunken stupor.

It appears that Debbie may have tried to get out, but was overcome by the smoke and fire. She was found just next to the couch in which she was lying on.

Although the fire had some possible indicators that it was intentionally set and gasoline was used as an accelerant (original lab results), the control samples explain this away. The control samples gave the same readings, indicating that the foam from the mattress and chair was producing the readings.

If you take the experts opinions that it was a smoldering fire that took some time to develop into a flame and started in the bedroom on top of the bed, if gasoline was used as an accelerant, then it could not have been a smoldering type of fire.

Also consider the witness who observed Debbie in the bed with a cigarette in her mouth from his trailer, which was 21 feet from her bedroom window. Although Probst stated they were never in the bedroom, he was obviously intoxicated. This witness is an impartial observer who has no reason to make up what he saw. Probst, on the other hand, was extremely intoxicated and just had a traumatic experience. Probst's blood alcohol content was .189 percent.

I believe that Probst's severe burn injuries were sustained because he had passed out or fallen asleep before the fire started. It would be very hard for him to self-inflict these injuries or get them accidently. Probst spent more than three weeks in the hospital and also had months of continued treatment for his injuries.

There were no drugs found in Debbie's system at the autopsy and she had no signs of injuries (no bruises, cuts, etc). So it does not appear Debbie was incapacitated or drugged at the time of the fire, as some individuals had mentioned. The fire was absolutely not set in order to cover a murder. A specific sedative-hypnotic drug screen was negative. Debbie's carbon monoxide level was 58 percent—5 percent to 10 percent is the norm for heavy smokers. This extremely high level of carbon monoxide would show that she was alive and breathing while the smoke and fire engulfed the trailer. This supports the fact that she was sleeping or passed out on the couch and not already dead.

The area in which Debbie was found is consistent with Probst's statement that Debbie was laying on the couch. It appears she tried to exit, but more than likely, was overtaken by smoke.

It is debatable how hard Probst tried to get Debbie out. However, he stated he tried to awaken her before exiting himself. Witnesses stated he did ask about Debbie and told people she was inside the trailer. According to one witness, Probst tried to re-enter the trailer to get Debbie, but the witness restrained him from doing so.

Although Probst had admitted he started the fire to a handful of people, it is my opinion he did this to make himself look "tough." I have little doubt that Probst is capable of murder and or other violent acts; however, it appears to me that he was also a victim in this fire.

Please consider the following statistics relating to cigarettes and house fires:

• Cigarettes are the leading cause of home fire fatalities in the United States, killing 700 to 900 people—smokers and nonsmokers alike—per year.

• Mattresses and bedding, upholstered furniture and trash are the items most commonly ignited in smoking-material home fires.

• Between 1999 and 2003, almost half (43 percent) of fatal home smoking-material fire victims were sleeping when injured; one-third (32 percent) was attempting to escape, fight the fire or rescue others.

Source: NFPA's Fire Analysis and Research Division

The totality of the facts indicates, in my opinion, that this was an accidental fire more than likely started by a lit cigarette that was unintentionally discarded on the bed.

The medical examiner also agreed with my findings: According to forensic pathologist Isidore Mihalikas, M.D., his opinion was:

> *"After review of the history and complete autopsy of the body of Ms. Deborah Marchese, death is attributed to conflagration and consequences thereof. Based on the currently available medical history and based on the autopsy findings, there is no evidence of any trauma or injury other than that directly related to the fire and consequences thereof. Ms. Marchese was intoxicated at the time of her death as evidenced by the whole blood ethanol and she consumed alcoholic beverages within the hour prior to her demise. The manner of death is accidental."*

When I was requested to look into this case by the victim's daughter, she praised me up and down for looking at the case. I had to convince my boss, the district attorney, why this needed to be done. I convinced him and reviewed the case for the victim's daughter.

However, when I told her of my findings, she wouldn't even finish her conversation with me.

Now, I completely understand her feelings and how she feels that she never had closure. She feels that a murderer is walking the streets. However, I cautioned her in the beginning that my findings are unbiased and that she should not get upset if she didn't agree with them. At the time, she completely understood and sang my praises to anyone who would listen. She was so happy that someone actually listened to her and looked into the matter.

But again, when she didn't get the answer she wanted, her attitude and opinion of me changed. I don't fault her. I finally told her that this is my opinion only. I'm fallible and it is just my opinion. If she doesn't agree with my opinion, please have someone else look at it because I am sure she will find someone else who disagrees with me. It happens all the time. She even started a petition to have me re-examine my own findings. I am completely OK with this. I do not take her anger toward me personally. She lost a mother. I have nothing but empathy and respect for her and her determination to find closure.

Regardless of my opinion that it was an accidental fire or someone else's opinion that it was arson, one thing will never change. That a very beautiful, young soul died that night and that is what should not be forgotten.

This is to certify that this is a true copy of the record which is on file in the Pennsylvania Division of Vital Records in accordance with Act 66, P.L. 304, approved by the General Assembly, June 29, 1953.

(Fee for this certificate, $3.00)

Charles Hardester
Charles Hardester
State Registrar

WARNING: It is illegal to duplicate this copy by photostat or photograph.

JUN - 7 1988
Date

C892877
No.

COMMONWEALTH OF PENNSYLVANIA
DEPARTMENT OF HEALTH
VITAL RECORDS
CERTIFICATE OF DEATH
(Coroner)

048319

D. Marchese

STATE FILE NO.

Name of decedent: DEBORAH J. MARCHESE
Sex: Fe
Date of death: 5/27/85

Race: White, Black: W
Age last birthday: 22
If under 1 yr.: Mos. Days
If under 1 day: Hours Min.
Date of birth: 1/30/62
State or foreign country of birth: PA
County of birth: Lycoming
City, Boro, or Twp. of birth: Winsor

County of death: Lycoming
City, Boro, or Twp. of death: Armstrong Twp
Hospital or Institution: RD #4 - Box 477
If Resp. or Inst. indicate D.O.A., O.P./E.R., or Inpatient (specify)

Decedent's Mailing Address: RD #4 Box 477 Williamsport PA 17701
State: N/M
Marital Status:

Was decedent ever in U.S. Armed Forces? No
Usual Occupation: LABORER
Kind of business or industry: CHAIR

Where did decedent die at: Pt
County: Lycoming
Usual Occupation: Armstrong

Father's name: LARRY MARCHESE, JR.
Mother's maiden name: MARY STOPER

Informant's name: LARRY MARCHESE, JR.
Mailing address: 704 SHERIDAN ST WILLIAMSPORT PA 17701

Date of burial: 5/30/85
Name of cemetery or crematory: RESURRECTION CEMETERY
Location: FAIRFIELD TWP PA

FD-0110645-G

ALLEN-MCCULLOCH'S REDMOND F.H. INC.
331 ELMIRA STREET
WILLIAMSPORT, PA. 17701

Signature: Miriam B. Johns
41398
May 29 1985

May 27, 1985
Hour of death: 1130
5/27/85 Pronounced

George W. Gedon 2101 Northway Rd Williamsport PA

IMMEDIATE CAUSE:
(A) Massive Burns of Body and smoke inhalation
(B) Trailer Fire

PART II Other Significant Conditions: Possible intoxication

Accidental
Date of injury: May 26, 1985
Hour: 12:30 A.M. Apprx.
Describe how injury occurred: Trapped in burning trailer

Marchese Death Certificate where death was ruled accident

Deb Marchese

Deb Marchese smoking

Deb Marchese

Man charged
in second homicide

WILLIAMSPORT, Pa. (AP) — The investigation of a Lycoming County man's knifing attack on his girlfriend has led to charges he killed another girlfriend in a fire three years ago.

Randall L. Probst Sr., 36, was charged Thursday with setting the fire that killed Deborah J. Marchese in her Armstrong Township mobile home in May 1985.

Evidence against Probst in the Marchese death came to the attention of Williamsport police Detective William Dalton and Lt. Phillip Preziosi during their investigation of the knifing case, District Attorney Brett O. Feese said.

State police Fire Marshal Woodrow W. Shaner then reopened the investigation begun in 1985 by another fire marshal, Trooper James DeVore.

Probst suffered serious burns in the fire, but an affidavit filed by Shaner alleges he was injured "because he fell asleep after starting the fire."

Probst reacted in shock Thursday when escorted by Shaner and other state police personnel to the Old Lycoming Township office of District Justice James H. Sortman for arraignment.

"Charging who?" he asked as William Miele, chief county public defender, tried to explain.

"I tried to get her out of there," Probst said to the attorney.

But in the affidavit, Probst is quoted as telling one woman, "I don't know if you're going to be able to handle this or not. It's real cruel and hard-hearted and it don't bother me. The fire I was in where Debbie burned up, I did that."

Probst charged with the murder of Deb Marchese

pouce Capt. John Sheenan said. He   ond chance.   down forced autos and trucks to de-

Man carves crosses
on girlfriend's back

WILLIAMSPORT, Pa. (AP) — Bail has been set at $170,000 for a man who police say carved crosses and foot-long cuts into his girlfriend's back and buttocks with a knife, then left her bleeding.

Randall L. Probst Sr., 34, was arraigned Thursday on an attempted homicide charge and two counts of aggravated assault before District Justice Allen P. Page III.

Probst is accused of cutting Nicole Diemer, 25, and leaving her on the floor for what may have been as long as 16 hours last Sunday, according to an affidavit.

The affidavit said police thought Diemer was dead when they discovered her Sunday night on the floor of the apartment she shared with Probst, but paramedics determined she was alive. She was taken to Divine Providence Hospital in critical condition and could not be questioned until Thursday.

Medical personnel at the hospital later told police Diemer "suffered a loss of over 50 percent of her blood," the affidavit said. She remained in the hospital's intensive care unit Friday in guarded condition.

Detective William Dalton described numerous injuries suffered by Diemer, including five "evenly spaced" horizontal cuts across her back, each "approximately 10 to 12 inches long" and two cuts on her right buttocks forming "the shape of a cross."

Other injuries described were a bruised left eye, three cuts on the side of the face, cuts on the right side of the face, a vertical cut on the left buttocks, a vertical cut on the back of each thigh and several other long cuts.

District Attorney Brett O. Feese asked for bail in excess of $200,000 because of "the calculated and brutal facts" of the case.

"The defendant is a threat to the community and to himself," Feese said, "and he certainly is a threat to flee."

Also present at the arraignment was an attorney from the county public defender's office.

According to the affidavit, Lt. Phillip E. Preziosi and detective Dalton interviewed Ms. Diemer. She was able to answer only by writing down the answers.

The affidavit states Ms. Diemer recalled Probst pulling her by the hair up the stairs to their second-floor apartment when they returned home about 3:30 or 4 a.m. Sunday. Ms. Diemer's last recollection is that "Randy Probst kicked her," the affidavit said.

Probst was taken to police headquarters Sunday night for questioning and was later admitted to the Divine Providence Hospital mental health unit. He subsequently was admitted to the Danville State Hospital, where he was arrested Thursday after police learned he was to be released.

Probst assaults girlfriend article

CAREY MAE PARKER
MISSING PERSON

"I recently photographed a wonderful man with a passion for solving cold criminal cases: Detective Kenneth Mains. This man has a good heart, a humble soul and a mind that seems to never stop processing."

Heather Hiller

I was contacted on Aug. 4, 2015, to assist on the missing person case of Carey Mae Parker. I have been in regular contact since that time with Patricia Gager, Carey's younger sister, in order to determine facts surrounding this case and her disappearance on or around March 17, 1991.

The following is only my opinion based on my investigative experience and training with the limited facts that I was provided. If additional facts are presented to me, it may change my opinion as to what ultimately happened to Carey in Quinlan, Texas.

This case is unusually difficult because of the lack of information made available to me in form of police reports and other law enforcement documentation. Every bit of information gleaned was provided by Gager or my own research and investigative techniques.

With the limited information I was provided, the following assessment was articulated and formulated to assist Carey's family in their attempt to find closure in knowing what may have happened regarding her disappearance.

A timeline is significant in order to visualize and construct movements, activities and whereabouts. In the case of a missing person, we need to concentrate on the past month and pay particular attention to the last 24 to 48 hours of activity of that missing person.

This is a particularly hard assignment because I have almost no information as to what Carey did before her disappearance. For example, did she leave work early; did she even make it to work? Her disappearance is almost a complete mystery simply because law enforcement did not follow up until four months had passed, and even then, they treated it as a welfare check, not a missing person.

8-24-89   Carey was issued three citations for speeding, having no insurance and driving at an unsafe speed.

2-9-91   Carey failed to appear at her court date or never made good on the citations and a formal process in court was initiated against her (called failure to appear).

2-15-91   A warrant was issued for her arrest for the 8-24-

89 citations.

| 2-21-91 | Arrested for "failure to appear" warrant, booked in jail. |

2-21-91   Arrested for "failure to appear" warrant, booked in jail.

2-22-91   1980 Buick impounded.

2-22-91   Released on signature bail

3-17-91   Last seen, possibly at work. This needs to be verified.

3-28-91   Failure to appear charges filed for 2-9-91.

7-16-91   Missing person report filed, but was classified as a welfare check by the Hunt County Sheriff's Office by Patricia Parker (Gager). Because of this crucial mistake, neither Carey nor her car was ever entered into NCIC database. This is the database where missing persons are entered.

5-15-10   Official missing person report filed by Brandy Hathcock (Carey's daughter).

Victimology

Victimology has many different meanings. Some will say victimology is the study of victimization, including the relationships between victims and offenders. I like to say that it is simply getting to know your victim, in every sense of the word. Knowing how the victim will react in a given circumstance could lead you to the offender.

In this case, the victim is Carey Mae Parker, a 23-year-old white female who went missing on or around March 17, 1991. By all accounts, Carey was very temperamental. If faced with a fight or flight situation, she would fight. This is important because it allows us to know what she will do when given a certain type of situation.

Carey was the oldest of four children to Howard and Mrs. Parker. She had two sisters and a brother. Carey's childhood could be described as problematic. Her mother had been sickened with multiple sclerosis and would later become bedridden. Her father sexually abused her and her female siblings while they were teenagers. It is unknown when the sexual abuse began or ended with Carey, but one at least one occasion, she was observed as a teenager engaging in intercourse with her father. She was also sexual abused by her father's brother as a teenager on at least one occasion.

Carey dropped out of high school in the ninth grade and left home by the age of 16. She had her first child at this time to Guadeloupe Galan, an older Mexican neighbor. That was followed by two more children to Leonard Goode and his brother, Arvin Goode.

By all accounts, Carey was treated differently by her father. This may be because he had a special bond with his oldest daughter or maybe it was because he was scared of her violent temper. When Carey got angry, she would throw things, scream at the top of her lungs and be ready to fight. Exactly where this compulsion came from, we will never know, but it gives us insight into her psyche.

Her relationship with her family was strained; people are described as "walking on eggshells" around her, afraid to set her off.

Carey was not much of a housekeeper as she had dirty dishes in the sink with mold growing on them and dirty diapers and clothing strewed about.

Children Protective Services had been called to investigate the safety of Carey's three children; none of her kids were living with her at the time of her disappearance.

Carey was committed to a mental institute as a teenager, presumably due to her violent outbursts and rebellious attitude. It is probable that this was because of the sexual abuse she was enduring. She stayed there for approximately six months.

Again, Carey was observed having sexual intercourse with her father around the age of 15. Although her father sexually abused his other daughters, it does not appear he had actual intercourse with the others—but he did with the oldest, Carey, and this gives us insight into her relationship with him.

Carey was also caught as a teenager with her uncle on top of her by her aunt. After she was caught and returned home, Carey was observed thrashing about and she stated she was slipped a drug. Most likely, this was a defense mechanism by Carey because she knew she was in trouble.

Carey smoked marijuana with her father as well. This demonstrates the lack of morality associated between father and daughter as well as the "comfortability" between the two.

Although Carey was not responsible, she was able to hold down a steady job for about a year previous to her disappearance.

Carey was a known drug user, or at the very least was running around in that circle. On one occasion, she was looking to obtain prescription pills illegally.

So, what about Carey's victimology helps us get closer to solving her mysterious disappearance?

1. If confronted by someone and she felt disrespected, frightened or jealous, Carey would fight. Carey would not disengage from the confrontation and I think this is important.

2. Although she was known to be temperamental toward male and females alike, she was closer to older male figures and was more likely to be in the company of males versus of females. From this alone, we can deduce she was probably either in the company of a male when she disappeared or she was alone.

3. Carey would not rat on a male, especially one she had the slightest feelings for. This can be easily deduced by her refusal to report her father or uncle for the sexual abuse she was enduring. Because of this, I think we can rule out any likelihood she was murdered to keep her mouth shut about any possible drug dealings she or her friends were involved with. Yet, it remains a possibility, however slight.

4. Carey was searching for a father figure in the men she dated. That is why she went from one boyfriend to the next with no time in between to be single. She did not want to be alone and wanted and loved the attention from men, which she learned from an early age that she could achieve through sex. This undoubtedly would lead to tense or jealous relationships with other female acquaintances. Therefore, we cannot rule out Carey's disappearance being associated with another female.

5. Carey had zero sense of responsibility. This is apparent for her lack of parenting and involvement with Child Protective Services to her failure to purchase/maintain financial insurance

on her vehicle and her failure to appear for court. From this lack of responsibility we can deduce the possibility she could walk away from her life without any regard or apathy.

Suspects

When determining suspects, we must account for individuals in Carey's past and present who had means, motive and opportunity to perpetrate a crime against her.

Although almost anyone can be a suspect, we must start with the ones closest to Carey and work our way out toward lesser-known associates and, finally, to strangers.

We can then use a process of elimination to deduce the likelihood that one of them committed this crime, if there was a crime. One of the obvious, surefire ways to eliminate a suspect is through an alibi. In this case, I have no documentation that anyone had an alibi. Therefore, the following individuals I believe should be considered suspect.

1. Howard Parker (father): Carey's sister confirmed that Parker sexual abused Carey. Not only did he abuse Carey, but all of his daughters. This alone makes Parker a person of interest. Carey had moved on from this abuse, at least outwardly. As an investigator from the outside looking in, I would initially dismiss Parker as a suspect based upon his and Carey's relationship, which was not contemptuous. However, I am concerned about the following:

According to Carey's sister, Parker was possibly the last person to see her before she went to work the day in question. He said she stopped by his house to pick up laundry. Carey was upset. She and Cody Songer (her on/off boyfriend) had a big fight. She threatened to "turn state's evidence" and said Songer was digging a hole out on the septic property that was "too big for a septic." This statement troubles me as if Parker is already pointing the blame at Songer *before* Carey even disappeared. I find it extremely odd that Carey would make this statement about a "hole" being dug "too big for a septic." To me, the statement is too convenient and shifts the focus or blame from Parker to Songer. This is a common tactic used by a guilty party who wants to turn the attention off of them as a suspect.

2. William Cody Songer (boyfriend): Carey allegedly had a big fight with Songer prior to her disappearance, at least if you believe the statement by Carey's father. It is alleged that Songer was coming back with drugs to sell and was pulled over in Dallas and the drugs were confiscated. It is unknown if this was the source of contention and led to the big fight. I would surmise that Songer and Carey, because of her temperament, had a lot of big fights and I don't believe this fight would be any different than the others.

Though Songer's supposed excavating activity (backhoe digging) is suspicious given the timeframe referenced to Carey's disappearance, I am not sure it is unusual. I am not certain that particular activity at a sewer installation business is odd. It is very possible the digging with a backhoe could have been relevant to the business. Yet, we cannot ignore coincidences when it comes to missing persons.

Songer had an intimate relationship with the missing person. Carey's car was also missing. Songer had access to a backhoe and was seen digging on his property near the time of disappearance. This is a coincidence that should not be ignored. In addition, Songer has multiple arrests from Texas to Oklahoma. Although arrests do not mean that the person has a propensity to kill, his arrest in 2010 for domestic abuse, assault and battery is alarming nonetheless. Accordingly, Songer is a suspect until he can be eliminated.

3. Ronald Noel (police officer): It is alleged that Carey was also dating Noel. My research has shown very little about Noel other than he did have a post office box registered to him in Quinlan, Texas, in 1991 and is living in Garland, Texas. He should be interviewed as he could shed light on Carey's state of mind and dating situation during the time of her disappearance. Again, if he was an intimate partner of Carey's, he has to be eliminated and I do not have the documentation to do so.

4. Guadeloupe Galan (oldest child's father): Although he was a part of Carey's life, there was no custody or child support issues that would lead me to believe Galan was involved in Carey's disappearance. Yet, I do not know enough about Galan to eliminate him as a suspect. I would want to know

more about his relationship with Carey to eliminate him. Child support, custody and the well-being of a common child are often the source of unexpected violence between former spouses and parents. Because of this relationship, he should be looked into further as a viable suspect.

5. Leon (uncle): Leon was caught by his wife "on top" of Carey. It is not known what happened between the two, but it was a significant event that led to Carey not spending the night at the uncle's house as previously planned and it caused a rift between Carey's father and his brother. It is probable that Carey was having a sexual relationship with her uncle. I would want to look into his background further in order to eliminate him as a suspect.

6. Leonard Goode (second child's father): Although he was a part of Carey's life, there were no custody or child support issues that would lead me to believe Goode was involved in Carey's disappearance. Yet, I do not know enough about him to eliminate him as a suspect. Child support, custody and the well-being of a common child are often the source of unexpected violence between former spouses and parents. Because of this relationship, he should be looked into further as a viable suspect.

7. Arvin Goode (third child's father): Although he was a part of Carey's life, there were no custody or child support issues that would lead me to believe Goode was involved in Carey's disappearance. Yet, I do not know enough about him to eliminate him as a suspect. Child support, custody and the well-being of a common child are often the source of unexpected violence between former spouses and parents. Because of this relationship, he should be looked into further as a viable suspect.

8. Unknown co-worker: This is a plausible suspect, yet we do not know if Carey left with a co-worker the night in question or even if she had a relationship with a co-worker. If she made it to work and worked a full shift, it is possible she had plans with one of her co-workers. Carey had worked there for a year; therefore, she undoubtedly made friends and relationships there. I would look extremely hard into this area for a suspect,

with a particular attention to a married male co-worker.

9. Dan Robertson (justice of the peace): It is rumored that he was involved, but there is no credible source of this rumor. It is rumored that he was the source of drugs being sold by Songer. Again, I have found no information of the sort.

10. Unknown stranger: The possibility that a stranger abducted, kidnapped or killed Carey is a distinct but lesser possibility, in my opinion. My research shows no other missing persons or homicides in Hunt County around this timeframe.

In all of my cold case homicides, I want to revisit the scene. It is paramount in order to understand everything that was taking place in that homicide. This is not relevant to this case because we do not have a crime scene.

Yet, it would be beneficial to drive the various routes Carey could have driven the night of March 17, 1991. Particular attention should be made to areas of the road that have steep banks or bodies of water in close proximity.

Possible Scenarios

There are only four possible scenarios in which could account for Carey's disappearance: accidental death, suicide, homicide or voluntary walk away. Let's examine each in detail:

1. <u>Accidental death</u>

We must consider this as a possibility for her disappearance. Carey had a history of bad driving to the extent of receiving at least one speeding ticket and one minor traffic accident. Her route to and from work is full of bodies of water, from creeks to ponds to large lakes. This isn't an uncommon possibility:

Law enforcement officials from multiple agencies examine the two cars pulled from a lake in Foss, Okla., on Sept. 18, 2013.

In 2013 a car was pulled from a body of water that contained three bodies. The car and its occupants were reported missing in 1970. Their deaths were an unfortunate accident and most people suspected foul play.

If Carey were driving alone, had an accident and her vehicle became submerged in a body of water with her in it, it may not be found unless all of her possible routes—areas within a certain radius—are checked by sonar or a scuba team. This scenario, because of her driving history, it being nighttime, it being St. Patrick's Day and her car never being recovered is a very good possibility. We must look at this as a possibility and not subject someone to the scrutiny of foul play without exploring all options. In both of these cases, foul play was suspected and suspects were put through years of public scrutiny. Although this is an unavoidable repercussion of a proper investigation, it also ruins the suspects' life as they are forever shunned and tarnished by law enforcement and, more importantly, the public—and for no reason. So, although this is unavoidable, we must try to minimize this damage and seek all possible explanations to one's disappearance.

Another accidental possibility is an overdose on drugs. There is a recent rumor that Carey died of an overdose. This information was given to Carey's sister by a former girlfriend of Songer's and is a new development. This information is possible, due to Carey's history with prescription pills and her past boyfriends' history with intravenous drugs. This new information is that a man in a wheelchair was with Songer and Carey when she overdosed at the Songer trailer.

Although this information may be true, the veracity of it should be challenged. First, if the guy in the wheelchair was there, how did he get there? He was described as crippled. A crippled person in a wheelchair cannot drive, so how did he get to the Songer residence?

2. Suicide

There is no indication that Carey was suicidal. This is a possibility as with any disappearance, but is highly unlikely. In order for her to commit suicide, she would have had to make her car disappear as well. She could accomplish this by driving her car into a lake, but this is not consistent with how a person would commit suicide. Of all the scenarios possible to explain her disappearance, this is the least likely.

3. Homicide

When a person goes missing, homicide must be adequately investigated as a possible explanation. We know through victimology that Carey was a moderately high-risk victim. By this, I mean her lifestyle and background made her a bit more susceptible to being a victim than others. An example of a high-risk victim would be a prostitute. An example of a low risk victim would be a priest, nun or a small child.

Carey's involvement with a variety of men, all of whom were drug users or dealers, and her own probable addiction to, at the very least, prescription pills causes her to have an elevated risk of being a victim.

When determining if a homicide occurred we must not only look at victimology, but we must know why. Because Carey was somewhat promiscuous, had sexual relationships with her father and uncle when she was a teenager, was institutionalized and had a hair-trigger temper, increased her likelihood that she became a victim of a homicide. Why would someone want Carey dead? The most plausible reasons people commit homicides are for sex, revenge and greed.

a.   Sex

I believe Carey, because of her childhood riddled with sexual abuse, liked to please other men. She realized she could use sex to either get what she needed in addition to making things go away. She used this strategy with her father. She gave into his sexual demands not because she wanted to or liked it, but because it allowed the act to stop.

In addition, Carey was attractive and could have been the target of a co-worker who wanted to date her or party with her. It is possible she was at a St. Patrick's Day party and met a man who had more than sex on his mind. It is also conceivable she was having an affair with a married co-worker.

b.   Revenge

Carey could have been the target of a jealous spouse or significant other. It is possible, if she was mixed up in the drug distribution scene as some have suggested, the unsavory characters of this shady world may have murdered her because they were afraid she was working with the police or simply killed to be made an example.

c. Greed

The act of greed can take many forms. It can be greed over financial proprieties, wanting what is not yours or the selfishness of taking what you don't need. In this case, money is not the root of this disappearance. Carey did not have money and did not come from money. She worked a menial job and did not own or even rent a home. Instead, she chose to live with friends.

4.   Voluntary Walk Away

Although this idea has to be investigated, it is not likely. She had very little to no money and never picked up her last paycheck. In addition, although she wasn't the greatest mother according to some, she still had contact with her family and children. There has been zero contact in 24 years. Carey did not walk away voluntarily and this theory can be discounted.

Investigative Strategies

This is probably the most important section, yet maybe the most redundant. The reason for this is because I do not know what the jurisdicting law enforcement has done to properly investigate this case. Therefore, I can only speak on what I would do if I had full access to witnesses, reports, etc. and what I would do if I were investigating this case.

1.   Scuba divers should be searching boat ramps where roads run into the water. Not only there, but also anywhere the road Carey may have traveled crossed over a body of water.

2.   Ground penetrating radar (GPR) should be utilized over the ¾-acre lot the Songers owned in March 1991. I would not limit the use to just the ¾-acre area, but would certainly start my efforts there due to the fact that information has been gleaned that a backhoe was being used on that plot of land around the time Carey went missing. There may be a reasonable explanation as to why a backhoe was needed, but I would still want to check this out. GPR uses a high-frequency radio signal transmitted into the ground and the reflected signals are returned to the receiver. The computer measures the time taken for a pulse to travel to and from the target, which indicates its depth and location. I have used GPR in the search of human remains so it no doubt will work unearthing a large vehicle if buried below the surface.

There has been at least one cold case solved in the past where a car from a missing person was buried. Lisa Kimmel was reported missing and later found buried with her car on a suspect's property.

Remember, you *do not* need law enforcement to do this. You have every right as an American citizen to respectfully ask the owner of this ¾-acre plot of land to allow you and a GPR unit to come drag the machine over the land in order to include or exclude that Carey or her car is on that property. The GPR unit will not disturb the area one bit and is totally non-intrusive.

3.   Dig deeper into Vonda Noland (Carey's friend) and Kenneth Cotton and ascertain additional information. Her reluctance to even acknowledge she knows Carey is troublesome if there is corroborating information that the two did know each other. The relationship between Vonda Noland and Carey needs to be determined. This is crucial. If it can be corroborated that they knew each other and Vonda has denied this, Vonda becomes an immediate person of interest. You do not deny knowing someone when you do—unless you want to disassociate yourself from that person. If this is the case, there is a reason why Vonda wants to disassociate herself from Carey and that needs to be investigated fully.

4.   Determine the name of the man in the wheelchair. By obtaining his name, you can then talk to his friends and relatives to see if he talked about Carey and/or her disappearance and whether it was tied to an overdose.

5.   Locate and speak with co-workers. This is a very crucial element of this investigation and must be followed up on. I would suggest placing an ad in the Terrell newspaper asking people who worked with Carey to come forward with what they may or may not know. The co-workers may have been the last people to see her alive. Carey may have been observed acting in a certain manner, which to them may not be important, but to the investigation, it could be relevant.

6.   Use a cadaver dog on any property in which Carey's remains may be. I would certainly begin on the ¾-acre plot of land. Again, law enforcement is not needed for this. All that's needed is the permission of the landowner. Cadaver dogs have

had success in detecting human remains decades after a person's death and burial.

7.	Review aerial maps of Quinlan as close to March 1991 as possible. Look for changes in the topography or objects that may be submerged in water. These maps are very common and can be found at libraries or on various websites.

8.	Interview neighbors. This is a must. Not only should every neighbor of Songer's be interviewed, it must be done ASAP because the more time passes, unfortunately so do memories and people. Every neighbor around Vonda Noland's home should be interviewed as well. You never know what they saw.

9.	Get this case in the public. Local newspaper and television outlets must be contacted and shown a picture of Carey and her car. This was never done to my knowledge and it needs to be. The Facebook page for Carey's case is a great start.

10.	Interview all known associates of Carey. They need to be identified and then interviewed because in that circle, the truth hides. The drug culture talks. The drug culture knows. If Carey died as a result of an overdose or a homicide by someone in this circle, they have talked. In particular, in my experience, I know that individuals who take meth or cocaine like to talk. If a homicide or overdose occurred, it has been talked about and someone knows. My experience in cold case work shows that people want to talk, but they won't take the step to come forward. Yet, if they are asked, they want to relieve themselves of that secret and tell someone—they are just waiting for the right person to ask them.

11.	Look for the pink laundry basket and clothing Carey may have had in her car when she disappeared. If Carey's car went into a body of water, the contents of her car may have floated out over the years. This is a long shot, but in a case where there are no leads, this is a possibility. Law enforcement officers should go back through their files and look for found property to see if anyone reported this.

12.	Where was Carey doing her laundry? If her father is telling the truth and she was going to do laundry before she disappeared, where was she going? Was there a laundromat nearby? If so, the employers should be tracked down and at the very least shown a picture of Carey and be interviewed.

13.   If Carey were having an affair with a married co-worker, hotel registrations need to be examined in the surrounding areas.

If I were the investigating officer or a private investigator, those are the things I would be doing to solve the case.

Conclusion

So what happened to Carey? This is impossible to determine with any given certainty at this juncture in the investigation. There simply is not enough documentation to ascertain even when Carey went missing. Purportedly hours before her disappearance, Carey was working at the Flanders Precisionaire in Terrell, Texas, on a 2–10 p.m. shift on Sunday, March 17, 1991. St. Patrick's Day is routinely celebrated and usually an alcohol-infused party night. This fits Carey's victimology as a night where she would have been partying.

So what is known about Carey's last known days? It is unknown whether she worked this shift at all or if she left the shift early to attend a St. Patrick's Day party. I would surmise that she worked her full shift, leaving at 10 p.m. or very close to that time and went somewhere to change from her work clothes to her evening clothes. She may have even changed at work or in her car. Carey had just got done doing laundry, so she would have changed. We know from her victimology she always tried to look good by dressing up and wearing makeup. The problem is, this is as far as we can go in the investigation because we do not know where Carey went. I would surmise she went to a friend's house, either Noland's or Songer's, to change clothes before going out, most likely to a party. She may have made it to the party and a horrific event took place there that took her life. Carey's violent temper may have been her downfall. It is very conceivable that she got into an argument with someone at a party and Carey, not ever backing down, was murdered out of rage/jealousy.

It is very possible she was intoxicated, either by drugs or alcohol or a combination of both, was driving to the next party or to where she was staying, got lost and accidentally drove into the lake. This is a very distinct possibility and should not be discounted.

If she did have an accident and was returning to Quinlan from Terrell, we must take in account her travels, which are a complete guess in itself. Although she was a moderately high-risk victim and she ran in a drug circle, I would surmise an accident is a very likely scenario.

It takes approximately 24 minutes to drive from her place of employment to Quinlan taking the following route to Songer's residence.

W Moore Ave to 9th St - 2 min (0.6 mi), Turn left onto 9th St - 3 min (1.2 mi), Take FM986 and FM1565 to Co Rd 2412 in Hunt County - 17 min (14.6 mi), Turn right onto Co Rd 2412 - 2 min (0.9 mi), 3815 Pvt Road 2410 Quinlan, TX 75474

If, in fact, Carey were living with Noland and Cotton in a trailer off Highway 34 in Quinlan, Carey would have just followed Highway 80 to Highway 34 South all the way to Terrell. This is the most direct route. However, Noland claims to not even know Carey when Gager called her on Sept. 14, 2015. Unless Noland was almost directly involved in Carey's disappearance, she would have no reason to distance herself from Carey. I cannot make a determination if Noland is lying or not because I do not have enough facts about any type of relationship between Noland and Carey.

There is an alternate route that is from Highway 751 to 429 to 80, but it would have been out of her way from her friend Noland's residence off Highway 34. This route has to be taken into consideration because we do not know where Carey was going after she got off work. Nevertheless, it was St. Patrick 's Day and we have no idea if she even went home.

I am very concerned with the proximity between Songer's residence and the large body of water all around. I find it very disturbing that if Songer or any of the Songers were involved in Carey's disappearance, how easily a body and/or car could be disposed of in this lake. Examining aerial maps of that area, there are numerous roads and trails that lead right into the water. These roads must be identified and each one examined.

Carey's father said she stopped by the house that day. She was going to do her laundry and get ready for work. He said that Carey was upset about a big fight with Songer, she threatened to "turn state's evidence" and that Songer was digging a hole out on the septic property that was "too big for a septic." Now, if this is true there are only two explanations. Either Songer was digging a hole to bury Carey and her car, which would clearly show premeditated murder, or the digging of the hole was coincidental and had nothing to do with the disappearance. If this information is true, it changes the whole dynamics of this investigation. I originally assumed Songer was observed digging the hole after Carey's disappearance, however this statement of him digging the hole came from Carey herself. Therefore, I would opine that Carey and her car would not be buried on this property and the digging of the hole was coincidental or at the very least, work related if the information Carey's father gave was in fact true.

Conclusion

Investigators took a report from Carey's sister, Patricia, four months after Carey was purportedly last seen. Investigators reportedly checked with Carey's place of employment and found nothing to indicate suspicion in their eyes. It must be noted that this report was classified at the time as a welfare check and not a missing person. So, between St. Patrick's Day, 1991, until July 16, 1991, a span of four months, no investigation was done to find Carey. Although this is tragic, it isn't irrevocable.

In 2010, when a family member inquired into the status of the case, it was revealed that Carey was never entered as a missing person and that the July 16, 1991, report was logged in as a welfare check, which is very damaging to the investigation. Mistakes will happen, yet we cannot work backwards and place blame. It is very probable that because Carey came from a dysfunctional family and she obviously was of age, no one cared that she disappeared, maybe assuming she would show back up someday. It wasn't unusual for her to leave her kids with family or even with CYS in which she did once say to CYS, "You take them," referring to her children.

Yet, the tragedy doesn't lie in the mistakes. The tragedy lies in the demeanor of law enforcement who failed, when given a second chance, to solve the case. The tragedy lies with the law enforcement entities that refuse help and instead offer excuses.

Those are the tragedies that cannot be overcome. However, we now must speak for that victim; we must move forward and work together with other like-minded individuals to solve the case.

Foul play is a very possible explanation for Carey's disappearance as is an unfortunate accident. I firmly believe that it is one of these two possibilities that explain Carey's disappearance. Yet, without more documentation or the ability to interview potential witnesses and suspects myself, I cannot determine which one ultimately led to Carey's disappearance.

Again, I want to emphasize that this is only my opinion as to what may have happened regarding the disappearance of Carey Mae Parker. It is not a fact and should not be concluded as such. Yet I feel strongly about this assessment and the investigative strategizes I provided, which need to be followed up on—either by law enforcement or another investigative entity in order to solve this cold case. With the limited facts I was provided, this is the investigative opinion I have formulated.

MICHELLE JOLENE LAKEY
MISSING PERSON

*"You have done an amazing job!! Just amazing! I am
proud to be affiliated with you and your work."*

Mary Ellen O'Toole, former FBI criminal profiler

I was contacted on Sept. 22, 2015, to assist on the missing person case of 11-year-old Michelle Jolene Lakey. I have been in regular contact since that time with Justina Forsythe, Jolene's sister, in order to determine facts surrounding this case and her disappearance on Aug. 26, 1986 in Scranton, Pa.

This case, too, is unusually difficult because of the lack of information made available to me in form of police reports and other law enforcement documentation. In fact, the only information I used were victimology and questionnaire forms filled out by the family as well as newspaper articles. In addition, I was able to read some hand-written, personal letters from a person of interest in this case. Every bit of information gleamed was provided to me by Forsythe, Jessica Dutter, who had assisted the family, or my own research and investigative techniques.

With the limited information I was provided, the following assessment was articulated and formulated to assist Jolene's family of in their attempt to find closure in knowing what may have happened regarding her disappearance.

This is a particularly difficult assignment because I have almost no information as to what Jolene did prior to her disappearance, other than walking to the hospital to visit her mother. We cannot intelligently discuss the timeline of Jolene's disappearance without talking about a few other missing persons and homicides that happened in the area during that time. Although serial killing is looked upon as somewhat rare, especially in this section of Pennsylvania, it is a possibility that must be examined.

12-7-78 Joanne Williams missing. She was 5 feet tall and weighed 95 pounds, which is important. Williams was last seen at her dance school in Chinchilla.

Williams left her residence in her red 1977 Datsun 200 SX with white racing stripes, in route to an exercise class. She was last seen at her dance school located on Route 6 at 10 p.m. Her vehicle was located on Dec. 16, 1978 at Lafayette Street and North Everett Avenue, West Scranton, unlocked with her purse and contents located in the vehicle.

8-26-86

12 p.m.   Jolene visits her mom in the hospital with sister

Rose.

3 p.m.   Jolene leaves hospital with Rose in route to Doreen Miller's home.

5:30 p.m.   Jolene leaves Doreen's home in route to her home.

-    Pennsylvania Power & Light Co. workers see Jolene at corner of Larch and North Washington St., less than one block from her home, and hear her say to the driver of a "yellowish" car something to the effect of, "I haven't seen you in a while."

-    Jolene is never seen by family again.

12-11-87   Laureen Finn, age 19, is murdered. The Elizabethtown, N.J., woman was last seen walking through Scranton's Hill Section after leaving a party in a student's apartment. Her badly burned body was found in an alley between two houses when neighbors who smelled something burning called in an alarm to Scranton firefighters. She, too, is of small to average build.

5-14-89   Renee Waddle, 9, is raped, beaten and murdered. A security guard for Pennsylvania Power & Light Co. saw a girl with long hair behind Frank's Auto and Truck Sales about 7:15 p.m. A newspaper account also said Frank Osellanie was having an affair with a woman and took her parking in the wooded area just off Pennsylvania Route 307, where the girl was found. Waddle, whose burning body was found about 11:30 p.m. on a private road in Roaring Brook Township near Lake Scranton. According to the state police's affidavit, Osellanie saw Renee Waddle walk past Frank's garage twice early this year and said he would like to engage in anal sex with the girl, according to a former employee, Scott Sebring. Osellanie told police he had never seen the child. Osellanie was charged in the murder after his wife, Cheryl, found a purple clam-shaped earring on the floor of his garage and turned it over to police, according to the affidavit. On the day of her murder, Renee Waddle was wearing purple, earrings she had received the previous day from her stepfather, police said. Renee died from blunt trauma to the head, was raped and had an earring ripped from her pierced lobe, the autopsy showed. Osellanie was held without bail in Lackawanna County Jail on the murder charges.

Osellanie was also accused of the sexual abuse of two girls in 1983.

Victimology

Victimology has many different meanings. Some will say victimology is the study of victimization, including the relationships between victims and offenders. I like to say that it is simply getting to know your victim, in every sense of the word. By knowing how the victim will react in a given circumstance, could lead you to the offender.

In this case the victim is Michelle Jolene Lakey, an 11-year-old female who went missing on Aug. 26, 1996, presumably around 5:30 p.m. By all accounts, Jolene was very happy. If faced with a fight or flight situation, she would fight though. This is important because it allows us to know what she will do when given a certain type of situation. She was raised by her mother, Louis Dunham, and was surrounded by three biological siblings:

1. Louis Lakey, age 14 at the time of the disappearance.
2. Justina, 13 at the time of the disappearance.
3. Israel Lakey, 12 at the time of the disappearance.

Also in the home were four stepchildren:

4. William Loney, 16 at the time of the disappearance.
5. Rose Loney, 13 at the time of the disappearance.
6. Berea Loney, 9 at the time of the disappearance.
7. Thomas Loney, 7 at the time of the disappearance.

In addition, there were several friends and boyfriends living in the home during the time of her disappearance:

8. Apache (nickname, real name unknown)
9. Buffalo (nickname, real name unknown)
10. Jerry Meade
11. Tommy Donovan
12. Dennis Donovan

Jolene liked to be different and would stand up for what she believed was right, even at her young age. She once called her stepfather a "perverted old coot" to his face. Although she was young in years, it appears she was forced to grow up rather quickly. She never wanted to upset her mother and would do things just to make her happy. She came from a broken home in which a sibling alleged that she was "encouraged" to date older guys. By dating, it is inferred that she was having sex with some of the guys who lived at the Dunham/Lakey home. Jolene also had an older teenaged boyfriend at the time of her disappearance, Larry Trygar.

Jolene was outgoing and a devoted animal lover. Jolene and her family were poor and oftentimes did not have a lot of food; therefore, she was a bit malnourished, which led to her being sickly. She had little to no contact with her biological father and hadn't seen him for a couple years, according to at least one account. Although she was described as very happy, she was prone to frequent violent outbursts, which could be the result of sexual molestation within her own home.

Her mother said Jolene was afraid of the dark. This isn't anything out of the ordinary for an 11-year old girl, yet it could offer some insight as to her making it home before dark.

So, what about Jolene's victimology helps us get closer to solving her mysterious disappearance? We can deduce a number of things from just Jolene's victimology alone.

1. She would speak to strangers, which leads to her vulnerability to be coaxed into a vehicle for a possible abduction. She was trusting. We can deduce this because of her outgoing nature and the fact she was often around older men introduced to her by her mother. She believed her mom would not do anything to hurt her.

2. She would/could be tempted into danger if an animal was used as a decoy or bait. This can be deduced from her admiration of animals. For instance, if someone approached her saying his or her dog was sick, would she go look at it; she would go.

3. She was trusting. Although it appears she would be very non-trusting if the allegations were fact that she was molested by a relative and was forced to have sex with the older men in her home, she didn't know that it was wrong or at least

frowned upon. To Jolene, it was normal—therefore she trusted adults, namely men.

Suspects

When determining suspects, we must account for individuals in Jolene's past and present who had means, motive and opportunity to perpetrate a crime against her.

Although almost anyone can be a suspect, we must start with the ones closest to Jolene and work our way out toward lesser-known associates and finally to strangers.

We can then use a process of elimination to deduce the likelihood that one of them committed this crime, if there was a crime. One of the obvious, surefire ways to eliminate a suspect is through an alibi. Yet, in this case, I have no documentation that anyone had an alibi. Therefore, the following individuals I believe should be considered suspects.

1. Frank Osellanie: Frank was a mechanic who lived near and operated a garage within walking distance from Jolene's home, at the very corner of the intersection where was last seen. He told original police investigating the case that he knew Jolene and would give her rides home. Osellanie was arrested with the sexual molestation of his two stepdaughters aged 7 and 8 at the time of the incident. Through reading his personal letters, I feel he is a classic example of a sociopath. Although I am not a psychologist, I know that he shows no remorse nor does he take responsibility for any of the murders he has been convicted of.

2. Stranger: A stranger abducting Jolene is obviously a possibility and has to be considered. Through my research, the only murdered missing girls from the Scranton area during this timeframe either knew their killer or had some sort of contact with them.

3. Live-in friends: This refers to the many men who were purported by a sibling of Jolene's to have lived in their home during this timeframe. These men, mainly recently released from jail, were invited by Jolene's mother to live in the home. The reason is unknown, but we can speculate that the men helped satisfy monetary needs by Louis Dunham in some

fashion or arrangement. In most missing persons or homicides, we must start with the individuals who have the easiest access to the victim. This list includes Buffalo, Apache, Jerry Meade, Tommy and Dennis Donovan. It is possible, if not probable, that these men at some point had sexual contact with Jolene. Individuals close to Jolene have hinted at this, but no actual proof exists. The allegations alone make them suspects in this disappearance, in my opinion.

4.   David Griffin: Jolene's uncle, who is alleged to have sexually molested all of the Lakey children. This fact alone makes him a suspect.

5.   Bob Douglas: Close friend of the family who allegedly had been in and out of mental hospitals. He is referred to as a pedophile by a sibling of Jolene's.

6.   Larry Trygar: He was alleged to have been Jolene's older boyfriend at the time of her disappearance. Because of his closeness to the victim, he has to be considered a suspect.

In all of my cold case homicides, I want to revisit the scene. It is paramount in order to understand everything that was taking place in that homicide. This is not relevant to this case because we do not have a crime scene.

Yet, if this were my case, it would be beneficial to walk the route Jolene would have taken the night of Aug. 26, 1986, just to get the feel for the area. I would pay particular close attention to street lights that were in place on that date as well as homes close to that intersection in which she was last seen.

There are only five possible scenarios in which could account for Jolene's disappearance: accidental death, suicide, homicide, abduction or voluntary walk away. Let's examine each in detail:

1.   Accidental death

This scenario is highly unlikely due to the fact she was last seen walking down a street in the city. If she were the victim of a hit and run, for instance, it most likely would be witnessed and her body recovered. This scenario has a bit more credibility if she went missing from a rural or secluded area, but that is not the case here. For that reason we can rule this out.

2.   Suicide

Of all the scenarios possible to explain her disappearance, this is the least likely. Although through victimology it has been alleged Jolene was "encouraged" to date and possibly even have sex with older men by her mother, she was not depressed about the situation. To the contrary, all accounts have her being a happy, normal acting pre-adolescent. I would rule this out.

3.   Homicide

When a person goes missing, homicide must be adequately investigated as a possible explanation. We know through victimology that Jolene was a moderately high-risk victim. By this, I mean her lifestyle and background made her a bit more susceptible to being a victim than others. An example of a high-risk victim would be a prostitute. An example of a low risk victim would be a priest, nun or a small child with a normal upbringing.

Jolene's involvement with a variety of men of all ages and with other "strange" men living in her home causes her to have an elevated risk of being a victim.

When determining if a homicide occurred, we must not only look at victimology, but we must know why. Because Jolene was surrounded by sex at such a young age, was probably molested by some of the men living in her house and would stand up for what she felt was right increased her likelihood that she became a homicide victim. Why would someone want Jolene dead? The most plausible reasons people commit homicide is for sex, revenge and greed.

a.   Sex

I believe Jolene's life was riddled with sexual abuse. There was a suggestion from a family member that she was possibly pregnant. Although there are no facts on which to base this idea, it confirms she was sexually active at such a young age. It is my belief that sex was the underlying motive in the disappearance of Jolene.

b.   Revenge

There is no indication that anyone had any revenge plotted against Jolene. It is possible, but certainly not probable that her birth father had a motive to kidnap her. I believe this can be ruled out as well.

c. Greed

The act of greed can take many forms. It can be the greed over financial proprieties, wanting what is not yours or the selfishness of taking what you don't need. In this case, money is not the root of this disappearance.

4. Voluntary walk away

Although this idea has to be investigated, it is not a likely scenario. There has been zero contact in 31 years. Jolene did not walk away voluntarily and this theory can be discounted.

5. Abduction

This is a very possible and most probable explanation. The reason for this is simple; she was last seen talking to someone in a "yellowish" car. Although I do not have any police documentation, this is information that was relayed from Jolene's mother and printed in the newspaper at the time.

Investigative Strategies

This is probably the most important section, yet maybe the most redundant. The reason for this is because I do not know what the jurisdicting law enforcement has done to properly investigate this case. Therefore, I can only speak on what I would do if I had full access to witnesses, reports, etc., and what I would do if I were investigating this case.

1. Continue to keep the case public. That is the only thing we can do in order to keep the pressure on the suspect. This not only allows for potential witnesses to come forward, but also lets the offender know we haven't forgotten about the crime.

2. Re-interview everyone within a block of that intersection in which she went missing. People want to tell someone what they saw, but are usually hesitant to come forward. However, if they are asked, they will talk.

3. Interview Osellanie's relatives and friends. Over time, relationships dissolve and loyalties wane; this is where a majority of cold cases get solved.

4. Determine who drives a yellowish car who Jolene *knew*. Not a stranger, but someone who was at least an acquaintance.

5.   Locate the PP&L workers who saw her talking to someone in the "yellowish" vehicle. Place an ad in the newspaper or on social media asking them to come forward.

6.   Get Jolene's medical records. I would do this just to determine what she was had been seen for. The pregnancy rumor could be confirmed or denied by this.

7.   I would like to know the vehicles that Osellanie had access to. He owned a garage, so he could have used any of the vehicles there that night to abduct Jolene. I am sure the police did this, but one must still check again.

8.   Go to the police immediately and ask if they know about Jolene being overheard saying to the driver of the "yellowish" car, "I haven't seen you for a while." To me, this is a huge lead that could change the course of this investigation and must be followed up on.

Conclusion

This is impossible to determine with any given certainty at this juncture in the investigation. There simply is not enough documentation available to me to ascertain conclusively, without question what happened to Jolene on Aug. 26, 1986. Yet, through the documents I have examined, victimology and my experience, I can tell you the most likely scenario.

I cannot overlook the fact that at least one young girl, Renee Waddle, age 9, was murdered within three years of Jolene's disappearance and lived in the same area. That murder was solved and the killer of this girl was without question Frank Osellanie.

In addition to Renee Waddle, Laureen Finn was murdered one year after Jolene went missing. The same type of fuel was used (Coleman) to burn both bodies, according to published accounts. That fuel, a typical cleaner used in garages, was linked to Osellanie's garage.

The probability, in my experience, tells me that Osellanie murdered Laureen in 1987 and Renee in 1989. He was convicted of these murders. Now that we have established Osellanie as the murderer of at least two young females, let's now talk about other probabilities that relate now to Jolene.

Osellanie knew Jolene, which established through the Lakey family and Osellanie's own admissions. Osellanie's garage was one block from her home at the very intersection from where she was last seen. It has been reported that Jolene, an animal lover, would pet Osellanie's dog in his garage on occasion. This coincides with her victimology, which acutely describes her as an animal lover.

In addition, it was determined through Jolene's mother that Frank had given her kids, including Jolene, rides home. This is a key fact because of the PP&L workers who heard Jolene say to someone in a yellowish car, "I haven't seen you in a while." According to Jolene's mother, this statement made sense because it was the summer and Jolene was not walking past his garage as much due to school being out.

When you don't have a lot to go on in an investigation, you will take any lead you can get. The fact that Jolene was seen talking to someone in a car and those were the words she spoke, to me, this is a huge lead. If these were, in fact, her words, I cannot overstate enough how important this lead is. This information should be taken to police immediately and at least brought to their attention so they can either confirm or deny that Jolene was overheard saying this.

Osellanie's garage was located at 417 Walnut St., which is located on the same block that Jolene was last seen on North Washington Avenue and Larch Street. We must take in consideration the time the disappearance took place as well, 5:30 p.m., when businesses are closing. It is probable that Osellanie was also closing and heading away from the business when he encountered Jolene at the intersection, only a block from her home at 1372 N. Washington. We must also take into consideration his past acts, which include the sexual assaults of his young stepdaughters. So, his proclivity is not just young smallish or petite girls, who may be his preferred, but it is sexual in nature, period.

Now, if we take all of these probabilities into account, we can deduce that the most logical and probable conclusion is that Osellanie abducted, raped and murdered Jolene on Aug. 26, 1986, and his reason for committing this murder was sexual in nature.

I would also surmise, based on his burning of the bodies of at least two other victims, he most likely did the same to Jolene's body. However, he allegedly stated to Trooper Carlson who investigated this case, "Why would I burn this one and the other one, if I buried the first two?" If this were, in fact, the incriminating statement Osellanie gave, it would indicate he buried Joanne Williams (1978) and Jolene (1986) and burned the bodies of Renee (1989) and Laureen (1987). Where he did this is the biggest question in my mind.

The murders of Renee and Laureen took place after Jolene's disappearance. Therefore, he had already gotten away with murder(s) and may have become sloppy or at least not panicked. This could be gleaned by evidence that he burned Renee's body in an area that was not secluded. Her body was found burning between two homes, as I understand it. That is very brazen and tells me he didn't plan. When a year passed since he murdered Jolene, he was a bit more confident that he got away with at least one murder and became somewhat more brazen in his murders of Laureen and Renee by leaving their bodies in non-secluded areas. I would hypothesize that he took Jolene's body to a secluded wooded area to dispose of it and not in the inner city of Scranton.

A prison inmate who met Osellanie said he told him, "They have me on the two burnings. But on the others, without the bodies, they have nothing." Now, you can take information from another inmate and toss it aside if you are inclined because of the source, but this statement just happens to coincide with Osellanie's statement to Trooper Carlson.

Foul play is a very possible and most likely explanation for the disappearance of Michelle Jolene Lakey, in my opinion. Yet, without more documentation or the ability to interview potential witnesses and suspects myself, I cannot conclude with 100 percent certainty what ultimately led to Jolene's disappearance. However, with what I have reviewed and from my experience with hundreds of cases like this, I would surmise that Jolene died on the day she went missing and was most likely murdered by Osellanie acting alone as a violent sexual predator.

If Jolene went missing due to the acts of her own family or a family friend, then why risk taking her from the street? The family Jolene came from was poor, peculiar and made some odd statements that certainly raise red flags. Yet, this does not ultimately make family members responsible or guilty for Jolene's disappearance. If Jolene got into a yellow car as has been documented, then who owned this car? It had to be someone she knew due to the statement she was to have allegedly made, "I haven't seen you in a while." Yet, she was observed by PP&L workers as getting into this car. Why? If someone involved with the family who was molesting her intended on harming to her, why not wait until she got home? Why pick her up one block from her home and risk being identified?

It makes more sense that Jolene got into a vehicle operated by someone she knew, but did not live with her, and that person took advantage of her trust and innocence.

Sometimes, there is no smoking gun. Sometimes, there is no body or evidence that a crime was even committed. However, when you take all the circumstantial evidence and all the possibilities and probabilities and tie them together, you have what is called the totality of circumstances. With everything added together, I think it is more probable than not—and even most likely—that Osellanie is singularly responsible for Jolene's disappearance.

Again, I want to emphasize that this is only my opinion as to what may have happened regarding the disappearance of Michelle Jolene Lakey. It is not a fact and should not be concluded as such. Yet I feel strongly about this assessment and the investigative strategizes I provided, which need to be followed up on—either by law enforcement or another investigative entity in order to solve this cold case. With the limited facts I was provided, this is the investigative opinion I have formulated.

Jolene Lakey

THERESA CORLEY

"Kenneth is a highly devoted investigator and has done a tremendous job in founding the AISOCC. His tenacity in finding forensic professionals to solve cold cases and bring order where chaos reigns deserves recognition. The skill set he possesses with networking, investigations, latent crime scenes and bridging the gap between investigative jurisdictions and the AISOCC has been an honor."

Anthony Meoli, MFP, J.D., DACFEI

I was contacted on Sept. 3, 2016, to assist on the homicide case of Theresa "Terry" Corley. I have been in regular contact since that time with Gerri Houde, Terry's sister, in order to determine facts surrounding this case and her homicide.

This case is unusually difficult because of the lack of information made available to me in form of police reports and other law enforcement documentation. In instances like this, as a reviewer you have no idea what evidence the investigating agency has, what was said during interviews or if any forensic analysis was attempted. In fact, the only information I used to complete this review were victimology and questionnaire forms filled out by the family as well as newspaper articles. In addition, I was able to read some hand-written, personal notes from Houde as well as documentation provided to me by Dr. Sarah Stein, a private investigator who has been assisting Houde with this case.

With the limited information I was provided, the following assessment was articulated and formulated to assist the family in their attempt to find closure in knowing what may have happened regarding Theresa Corley's homicide. Again, if I was privy to additional information that was not provided to me, my opinions could change.

In any homicide or missing person's case, we need to concentrate on the past month and pay particular attention to the last 24 to 48 hours of activity of that individual. In cold cases, it is very important to separate fact from fiction. As time goes by, rumors, conjecture, opinions and innuendos propagate, thus supplanting the most important aspect of the case and that is the facts.

Yet, this is a particularly difficult assignment because I have almost no information as to what Terry did prior to her disappearance other than what she did the night and early morning hours of her disappearance/murder. I am relying solely on interviews conducted by family members, Dr. Stein and newspaper articles.

As it relates to Terry's last-known movements from documented sources, the following timeline can be constructed: All times are approximate.

Dec. 4, 1978

- 3–7 p.m. – Terry works at Penthouse Sales and says she is

going to a party later in the evening.

(Source: Terry's mother in 1978 newspaper)

-   At some point before going to a bar, she is drinking at Jimmy Galvin's apartment.

(Source: Steve Ross interview, 3-25-15)

-   10:30 p.m. – Terry arrives at the Train Stop Bar to celebrate a friend's birthday.

(Source, Mike Ballard, 4-18-16)

-   11:30 p.m. – Terry departs Train Stop Bar after getting into argument with her boyfriend, Rick Cogliano.

(Many Documented Sources)

There is some discrepancy as to whether she hitchhikes or is given a ride from the bar, but she ultimately ends up at the Presidential Arms Apartment Building. In Dr. Stein's documentation, Terry is picked up by Ronnie Moore, Donnie Moore and Michael Millette in front of the Dairy Queen, 21 N. Main St. If this is the case, I do not know how she got from the Train Stop to the Dairy Queen. Other sources say she was given a ride with individuals named Cohn, Thornhill and Thibodeau to the Presidential Arms Apartments, 491 W. Central St., Franklin, Mass., where a party is taking place. It is my belief she got a ride by three male acquaintances who were either leaving the bar or already at the bar.

(Source: Mike Ballard, 4-18-16, and 7-14-02 newspaper)

December 5, 1978

-   4–4:30 a.m. – Terry leaves the Presidential Arms apartment. There is a discrepancy as to why she leaves. It is suggested she is angry that a possible sexual assault or sexual assault attempt occurred or for other unknown reasons. Regardless, Terry leaves the apartment with mismatched shoes (one male and one of her own). This could be because of her intoxication level, her haste to leave or simply because it was dark. I believe it was most likely a combination of all three. What occurs here during this approximately four hours is speculation.

(Source: Newspapers, 1979 and 2002)

- 4–5 a.m. – Terry is observed sitting on a guardrail on Route 140 and is picked up by Garelick Farms truck driver. He drives her to the entrance of his employer, 1199 W. Central St., Franklin.

(Source: 1997 newspaper)

- 5 a.m. – She gets a ride by a second Garelick Farms driver, who drops her off in front of the police station at the intersection of Route 140 and Route 126.

(Source: 2005 newspaper)

- 5:30 a.m. – Terry is observed by three men carpooling to work at the General Motors plant walking past the Dairy Queen toward Hartford Avenue. This is the last known sighting of Theresa Corley alive.

(Source: 1986 newspaper)

December 8, 1978

- 4:30 p.m. – A call is placed to police about a body being located. Caller identified himself as John Burlington from Connecticut. Theresa Corley's body is recovered in a gully off the northbound lane of Interstate 495.

Victimology

Victimology has many different meanings. Some will say victimology is the study of victimization, including the relationships between victims and offenders. I like to say that it is simply getting to know your victim, in every sense of the word. By knowing how the victim will react in a given circumstance, could lead you to the offender.

In this case, the victim is Theresa Corley, a 19-year-old white female who was last seen alive on Dec. 5, 1978, presumably around 5:30 a.m. By all accounts, Terry was very happy at this juncture in her life. If faced with a fight or flight situation, she would fight. This is important because it allows us to know what she will do when given a certain type of situation. She worked as an attendant at Penthouse Sales, and was attending Holliston Junior College. She had previously worked as a cashier at Star Market. She was raised by her mother. Her father has been described as an abusive alcoholic. Terry had eight biological siblings. From Dr. Stein's interviews, the following has been determined:

> *Theresa was a free spirit and very laid back. Ms. Houde indicated Theresa was not easily intimidated and was not fearful of falling victim to any type of violent crime. Further, Theresa's family once lived in a predominantly African American community in the Boston area and then moved to Bellingham as Theresa's parents felt it would be safer to raise children there. Given this fact, Ms. Houde mentioned that Terri perhaps had a "false sense of security" given that Bellingham is a small, rural town as compared to the area where the family used to live. Theresa's ultimate professional goal was to be a pediatrician, but she was enrolled at classes at Holliston Junior College at the time of her death to become a medical assistant. Theresa had only moved to Bellingham a couple years prior to her death and as such did not develop many significant friendships or intimate relationships.*

So, what about Terry's victimology helps us get closer to solving her murder? We can deduce a number of things from just Terry's victimology alone.

1. She would speak to strangers, which leads to her vulnerability to be coaxed into a vehicle for a possible abduction.

2. She was trusting. We can deduce this because of her outgoing nature and the fact she hitchhiked often.

3. She was tough. She believed nothing bad would happen to her, especially as it related to her walking and hitchhiking.

4. She was not a heavy drinker. She did smoke marijuana, but that was the extent of her drug use. Her small body frame, 5 feet 4 inches and 120 pounds, would have an effect on her intoxication level when drinking.

5. Her sexual history indicates two known partners. If this is true, an account of consensual sex while at the Presidential Arms with multiple partners can be called into question. However, it would confirm her intoxication level.

6. She was attractive, in good physical shape and walked a lot.

7. She may have been a victim of a past sexual assault by a neighbor.

8.   She had a good relationship with her family and her mother and would call home if in trouble.

In all of my cold case homicide reviews, I want to revisit the scene. It is paramount in order to understand everything that was taking place in that homicide. This is not relevant to this case because we do not have a crime scene—but we do have a body dump location.

We can tell a lot by where Terry's body was recovered. The location is along the northbound lane of Interstate 495, which is a busy major road. The exact location was approximately 25 to 35 feet down an embankment in a small gully. Therefore, she wasn't dumped out of a vehicle. She was dragged or carried to her final resting spot.

Suspects

When determining suspects, we must account for individuals in Terry's past and present who had means, motive and opportunity to perpetrate a crime against her.

Although almost anyone can be a suspect, we must start with the ones closest to Terry and work our way out toward lesser-known associates and finally to strangers.

We can then use a process of elimination to deduce the likelihood that one of them committed this crime. One of the obvious, surefire ways to eliminate a suspect is through an alibi. Yet, in this case, I have no documentation that anyone had an alibi. Therefore, the following individuals I believe should be considered suspects initially.

1.   David Cohn: According to an interview with Dr. Stein, David, who she believed was "being honest and forthright," was present at the Presidential Arms apartment with Terry. She went into his room to sleep. He admitted that John Kelly, Ronnie Moore, Donnie Moore and Steve Frechette went into that room and tried to assault Terry. Cohn claimed that no sexual assault took place and she ran out of the apartment. She was offered a ride home by Kelly and Cohn, but declined. Kelly left the apartment with Terry.

2.   Steve Frechette: Implicated by Cohn and former Massachusetts State Trooper Jim Redfern as trying to sexually assault Terry.

John Kelly told Redfern that Frechette was living in Medway at the time of the murder, left a few weeks later and was acting suspiciously. Toni Cook told Houde that Frechette came in their apartment and said he had been with Terry (had sex) when she was having an orgasm she scratched his face up. He stated it was his shoe she left with.

3. John Kelly: Implicated by Trooper Redfern as well. Implicated by Cohn as trying to sexually assault Terry and leaving the Presidential Arms apartment with her. Yet Terry is observed later on alone by two Garelick Farm truck drivers.

4. John Burlington: Identity used by the man who called the police to report finding a body. Burlington said when his car overheated, he pulled off the road and was urinating when he saw a body. He did not remain on scene and called when he got home, not utilizing 911 emergency system. Many believe that John Burlington is, in fact, Ronnie Moore.

5. Donnie Moore: Implicated by Cohn as trying to sexually assault Terry.

6. Ronnie Moore: There has been a lot made of Moore being involved in this murder. First and foremost, it was determined that he was present earlier in the evening at the Presidential Arms Apartment Complex, where there is speculation that Terry was sexually assaulted. Secondly, and more compelling, is that Moore found his way to the police station shortly after "John Burlington" placed a call to local law enforcement. Moore is implicated by one of the original police officers on the scene of the body recovery. Officer Haughey claims Moore was close to confessing on a couple of occasions.

7. Rick Cogliano: Terry's boyfriend. He had gotten into an argument with her earlier at the Train Stop Bar. It is believed that he was Terry's second sexual partner, according to victimology.

8. Karen Kosmenko: Rick Cogliano's girlfriend prior to Terry. Reportedly said she "had a dream something bad was going to happen to Terry that night." Terry left the Train Stop Bar because Cogliano was talking to Kosmenko. Kosmenko stated she would get physically ill when driving on Interstate

495 after Terry's murder.

9. John Toolin: Implicated by David Mancini as being present in a van with Terry when she was murdered. Mancini claims that Toolin once resided in Burlington, which is an obvious reference to "John Burlington," who placed the call to police after finding the body.

10. Tim "Jay" Hamelin: Implicated by Mancini as being present in a van with Terry when she was murdered. Mancini claims that Hamelin was suspected of other rapes near Bellingham at the time of Terry's murder. Implicated by Patrick Hammond and Mike Ballard. Ballard stated about two weeks after the murder, he observed Jay with scratches on his face. He stated that it was from female problems but then later changed that and said a cat scratched him.

11. Billy Heuklam: Implicated by Mancini as being present in a van with Terry when she was murdered.

12. Garelick truck driver no. 1: It is documented in newspaper articles he picked Terry up as she was resting on a guardrail on Route 140. He took her to the entrance of Garelick Farms, where he dropped her off. In 2015, he apparently told Houde he didn't even know Terry.

13. Garelick Farms truck driver no. 2: She told him that she was sexually assaulted. He also indicated she is intoxicated. He dropped her off in front of the Bellingham Police Station at the intersection of Route 140 and Route 126. He continued southbound after dropping Terry off.

14. Paul McIntyre: Was arrested in late 1981 for attempting to kidnap a 17-year-old girl in Bellingham who was hitchhiking on Mill Street, the same area Terry was last seen. He lived in Woonsocket, R.I., 8.8 miles from where she was last seen.

15. Stranger or unknown acquaintance: We must consider that because of the time of day, location of body and specific manner of death, that Terry was murdered by a stranger, lesser-known acquaintance or serial murderer.

Deducing Our Suspects

It is my opinion, based on my review, that the following people likely can be eliminated as suspects and most importantly, why I believe they can be eliminated:

1. David Cohn: Cohn answered questions posed to him by Sarah Stein rather accurately and truthful. He did not have to admit to an attempted sexual assault, but he did. It is my experience that generally, suspects will just deny. It is possible he is minimizing his involvement by admitting to a sexual assault attempt and not a homicide. However, it is my opinion he was being truthful. He did not offer any further questions to glean information from the investigation as if he were trying to determine what *we* know.

2. John Kelly: Former Trooper Redfern implicated Kelly as a major suspect, according to Houde. Cohn stated Kelly was one of the men trying to sexually assault Terry and he actually left the apartment with her. Yet, Terry is observed later on alone by two Garelick Farm truck drivers who gave her a ride. So, we can deduce that Kelly may have walked out the apartment with or behind Terry, but he did not follow her. Therefore, Kelly can be excluded as a suspect because if he wanted to kill Terry he could have done it right then and there. There would be no need to let her go, especially if a rape just occurred.

3. Rick Cogliano: As the current boyfriend who had argued with Terry that night, he had motive. Yet, because of where Terry's body was found and the condition and circumstances of her body, he can be eliminated as a suspect.

4. Karen Kosmenko: She had motive as Cogliano's former girlfriend and was the source of the argument at the bar. Yet, because of where Terry's body was found; how she was clothed or, in this case, lack of clothing; and how the victim was murdered, Kosmenko can be eliminated as a suspect in my opinion.

5. Billy Heuklam: I have seen nothing in the documents that I was provided that indicates his involvement other than rumors from one individual. He can be eliminated unless his background indicates he is a sexual sadist or predator who lived north of Bellingham. If either of those two conditions applies to him, he should be investigated further.

6. Garelick Farms truck driver no. 2: His story of dropping Terry off at the intersection of Route 140 and Route 126 as he continued south matches with him not driving her the remaining distance to her home. In addition, Terry was seen after he dropped her off.

Conclusion

This is impossible to determine with any given certainty at this juncture in the investigation. There simply is not enough documentation available to me to ascertain conclusively, without a doubt, what happened to Terry on Dec. 5, 1978. Yet, through the documents I have examined, victimology and my experience, I can tell you the most likely scenario.

My research has shown that there were nine murders during that timeframe (1977–1981) within 50 miles of where Terry was ultimately found. To my knowledge, these murders have not been solved, at least publicly. All of these victims share the same age and method of disappearance—they were hitchhiking or walking when the disappeared:

Karen L. Burton, 18

Vanessa Felder, 16

Mary Harvey, 13

Roxanne Robinson, 17

Lisa Arcudi, 17

Diane McKeller, 14

Diane Drake, 19

Mary L. Arruda, 15

Lisa Gail, 17

Michelle Kelly, 14

I cannot overlook the fact that these nine girls were murdered within a couple of years of Terry's murder and within very close proximity of each other. This is not including the unsolved murders that took place in the late 1980s of young women whose bodies were dumped off the highway in Bedford, Mass.:

Robin Rhodes, 28

Rochelle Clifford Dopierala, 28

Deborah McConnell, 25

Debra Medeiros, 30

Christine Monteiro, 19

Marilyn Roberts, 34

Nancy Paiva, 36

Deborah DeMello, 35

Mary Rose Santos, 26

Sandra Botelho, 24

Dawn Mendes, 25

If we include those unsolved murders, we have a total of 18 unsolved murders within 50 miles of where Terry was murdered. See the map at the end of the chapter for the distance between New Bedford and Bellingham.

Although I do not subscribe that all unsolved murders are the result of a serial murderer as some, it certainly needs to be investigated further in this case and area.

Victimology

We know through victimology that Terry was a moderately high-risk victim. By this, I mean her lifestyle and background made her a bit more susceptible to being a victim than others. This is mostly because of her age, physical appearance and especially her penchant for walking and hitchhiking. An example of a high-risk victim would be a prostitute. An example of a low risk victim would be a priest, nun or a small child with a normal upbringing.

When determining why a homicide might have occurred, we must again look at victimology. Because Terry may have been molested by her neighbor, according to her victimology, this could mean she would likely stand up for what she felt was right and fight back during any sort of attack against her. Although brave, this would increase her likelihood that she became a victim of a homicide. But why would someone want Terry dead? The most plausible reasons people commit homicides are for sex, revenge and greed.

a. Sex

Terry was found nude. Her clothing was beside her. This was a sexually motivated crime, without question. Because it was a sexually motivated crime, we can deduce and eliminate other suspects.

b. Revenge

There is no indication that anyone had any revenge plotted against Terry. It is possible that the individuals from the Presidential Arms apartment may have had reason to silence Terry if, in fact, a sexual assault occurred. However given the time of day that this took place, I find this unlikely.

c. Greed

The act of greed can take many forms. It can be the greed over financial proprieties, wanting what is not yours or the selfishness of taking what you don't need. In this case, money is not the root of this homicide.

Scenarios

I believe there are only two scenarios that would explain Terry's death: the incident at the Presidential Arms apartment and the hitchhiking/walking home aspect of the case. I will explore both scenarios.

Scenario 1: Presidential Arms

I believe, as most do, this is a likely scenario on why she died. I base this on two factors:

- Terry told Garelick truck driver no. 2 that she was sexually assaulted. He dropped her off in front of the police station. If she was sexually assaulted while at the Presidential Arms apartment building, there is the possibility the offenders wanted to silence her from reporting the crime.

- The many rumors from individuals at the party pointing the finger at each other, according to Officer James Haughey. Is it possible that when Terry left the apartment, a few of those guys went to look for her? This is a possibility and if this is the case, Frechette, Ronnie Moore and Hamlin would be the main suspects in her murder. In my opinion, Frechette and Hamelin first and foremost because of the indication they both had scratches on their faces. This is a very specific implication that I am sure is or should be easily determined in the police reports. If this is true, they will be the main suspects in this murder because we know through victimology Terry would scratch when she got into a physical altercation. However, I have investigated many cases where the scratches were from a completely different time period and the information gets lumped in with the timeframe when it actually occurred before or after the murders and is not even connected.

Nevertheless, we need to look at the Presidential Arms scenario a bit more in depth. Why was Terry there to begin with? She arrived at that apartment already intoxicated—some say highly intoxicated. She went to the apartment with at least three men. We do not know what she did while she was at the apartment other than she went to sleep in Cohn's bedroom. At some point, several men entered the bedroom. What happened in this bedroom is a mystery. Cohn stated that Kelly, Donnie Moore, Ronnie Moore and Frechette went in to sexual assault her, but no assault actually occurred as she ran out of the apartment. Others, James Schoener in particular, say she was having consensual sex with multiple guys the night she died. This goes completely against her victimology. Yet, with alcohol being brought into the mix and her intoxication level, it must be considered. Still yet, according to Houde, investigators said Terry was held down while the men tried to have sex with her. Investigators were told the man "didn't finish" or ejaculate. Later, the investigator denied saying this. In addition, a prosecutor at the district attorney's office stated it was more consistent with a "date rape" scenario then a sexual assault/ rape. In 1978, there wasn't such thing as date rape.

One aspect of Terry's time at this apartment is paramount: the amount of time she spent there. Terry was at this apartment for *four hours*. Terry was not there against her will. She was there voluntarily. If the men from the Presidential Arms Apartment Complex murdered Terry, then why risk abducting her from the street during close to daylight hours during a weekday when people were going to work? I think it is more likely than not that any sexual contact at the apartment complex was consensual to an extent. By this, I mean she may have had a consensual sexual encounter or flirted heavily with one person when others decided to try to join in because of her intoxication level. She had been drinking for at least six hours at this point. The reason I think this has to be considered is because if Terry was raped, why didn't she go to the police station since she was dropped off there? Why, at the very least, didn't she go home to take a shower as many rape victims do? Why didn't she call her mom or older siblings, who she loved and trusted? She had the means and opportunity to report this alleged crime, but she chose not to. This is very significant. It is very possible that she was embarrassed about the whole situation and did not want to report it to anyone.

Scenario 2: Hitchhiking/Walking Home

Very simply stated, this is where she is picked up by an acquaintance or stranger and murdered before daylight on Dec. 5, 1978. It is my opinion this is the most likely scenario. Now, through the art of deduction, we can see the suspect start to show himself to us.

Remaining Suspects

1. John Burlington: Is it possible he was telling the truth? Some say he did not call 911, which was unusual, and that he didn't wait on scene until police arrived. Instead, he called the local police department. In 1979, only 26 percent of the population of the United States had 911 services. So calling 911 was not that common. The caller couldn't have waited on scene; remember, there were no cell phones in 1978. He called when he got home or another location. I do not find this suspicious at all.

Look at the picture of where Terry was found. The end of the guard rail would be the most logical area for someone to pull over when a car was overheating, as he stated, and then to urinate just as the killer pulled in the exact area to dispose of Terry's body. Ronnie Moore showed up at the police station after the call came in that they found a body. This was deemed as suspicious since the call did not go out over the scanner. Yet, Moore's stepfather, Det. Mel Arcand, worked,, ,wpworke at the police department. He would have been informed of the body location and discovery. It would be big news that a body was found. I am sure after the call came in to the police dispatcher, within 30 minutes, many people knew a body had been found. Couldn't it be as simple as the stepfather being informed about the body while working and then, in turn, telling his stepson about the discovery? With that said, I cannot completely rule out Burlington as a suspect.

2. Ronnie Moore: If Ronnie Moore were responsible, what would be his reasoning for getting up on the interstate with a dead person in his vehicle? That makes zero sense. Moore was very familiar with the area. His family owned various businesses and properties in the area. If he murdered Terry as most surmise, it is my opinion he would have found a less traveled and secluded area to dispose of the body. He also would not have kept her clothing as a souvenir, as some of Terry's clothing was missing. From what I have reviewed, Moore can be eliminated as a suspect.

3. Truck driver: Truck drivers frequented Marie's restaurant and travelled Interstate 495 routinely in 1978. I strongly suggest that this possibility be investigated further as it remains the most likely scenerio to who committed this crime. If John Burlington was being deceptive about his true identity and he was responsible for the crime, I would suggest he is a truck driver from Connecticut who was passing through Bellingham. The following is from the FBI's Highway Serial Killings initiative.

In 2004, an analyst from the Oklahoma Bureau of Investigation detected a crime pattern: the bodies of murdered women were being dumped along the Interstate 40 corridor in Oklahoma, Texas, Arkansas, and Mississippi. The analyst and a police colleague from the Grapevine, Texas Police Department referred these cases to our Violent Criminal Apprehension Program, or ViCAP, where our analysts looked at other records in our database to see if there were similar patterns of highway killings elsewhere. Turns out there were. So we launched an extensive effort to support our state and local partners with open investigations into highway murders. They're frequently picked up at truck stops or service stations and sexually assaulted, murdered, and dumped along a highway. The suspects are predominantly long-haul truck drivers. ViCAP analysts have created a national matrix of more than 500 murder victims from along or near highways, as well as a list of some 200 potential suspects. Names of suspects—contributed by law enforcement agencies—are examined by analysts who develop timelines using a variety of reliable sources of information.

4.   Garelick truck driver no. 1 – He had already picked Terry up and given her a ride to his employer's entrance. It is plausible he picked her up again as she was walking on Route 126, depending upon where his next delivery took him or if he was ending his shift. She had already gotten one ride with him, so she wouldn't hesitate to get in with him again. It is also suspicious that Terry did not alert him that she was sexually assaulted, but did the other truck driver. Maybe she did and we do not know about it or it wasn't reported. All of this should be easily determined by his trucking records and interview he did with the police.

5.   Visitor to Bellingham: Someone from out of town staying at a hotel or with a friends or relatives and has a history of sexual assaults. Someone, who for some reason, was awake early on Dec. 5, 1978 and most likely lived north of Bellingham.

Quaaludes and Eggs

One of the most important and mysterious factors in this crime is the purported contents of Terry's stomach at her death. Although I do not have the autopsy report to review as it was not available to Terry's family or me, the memories of three of Terry's siblings indicate she had eggs and Quaaludes in her stomach at autopsy. They recall reading the autopsy report at some point in time and have recollections of their mother talking about this. This is hugely significant; not only the drug use, which was not in character for Terry, but also the undigested eggs. After you eat, it takes approximately six to eight hours for food to pass through your stomach and small intestine. Food then enters your large intestine (colon) for further digestion, absorption of water and, finally, elimination of undigested food. That would mean Terry either ate eggs while at the Presidential Arms apartment, possibly the Train Stop Bar or another location altogether. Unless she was held against her will for two days (possible, but not likely), we can narrow down when she ate these eggs.

She had to have eaten the eggs between 10 p.m. Dec. 4 and 5:30 a.m. Dec. 5, the last known sighting of her. We can eliminate Terry eating eggs at the bar. That leaves eating the eggs at the Presidential Arms apartment while she was there between midnight and 4 a.m. I think this is highly doubtful, but could be confirmed by interviewing the partygoers. That leaves her eating eggs sometime between 4 a.m. and 5:30 a.m. It is my belief it was closer to 5 a.m. after being dropped off right in front of Maria's restaurant that opened its doors at 5 a.m.

What Happened

Terry's night started out drinking at a friend's apartment. She ended up going to the Train Stop Bar with her friends and boyfriend. She continued to drink and it does not take her long to get intoxicated. She isn't a big drinker and her physical size enhances her intoxication level. Terry gets angry and jealous when she sees her boyfriend, Cogliano, talking to his ex-girlfriend, Kosmenko. By all accounts, Terry storms off angry. While leaving the bar, she is observed by men who invite her to a party. Terry is intoxicated, pretty and those guys knew it. I believe Terry was familiar with at least one of them, maybe not very well, but she knew someone enough to accompany them to the party at the Presidential Arms apartment. I do not believe she would have gone there with complete strangers. She accepts because as she said to her boyfriend, "I'll show you."

While at the Presidential Arms apartment, she drinks more alcohol. She may have voluntarily taken Quaaludes because of her intoxication level or they were given to her without her knowledge. The intoxication, time of night and Quaaludes have an effect on her body and she is tired. She went to lie down in the bedroom. Whether she went in that bedroom to have consensual sex or to sleep is unknown. Yet, she is in the bedroom and she takes off her shoes. Terry may have kissed or flirted heavily with one of the men while she was at the party, which enhanced every guy's perception that she could be an easy person to sleep with. It is possible she was interested in one of the guys and because of her intoxication level, did have consensual sex with a male.

Regardless of what took place, she eventually went into the bedroom and more than one man went in that room after her at some point. They went in the room to attempt to have sex with Terry. She rebuffed them and became angry. She storms out of the apartment and in her haste, intoxication and drowsy stupor, takes her shoe and a man's shoe and leaves. According to Cohn, she was asked if she wanted a ride home and refused. This is not something someone asks a victim of a violent sexual assault. I don't know if I would exactly agree with the assistant district attorney who equated it to "date rape" versus a sexual assault, because we do not know what happened in that bedroom. In no way am I condoning either form; it is still rape. I believe Terry said "no" at a certain point in the encounter and those guys continued. To what extent, we may never know. According to investigators, Cohn stated they did not "finish" or ejaculate. This is still rape. Yet, as coincidental it may seem—I do not believe it contributed to Terry's death.

Terry begins to walk and/or hitchhike, which she is very accustomed to do. At some point on Route 40, she sits down on a guardrail. She is picked up by a Garelick truck driver who takes her to the entrance the business, which is 2.3 miles from a police station. At the entrance of Garelick Farms, another truck driver picks her up. She tells this driver she was sexual assaulted. He describes her as cold, tired and intoxicated. At around 5 a.m., he drives her to the front of the police station. Next door was Maria's restaurant.

According to Sue Deslauries, who waitressed the restaurant in 1978, they opened at 5 a.m. and it was frequented "a lot" by truck drivers. **If** Terry was found with eggs in her stomach, which Terry's siblings remembered from reading the autopsy report, I surmise she went into Marie's to eat. This is a big assumption and I believe police would/should have considered this. Terry has the opportunity to use the phone here to inform someone about the sexual assault. She doesn't do that, which leads me to believe she was not truly sexually assaulted in her mind but was taken advantage of by young men because of her choices due to her intoxication level. Again, this by *no means* condones what happened to Terry at the Presidential Arms apartment by those men, but it goes to Terry's state of mind. She leaves the restaurant after eating eggs and is seen walking the half-mile from her home at 5:30 a.m. by three men carpooling to the General Motors plant in Framingham.

It is my professional opinion that someone at that restaurant or in the vicinity of that restaurant locked in on her and followed her. The offender may have offered her a ride home, even though she was very close already, and she may have accepted because it was very cold out. She may have declined the ride and was forced in a vehicle. I do believe it was someone she knew as only a general acquaintance or it was a complete stranger. It was not someone close to her. It may have been a co-worker at Penthouse Sales. I say this because of the ligature being thin and Penthouse Sales manufacturing plastic rope. This is consistent with the description of the wound on Terry's neck.

Her body was found off a major interstate heading out of town. There is *absolutely no reason* for someone to dispose of her body on the side of the interstate except that they were heading out of the town of Bellingham. I cannot emphasize this fact enough. If someone who lived in Bellingham abducted her, they would continue on Route 126 or one of the many other small desolate roads to dispose of her body. This is why I believe it was most likely a truck driver whose vehicle would look suspicious driving around unfamiliar desolate roads yet look very normal pulled alongside a major interstate.

From where she was last seen to where she was found, there are many wooded areas and paths. Someone from that area—or familiar with that area such as Ronnie Moore—would not discard her body along Interstate 495 as it was rapidly approaching daylight and risk being caught. This was a weekday; people are going to work. There is a lot of traffic starting to build on 495 as daylight approached. The only person who would risk that is someone heading out of town and/or was not familiar with the area. In addition, look at the newspaper article picture where she was found once again and compare that to the satellite map of the area. It will confirm that the guardrail ends right in the spot she was found. This is significant because it shows that whoever disposed of the body did it at the first available area on that interstate.

Ligature strangulation is not the most common form of murder. However, it is a common form for a sexual sadist or sexual predator. A ligature can also be a weapon of sheer opportunity as well. Yet, how many small, thin items can be used as a ligature that may be lying around someone's vehicle? It was reported that she had small thin line around her neck. This is not consistent with a belt, so that can be ruled out. Her own bra or pantyhose, which are used a lot by offenders, can be ruled out as it is reported she did not wear either. A shoelace is a possibility as well, but it would take time to take a shoelace out of the shoe to use it—unless it was already removed. Other than that, there are not too many weapons of opportunity that match this wound description. Therefore, it is more likely the ligature was made ahead of time for the distinct purpose to kill or incapacitate, which is common for a sexual sadist or experienced sexual predator.

Terry's body itself, being in the position it was in and absent of clothing tells us that this was a sexual crime without a doubt. There is no reason to remove her clothing if this wasn't a sexual crime—unless it was to destroy evidence, which is not the case as some of the clothes are discarded near her. The clothing that was discarded beside her tells us something as well. It means the offender did not want to increase his chances of getting caught, therefore, he disposed of her clothing at the same time he disposed of her body. However, it is what is not recovered that tells us the most. According to reports, only her jacket and pants were found next to the body. Where are her panties? Her shoes? Her socks?

According to the FBI's Behavioral Assessment Unit's publication "Serial Murder, Pathways for Investigations," 54 percent of serial killers removed *multiple items* from the victim's body and 48.5 percent of the time, they took the victim's shoes and other items of clothing.

It is my belief that Terry was not murdered by someone she knew intimately. It is possibly the offender was an acquaintance, but more than likely, it was a stranger who murdered her.

It was brought to my attention that some individuals with an interest in this case believe this homicide is not solved because of a police cover-up. When asked about this possibility, Officer James Haughey, who was first on scene of the body discovery, stated former Det. Arcand would never cover up this crime for his stepson, Ronnie Moore. I agree that there is no cover-up involving police. Although a former police officer indicated that corruption is rampant within the police department, there is no indication it is true as it relates to this particular case.

In my opinion investigators investigated this case appropriately for the time, from what I have seen. It appears that the re-opening of the case subsequently was done appropriately as well and with the best intentions. An assertion that a flood destroyed crucial evidence and subsequent fire is something I cannot answer. I have to believe that as sworn law enforcement officers, they are telling the truth and it is not a case that the department is embarrassed by lost evidence due to incompetence or oversight. In order to have a cover-up, there has to be specific intent and there would have to be a conspiracy between a myriad sworn law enforcement officers and officials. I do not believe at all that this is the case here.

Conclusion

Terry Corley was murdered by a complete stranger or at the very least a very casual acquaintance (possibly co-worker) who most likely was frequenting Maria's restaurant in the early morning hours of Dec. 5, 1978. The offender acted alone. I cannot determine the race of the offender because Terry grew up around African-Americans before moving to Bellingham according to her victimology. Therefore, she was not "afraid" of black individuals and would not be concerned to get in a vehicle with an African-American male at that time of the morning.

Although in 2010, the population of Bellingham was 91 percent white with only 1 percent being African-American, in 1978, the diversion of race was the same if not even more. That does not take in consideration that an African-American male truck driver or guest was passing through Bellingham that morning. Therefore, I cannot make a determination as to race of the offender and guessing as to this would be foolish. Regardless race, the offender may have offered her a ride at the restaurant and she refused or he simply saw her at the restaurant and because she was cold, tired, good-looking and intoxicated, locked in on Terry as a potential victim.

She would have started to walk home from the restaurant where the offender forced her in to his vehicle or used a ruse to get her in his vehicle. The situation quickly escalated when he drove Terry past her house at 145 N. Main St. to a semi-secluded area—not the interstate. This may have been a parking lot of a business. Dawn broke at 5:19 that morning, so daylight was rapidly approaching. The sun rose at 6:59 a.m. and before that happened, Terry was already raped, murdered and dumped. He raped her in a vehicle before strangling her with a thin ligature. He then started his drive out of town, stopping to dump her body at the first available area of Interstate 495 where he could pull off the road as far as possible. The offender dragged or carried Terry's body down the embankment about 25 feet from the interstate. He returned to the vehicle, retrieved her jacket and pants and discarded them near her body. The offender kept her panties, shoes, socks and shirt or some variation of these as souvenirs. The reason he keeps these items is for sexual gratification. When he sees and touches these items, he can relive that sexual gratification he felt when he raped and murdered Terry. The offender, after dumping Terry's body and clothing, leaves the area, driving north on 495 to his home or his next work assignment.

Without more documentation or the ability to interview potential witnesses and suspects myself, I cannot conclude with 100 percent certainty what ultimately led to Terry's death or who was responsible. However, with what I have reviewed and from my experience with hundreds of cases like this, I would surmise that Terry died very close to 6–6:30 a.m. on Dec. 5, 1978. She was most likely murdered by a male acting alone as a violent sexual predator, possibly being a truck driver.

Sometimes there is no smoking gun. Sometimes there is no body or evidence that a crime was even committed. However, when you take all the circumstantial evidence and all the possibilities and probabilities and tie them together you have what is called the totality of circumstances. With all everything added together, I think it is more probable than not, and even most likely, that a stranger who either saw her at Maria's restaurant or gave her a ride from that area raped and murdered Terry Corley.

Investigative Strategies

This is probably the most important section, yet maybe the most redundant. The reason for this is because I do not know what the jurisdicting law enforcement has done to properly investigate this case. Therefore, I can only speak on what I would do if I had full access to witnesses, reports, etc. and what I would do if I were investigating this case.

1. Continue to keep the case public. That is the only thing we can do in order to keep the pressure on the suspect. This not only allows for potential witnesses to come forward, but also lets the offender know we haven't forgotten about the crime.

2. Re-interview everyone within a block of that police station. People want to tell someone what they saw, but are usually hesitant to come forward. However, if they are asked, they will talk.

3. Interview relatives and friends. Over time, relationships dissolve and loyalties wane. This is where a majority of cold cases get solved.

4. Locate suspects who lived or worked north of Bellingham.

5. Interview everyone who frequented Maria's restaurant. Place an ad in a newspaper or on social media asking for them to come forward. Particular attention should be made to determine if she was there or if any truck drivers stood out to them.

6. Officer Haughey was first on scene to the body discovery. He stated that Terry was "displayed in a spread eagle fashion, face up and naked." This information was given to Dr. Stein on Jan. 25, 2016. If this is true, and she was "displayed," John Burlington moves up the list of potential suspects. It needs to be determined if she was truly "displayed." On Aug. 9, 2015, Officer Haughey told Houde when he found the body, her "head was facing downward below her feet and "I swear she had her clothes on." On Oct. 5, 2016, he stated it looked as if she was dragged to the location by her arms as they were straight out over her head and she was clothed. Because of these contradicting statements, I do not believe we can truly rely on Officer Haughey's memory at all. His information, unless corroborated, should be discarded.

7. Confirm where Frechette was living. Kelly told Trooper

Redfern that Frechette was living in Medway at the time of the murder and left a few weeks later. Medway is north of the body location and it is my belief that whoever did this was traveling out of town, or at least going north.

8. Examine vaginal smears and any other evidence. If evidence is available, my organization, the American Investigative Society of Cold Cases, would test these items pro mono.

9. Locate companies whose truck drivers traveled 495 regularly. The offender may have been unemployed, on a day off or working third shift. This can be deduced that he was awake at 5:30 a.m. on a weekday. It is not an absolute, put a possibility.

10. Identify any truck drivers who were serial killers on the East Coast. I would surmise this was not his first or last killing. I say that because of the amount of time that this assault and murder took place—within an hour, most likely—and the fact a ligature was used. It is not common for serial murders to start out with ligature strangulation in the research I have done. It is possible, but the totality of everything (time of day, ligature, nude body, location) leads me to believe the person killed before this and most likely after this.

11. Research people who frequented Maria's restaurant and may have been arrested for other crimes such as being a "peeping tom" and committing lewd acts or other sexual assaults within major cities near Bellingham.

12. Re-interview Toni Cook and determine exactly when she saw Frechette and heard him say he had sex with Terry and she scratched him. This whole interaction needs to be fully explored and timeframe narrowed down.

13. Look to establish case linkage between the Bedford Murders or any other of the unsolved murders of the females I mentioned earlier. If any of those cases were solved, the offender needs to be interviewed and asked about Terry's murder.

14. Look at Paul McIntyre as a suspect. McIntyre was

arrested in 1981 for attempting to kidnap a 17-year-old girl in Bellingham who was hitchhiking. This occurred on Mill Street, the same area Terry was last seen. He lived in Woonsocket, R.I., 8.8 miles away from where she was last seen.

Again, I want to emphasize that this is only my opinion as to what may have happened regarding the homicide of Theresa Corley. It is not a fact and should not be concluded as such. I am sure some of this assessment can be confirmed or refuted by the investigating police agency that is familiar with the case. Yet, I feel strongly about this assessment and the investigative strategizes I provided based upon the limited information I was provided, which needs to be followed up on, either by law enforcement or another investigative entity in order to solve this cold case. With the limited facts I was provided, this is the investigative opinion I have formulated.

Theresa Corley

Recovering Corley's body

Notice the end of the guardrail

Map of other unsolved murders possibly related to Corley

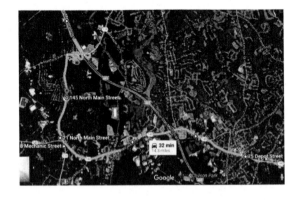

Corley's route night of her murder

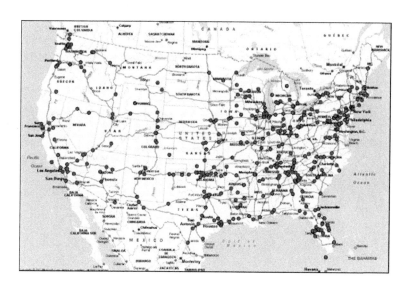

This map shows the more than 500 cases in our Highway Serial Killings Initiative database; the red dots mark where bodies or remains have been found along highways over the past 30 years.

CONCLUSION

"Forgive your enemies, but never forget their names."

John F. Kennedy

During my decade and then some of investigations, I have concluded one undeniable fact: you never know what people do behind closed doors! You can look a murderer in his face, shake his hand and never know that very hand was wrapped around the neck of a victim, choking the life from their very soul only minutes before.

As an investigator, you must be thorough and meticulous with every aspect of the investigations. You cannot allow outside influences distract or sway you from obtaining the truth. It is an ugly world when you look at it through the eyes of a detective. You see the worse in humanity. Yet, progressing through life, you come to slow down and accept this fact. You slow down in order to forget about the ugliness in people and look for the beauty.

The older I become, the more I enjoy life and its subtle beauties. I take enjoyment in getting up in the morning and wondering who I can inspire today or what case I can make an impact on. To me, that is what life is about, the small things. Helping others, listening to others and assisting others. Making a difference in a 10-year-old boy's life by giving him a badge or making a 55-year-old women smile because you held a door for her—that is life.

I am fortunate enough to be in a position to help others, so that is what I choose to do. Kindness is about character—integrity, honesty, thoughtfulness, generosity, moral courage and the like. More than anything else, it is about how we treat other people. I remember speaking with award-winning documentary filmmaker Joe Berlinger ("Metallica: Some Kind of Monster," "Brother's Keeper" and the "Paradise Lost" documentaries) about an upcoming television show he was producing. He had me look at several cases in which he believed there was a potential for the convicted person to be innocent. Because there was a potential, of course I looked at them. I specifically remember telling him, "Everyone in prison has a story. It's just my job to figure out whose story is the truth."

In truth, we can acknowledge our weaknesses and failures. I will always look at my failures before successes, because through those failures, comes change. I failed Dawn Miller because I never found her remains. I failed Gail Matthews because her killer still walks the same streets I do. I failed Tamara Berkheiser because her killer is allowed to see his own daughters grow up and she never will. I failed because their killers were never brought to justice under my watch. No matter how hard I tried to locate Dawn's remains, I couldn't. No matter how hard I tried to bring Gail and Tamara's killer to their day in court, I couldn't. These are failures. Rest assured though, I am still trying and will continue to try until I die.

Through those failures, I learned to succeed. Through those failures, I succeeded where it matters most—in life. The raising of my young daughter is done, with the experiences of my son's struggles a constant memory. I write this with a still-grieving heart. I am an intensely private person by nature. I rarely share emotions and I never show weakness. That is how I was raised and it is ingrained into my DNA to be this way. I am a leader and never a follower. I am a fighter for victims who have been silenced and I am a fighter in life. Yet, when something tragic takes a stranglehold on you in life, you try to fight just to cope.

In addition to coping, you wonder what life is about. Why are we here on this Earth and is there a God? Philosophical questions run amuck. Yet, I continue to believe. I believe in something greater and I believe in myself. I believe that man is basically good and righteous. You see, the older I get, the more things become clearer and take on a whole different meaning. No longer is an image or reputation important as it once ruled my space. No longer is it about me.

As you age and become mature, you become sentimental; you become more of a thinker, for lack of a better term. You philosophize about ideology and seek wisdom. You want your children to grow up better than you did and you live every day to see them smile. There is no greater joy in the world than to see a child laugh and smile.

I want other parents who have lost a child to know there is someone else who feels like they do. I don't want sympathy and I am not looking for applause. I want other parents to know that you didn't fail, although I know you believe you did. I know that no one will ever convince you otherwise and that is OK. But it is how you move on from that perceived failure that is important.

This is a father baring his soul, which is an extremely hard thing for me to do because that is not me. I should have seen it coming, but I didn't. I was blinded by optimism. My son never got a chance to grow up and that is what troubles me the most. All those life lessons, all that punishment to make him a better person when he was grown up—all for naught. That is the damnedest misery of it all.

I got the call on a chilly November night in 2013. "Erick is dead," were the words I heard on the other line. "What?" I said, although there was no mistaking what she had said. She repeated those horrible words again hysterically. I dropped the phone. It is a phone call no one ever wants and I pray no one ever gets. I wouldn't wish it upon my worst enemy. I hadn't talked to my son in almost a year prior to that call. Previous to this, we were inseparable. He was my buddy. He was my boy.

I will keep moving forward. I will continue to remember the very last time I actually saw my boy. Christmas 2012. He was wearing a light blue plaid shirt and ball cap. He had his son with him. He was skinnier than normal and I was hoping it was from exercise, but I knew better. Before he walked out the door, I gave him a hug and said, "I love you." He was taller than I am; he has always been taller. My head rested momentarily on his chest. As I breathed in, I caught his scent. I smelled it again after he had died. I smelled it in his room when I laid and cried on his bed, holding his sweatshirt.

So what can parents do to keep their kids on the right path? If I had that answer, my son would still be alive. That's the reality of it. I will forever miss my boy. I will forever miss his soft-spoken voice and coy smile. He was taken away from me way too early, just like millions of others. I cannot ever get him back and that is a hard pill to swallow. Yet his death made me a man. Everything I tried teaching him, he ended up teaching me. I was trying his whole life to make him a man. He made me one. How, you ask? Let me tell everyone who has never gone through something like this. Planning a funeral and delivering a eulogy for a dead child was by far the hardest thing I ever had to do in my entire life. No matter how tough, how hardened or how determined you are not to be affected, you will crumble. It will bring you to your knees and you will be flooded with emotions. That is how my son made me a man! I have memories of him flooding through my mind in rapid succession. Like snapshots flickering on a movie screen. Visions of him with his cousins, sled riding and singing. Visions of him sleeping in my tree stand asking me if he could go back to the car because he hadn't seen any deer and he was cold. All of these crazy, uncontrollable emotions. The love, hate, remorse, regret and numeous all other emotions are flooding into your body all at once. Dealing with these emotions was harder than Marine Corps boot camp; it was harder than the police academy; and it was harder than any physical fitness test I ever had to take. It will absolutely cripple you momentarily until you realize you have to carry on—somehow.

See, in the end, his death taught me. It taught me that life isn't about lessons . It is to live and love your family and friends every single minute of every single goddamn day! That is what I would tell parents. Love your kids; love and hug them every goddamn day!

My son was a great kid. He had an infectious personality and smile that brought joy to my life every single day. That smile lives on forever—in my memory and everyone else's memory who had the privilege of knowing him. Yet my very last image of my son, Erick Stephen Mains, is in a coffin, looking asleep, just as I had observed him for 21 years. Please don't let this be the last image of your child.

Learn from my mistakes. Talking to your kids is not enough. Be *more* involved in their lives. Know their friends. Know their inner demons. Know every single inch about your children. Take that extra minute to hug them and tell them how much they mean to you—because you never know when the last time will come. People will say, "There is always tomorrow," and "It can't happen to me." Trust me. I said both those things and now I have to live with that regret.

So what would I say to him today? The same thing I say almost every single night in my own head to him. I am sorry for not doing enough. I am sorry for not being there enough. I'm sorry I was too tough. I am just sorry! But please remember, I will forever love you, my beautiful baby boy. Yet as Ronnie Van Zant of Lynyrd Skynyrd bellowed, "Somehow, I've got to carry on ..."

Investigating other cold cases and knowing what to do and what not to do because of my life experiences is a lesson learned that helps me in investigating cold cases. It all works out in the end because that is the way life is. My failures will bring success where it matters the most—in life. Regardless of successes and failures, rights and wrongs or justs and unjusts, one thing remains constant: I can look myself in the mirror every single morning, knowing I am a good man. That, my friends, is called integrity and that is what life is all about. Life is also about taking everything that molded you and making it work for you. That is because all the hardships, the mistakes, the failures, the life lessons and the entire experiences that shaped me during my life plays a role in how I solve cold cases. That is why I don't give up. It is why I care about the victims and their family and friends. That is the reason I have been called one of the greatest cold case investigators in this country. That is why I succeed! That is why I am the best!

For the most part, I just want to be left alone. In the mountains, living a simple life with my family and doing some farming. I don't like the spotlight or the adulations. I just want to help law enforcement and victims' families solve their nightmares without creating a hardship for anyone. Yet, sometimes I notice if I get pressed, pushed, or thrown a cheap shot—I fire back with a vigorous fury. That's who I am. I approach my cases in the same manner—simple but with a violent wrath. That is how you effect change.

However frustrated I get over the justice system—and some of the people who work in it—I can take solace knowing I did my job to the best of my ability with the utmost integrity. I investigated the crime and I solved the case. That is my job. It isn't my job to determine whether a statement gets suppressed or whether a witness is credible. It's not my job to have friends or just maintain the status quo. It's not my job not to make sure I don't step on the toes of another investigating agency or upset a convicted murderer. It is not my job to make sure the prosecutors or investigators don't get their fragile egos hurt because I disagree with their case findings. It is my job to solve the case.

Call it passion, resolution, determination or perseverance. It's my job to solve the case. I can do that. I have the innate ability to do that. What happens after that—well, that's up to the system. At the end of the day, you must be able to look at yourself in the mirror knowing you have pride, integrity and you gave it your all every single day. That, my friend, is called success.

My name is not Kenneth L. Mains, savior of the justice system. My name is simply Kenneth L. Mains, detective.

Kenneth L. Mains, 2017

"The man who is anybody and who does anything is surely going to be criticized, vilified and misunderstood. This is a part of the penalty for greatness, and every great man understands it; and understands, too, that it is no proof of greatness. The final proof of greatness lies in being able to endure contumely without resentment."

Elbert Green Hubbard

Use this link to sign up for advance notice
of Kenneth L. Mains' Next Book:
http://wildbluepress.com/AdvanceNotice

Word-of-mouth is critical to an author's long-term success. If
you appreciated this book please leave a review on the Amazon
sales page:
http://wbp.bz/unsolvednomorea

Another Great True Crime
Read From WildBlue Press

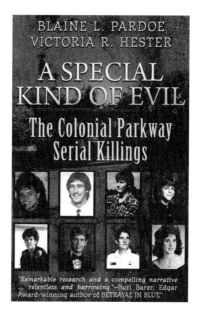

BLAINE L. PARDOE
VICTORIA R. HESTER

A SPECIAL
KIND OF EVIL

The Colonial Parkway
Serial Killings

"Remarkable research and a compelling narrative
... relentless and harrowing."–Burl Barer, Edgar
Award-winning author of BETRAYAL IN BLUE"

In the late 1980s, a predator stalked the Tidewater region of Virginia, savagely murdering his carefully selected his prey. He, or they, demonstrated a special kind of evil, and to this day have evaded justice. This is the first comprehensive look at the Colonial Parkway Murders and sheds new light on the victims, the crimes, and the investigation.

Read More: **http://wbp.bz/aspecialkindofevil**

WILD BLUE PRESS

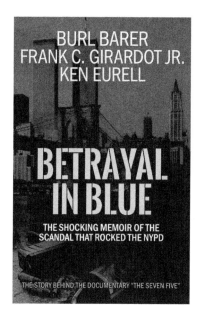

See even more at:
http://wbp.bz/tc

More True Crime You'll Love From WildBlue Press

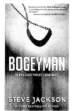

BOGEYMAN: He Was Every Parent's Nightmare by Steve Jackson
"A master class in true crime reporting. He writes with both muscle and heart." (Gregg Olsen, New York Time bestselling author). A national true crime bestseller about the efforts of tenacious Texas lawmen to solve the cold case murders of three little girls and hold their killer accountable for his horrific crimes by New York Times bestselling author Steve Jackson. *"Absorbing and haunting!"*(Ron Franscell, national bestselling author and journalist)

wbp.bz/bogeyman

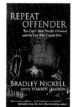

REPEAT OFFENDER by Bradley Nickell
"Best True Crime Book of 2015" (Suspense Magazine) A "Sin City" cop recounts his efforts to catch one of the most prolific criminals to ever walk the neon-lit streets of Las Vegas. *"If you like mayhem, madness, and suspense, Repeat Offender is the book to read."*(Aphrodite Jones, New York Times bestselling author)

wbp.bz/ro

DADDY'S LITTLE SECRET by Denise Wallace
"An engrossing true story." (John Ferak, bestselling author of Failure Of Justice, Body Of Proof, and Dixie's Last Stand) Daddy's Little Secret is the poignant true crime story about a daughter who, upon her father's murder, learns of his secret double-life. She had looked the other way about other hidden facets of his life - deadly secrets that could help his killer escape the death penalty, should she come forward.

wbp.bz/dls

BODY OF PROOF by John Ferak
"A superbly crafted tale of murder and mystery."– (Jim Hollock, author of award-winning BORN TO LOSE) When Jessica O'Grady, a tall, starry-eyed Omaha co-ed, disappeared in May 2006, leaving behind only a blood-stained mattress, her "Mr. Right," Christopher Edwards, became the suspect. Forensic evidence gathered by CSI stalwart Dave Kofoed, a man driven to solve high-profile murders, was used to convict Edwards. But was the evidence tainted? A true crime thriller written by bestselling author and award-winning journalist John Ferak.

wbp.bz/bop

Printed in Great Britain
by Amazon

81596998R00200